Dying to Stay

A Love Story. A Ghost Story. A True Story.

D.L. Meyer

APRIL 3, 2019

Creative Nonfiction

ISBN: 9781704571843

This is a fictionalized autobiography based on actual events. Some names, characters, places and incidents have been altered for dramatic purposes, to protect the privacy of others, or have been used fictitiously.

Cover design & candle photo: © Rachel Peterson

For Jim, Leonard, Esther, Bill, Pat,
Len, Mary and Chris.

Feel free to talk over the top of us. We're listening.

"Hereafter, in a better world than this,
I shall desire more love and knowledge of you."

William Shakespeare

Chapter Void: 1.3655976751203

Dying is a lot like being born. I've done both, so I can say this with authority. One moment I was in a safe, familiar place; the next I was spat out into the void.

My stomach fluttered, just as it had on April 16, 1958. My arms flailed, fingers splayed to grab hold of something—anything—solid and secure. I sucked in a big ol' lungful of air, unsure for a second what I was supposed to do with that sweet-sour thing filling my nose—the same way I had in the delivery room. And though I didn't know what it was called the day I took my first breath, I sure as hell recognized it as I neared my last: the silvery hit on my tongue was fear.

Yeah, fear. It's there at the beginning; it's there at the end. Cold, bitter and tasting like old pennies.

I shouted, too: a cry of surprise and outrage, the same sound on day one as on day almost-over. A yell for help to whatever Big Guy was out there waiting to catch me.

It probably sounds like I had ages to get all zen about death, doesn't it? Big no to that. The switch from *I am* to *I am not* can be flipped in less than a heartbeat. In fact, the only difference I can tell between being born and dying is timing. I've heard stories about women being in labor thirty-six hours. Trust me when I say, a finger snap can end it all.

Like now. You could be relaxing with what you hope will be a good book. Or pouring your first coffee of the day. Or about to jump into the car to run out for baby formula. You are going about your life as if you have all the time in the world.

You don't.

In my case, change came in less than two seconds. That's barely an eye blink —too short to count down, out loud, with that final desperate gulp of oxygen.

Less than two seconds to drop through the air to the ground.

To go from on to off to reset.

Let's be precise, shall we: 1.3655976751203 seconds to travel from the first place I knew as home to the one that would be my last.

Which turned out to be not so last after all.

Chapter One: Don't Call Me Ghost

I died two days before Christmas, December 23, 1983.

At least that's what it says on my death certificate. My synapses stopped firing on the twenty-second, but my wife agreed to leave me on the vent long enough for family to drive to Toledo for final goodbyes. The name on the obituary read "James Patrick Meyer." They forgot to add "Senior." Missed it in the news article, too.

You can call me Jim. Everyone does, except for a few childhood friends who hung on to "Jimmy" long after I stopped feeling like one. When you're a twenty-five year old married man with two kiddos under the age of three, your name should never sound that cute. Hell, I covered my chin with hair to get past that Jimmy thing. But beard or no beard, some folks just wouldn't give it up.

Whatever you do, do not call me Charlie Brown, the way my wife did a time or two before she became my wife. If she'd kept it up, I doubt I would have married her. Just kidding, hon. Oh, and do not even jokingly compare me to that middle Brady Bunch kid. I am—well—I hesitate to say studly, but definitely not cuddly. Besides. I never saw the resemblance. Call me by the P name at your peril.

More importantly, don't call me ghost.

If you're waiting for me to slide a penny up a door, or materialize in a halo of light to murmur "ditto" a final time to my true love, you're gonna be disappointed. This is not the movies—though if Fox comes a-knocking, honey, sign on the dotted line.

I'm not sure what I am, nor does it matter to me. Denise was the brainy half of our partnership, the one who could spend hours debating the hereafter. She could probably come up with a description stuffed with twenty-dollar words explaining Dead Me as some sort of esoteric construct: remnants of brain waves, thoughts and memories left over from my time on earth. A psychic presence, maybe. Who knows? She could be right. Our two sets of smarts were different. She thought things up; I made them happen. Good fit. But electronics was my field, building alarm systems for manufacturing equipment. I would never argue with her on a philosophical level. I picked my battles, people.

Uh-oh. That's got her scowling. See her? Sitting at her laptop, a little in front of me, to the left. Damn, she looks good. I'd say "for her age," but one scowl a day is more than enough. Sandy blonde hair, hazel eyes, long nose, stubborn jaw—and tall. She's got me by half an inch. Curvy like those Amazon warriors that end up carved out of marble in a museum. My Denny Lou, more beautiful than she believed, despite years of telling her. The woman I love, the mother of my children. Light of my afterlife.

Okay, she's laughing at me. And proving my point. That face comes alive when she smiles, doesn't it? Wow, woman. You still do it for me after all these years.

Anyway, where were we? Oh yeah. Who is Jim Meyer now that he's as late as he once was great? If you twist my arm behind my back? Force me to come up with a description? I'd say, "Alive, man. Just another kind of alive." I worked with electricity, so that's how I see the hereafter—a new form of energy. I told Denise this so often when I was still sucking oxygen, she can probably recite it in her sleep. Listening, hon? Start typing: "We are energy. And energy does not die. It can transform into something else, like heat, light, or sound. But it does not go away." So—sure, why not?—I really could be an eso-something psychic memory construct or other crazy thing.

Bottom line: I exist. My wife has heard me and seen my messages. Others have, as well. I would prove it by writing this story myself, but I no longer use language the way I once did. So, give it your best shot, Denny Lou. I give you permission to tell the story of my life, after my life.

Oh, one more thing. I may not communicate the way you're used to, but there's nothing wrong with my hearing. The Big Guy lets me eavesdrop, even after all this time. The longer I am separated from the people I love, the quieter their voices have become. Which probably has something to do with how seldom they need me now. But my ear is still to the wall.

Okay, babe, that about covers it. Get your finger off the delete key. The Peter Brady thing stays in. Right? Good.

And no wisecracks about ghost writing.

Chapter Two: The Road Less Traveled

I'm a pretty straightforward guy, so it should follow that
I'd start this story with In the Beginning and roll right along to The End.

Don't count on it. This tale is more likely to meander back and forth while it tries to get to the point. Why? First of all, because I am a testosterone-fueled cliche: the male who throws away the instructions manual and dives right in to all those shiny unassembled parts. It always made me laugh to see my wife's horrified face, and I never failed to declare, "*Destructions*? We don't need no stinking *destructions*!" I think she stopped snickering at that joke somewhere between the fifth and sixth telling. Hey, I always got it put together, didn't I? Eventually.*

Second of all, I am the same hormone-burdened male that refuses to use a map. The first time Denise and I set out on a camping trip to West Virginia with some of my brothers and their girlfriends, I let her hold the TripTik. (That's the Triple-A old-school equivalent of a navigational system, for those of you born post Google Maps.) I figured it would give my newly-declared-sweetheart something to play with on the long drive.

Now, *she* will tell you—incorrectly—that I got lost. I would point out that the exits were poorly marked, and I would have figured it out. (*See above disclaimer.) But she just kept trying to be *helpful*, telling me where I'd gone wrong, and where to stop, turn around and backtrack to correct the problem.

There was no problem.

Did she listen to me? Hell, no. Kept yammering on and on about how the map said this and the map said that. Would not. Shut up. About. The Map. Seriously, what was a normal, intelligent male to do?

I lost it (my temper, not my sense of direction) and shouted at my potentially-former girlfriend, "Okay then, the fricking map is *wrong*. Might as well throw it out the window for all the good it's doing us."

Do I have to fill in the punchline?

That TripTik is still littering a gulley somewhere between I Know Exactly Where We Are and Clueless. I ended up radioing my oldest brother Bill on the CB. (That's "Citizens Band," Millennials, smartphones yet to be a twinkle in Steve Jobs' eye.) Bill agreed with me that the exits were poorly marked but, just to be safe, I might want to stop, turn around and…

Well, anyway. I apologized to Denise. Not because she was right, exactly, but because we were slated to share a pup tent later that night, and the forecast was calling for rain.

Hmm, I wonder what happened to CBs? Would be useful for those of us who've passed our last earthly exit but still want to maintain contact. "Hey, Hot Pants. Angel Face here. Got your ears on? Come back. Over."

See. I digress. Often and without apology. You might as well get used to it.

So. Let's start at the beginning. Denise Tomanski and James Meyer Not-Yet-Senior met in 1962.

And 1973.

And 1977.

Probably a few other times in between we didn't know about. But officially in 1974. That was when we actually exchanged names and acknowledged the other's existence.

I tried out for my high school's junior class play, *Send Me No Flowers,* and Miss Tomanski, recent college grad and rookie English teacher, was directing.

Yep, you read that right. My wife was a Cougar before anyone had coined the term. Ahead of her time. I can smile at this because I am the lucky younger man in the equation. (Stop scowling, honey. It causes wrinkles. I'll save your reputation.)

Miss Tomanski was indeed seven years old the day I was born, but she did not come on to me during my formative high school years. More's the pity for me. Miss Tomanski was bright, funny, proper with a capital P... and scarcely noticed me before or after my audition. She did admit years later that in her notes of that afternoon it states: "James Meyer. Cute kid. Great smile. Nice comedic timing. Good at back-and-forth dialogues. Horrible at long speeches when he has to carry the bulk of the script. Possible small role."

I did get a part, by the way. Played an undertaker selling pre-paid funeral plans. True. You can't make up irony like that.

That was 1974. Those other years when we met? In 1962, my family who lived on the west side of town and her family who lived on the north side of town signed up for the same dentist. Downtown. Dr. Black (nice moniker for a tooth doc, right?) had an office in the same building as my dad, an OBGYN. They knew each other, hence the decision to become a patient there. Denise never found out why her folks chose the same out-of-the-way dentist. Point is: we probably bumped into each other and never noticed. Pain from drillings and fillings might have been an impediment to romance. That and the fact I was five and Denny would have been twelve.

In 1973, Denise moved out of her parents' home and into an apartment with her sister in West Toledo, only blocks from my folk's place. She wanted to join a local Catholic parish, and chose—drumroll please—my family's Catholic parish. Probably passed each other between genuflections, going and coming from Mass. Again, nary a notice.

By 1977, the couple-to-be had finally laid eyes on each other. Across the high school footlights, true; but the official meeting was behind them. Still, nothing came of it. That kid who looked like an escapee from the Brady Bunch had not yet learned how to leave a lasting impression. Nonetheless, God, Fate, Destiny, or some other spiritual chess player was throwing them into each other's path on a regular basis.

Need more proof? That year, my sister, Jan, gave birth to our family's first grandchild, Brooke. Same year, Denise's brother, Len, presented the Tomanski clan with their first grandchild, Danny. My father took videos of Brooke's christening, which was held in St. Clement's church, along with a large number of other baptisms. Denise's dad took videos of Danny's christening. Guess where? Years later over a bowl of popcorn, my wife sat up straight on our couch and scowled at the home movie we were watching. "How did your dad's footage of Brooke's baptism end up on this reel?" Turned out, it hadn't. Her dad and my dad had been standing side-by-side at the front of the church. One panned left over his own family and caught a second family smiling alongside them. The other panned right, and picked up the same smiling faces, in reverse.

Side by side. Almost identical footage. There I was. There she was. A dozen yards apart. Neither of us turned, noticed, or exchanged a smile. Footnote: in our wedding album a few years later you'll find Brooke and Danny again wearing white—this time as flower girl and ring bearer.

Now, do I believe God dictates the direction of our lives to such an elaborate extent? I do not. Even more so now that I've gotten a glimpse of how (s)he works from backstage. What I do believe is that like any caring parent, he or she tries to fill our lives with good choices to counter the bad. Eat your vegetables; they will make you strong. Don't touch the fire; it will hurt. A superior being doesn't have to push us around. Just give us a few important rules and let us make our own mistakes. That's how we learn. How we grow. Hopefully into good people. But becoming bad is entirely our choice, too. Without heavenly interference.

Denise and I traveled different paths: sometimes the road less taken, sometimes a highway worn smooth. Those paths crossed. And crossed. And crossed again. Until we looked up one day and something clicked. (Be patient. There'll be more about that click later.) In the end, it didn't matter who was older, or who was smarter, or who was more stubborn. We'd found the good, and decided to hold on to it.

Our choice. With an occasional signpost pointing in the right direction.

Even knowing how short our time together was going to be, we would make the same decision again. Just a guess, though? Denny would insist I use a map so it doesn't take so long to get where we were meant to be.

Chapter Three:
Conversation Interrupted

I have to ask. Are you reading this because it's a love story or a ghost story? Your answer could make the difference between telling you how Denny Lou and I clicked, or how I discovered I could speak to her from the other side. If this is going to be a good novel, it's gotta hold attention. You know, keep you turning the pages. So? Where to next?

I don't know good writing from Sanskrit. Denise was the reader in the family. Could devour a novel in two days when school was out for summer, burning off layers of skin cells while lounging on our airing deck with King or Grisham or Binchy. Me? Took two months to get through *Dracula*.

It's not that I don't enjoy reading; I have trouble with the mechanics. Denise thought I was dyslexic. Could be. I had to focus on individual words, often losing track of the sentence. *The Cat in the Hat Comes Back* was easier. Yeah, I was surprised, too. But all those broken up phrases and rhyming words sort of beg to be savored bit by bit, don't you think? I mean, some of them aren't even words at all, so it doesn't matter if you can pronounce them or know what they mean. It's all for fun.

Rachel and Jimmy loved my renditions of Dr. Seuss—even if I did stammer more than their mom. Then again, Rachel loved it when I read to her from a computer manual, so perhaps she wasn't a good judge.

Now do you understand? I'm clueless. So back to my original question: love story or ghost story? Ali McGraw and Ryan O'Neal or Demi Moore and Patrick Swayze? Am I showing my age? Make it Kate and Leonardo.

I'm betting ghost—even though I told you I'm not one. You're waiting for the scary stuff, some pee-in-your-pants, jump-out-of-your-seat goodness. That's okay. I can relate. *The Shining*. 'Nuff said? I couldn't sleep the night I saw it at the drive-in with my brothers. This was back when they charged you per person instead of by carload, so we smuggled my youngest brother, Joe, in for free. Grabbed him and locked him in the trunk. I don't think he slept that night either, but due more to the actions of his older siblings than the memory of Jack Nicholson waving a hatchet.

Where was I going with this? Oh, right. Ghost story. Goosebumps. Save the warm tinglies for later.

So be it.

I told you I died on December 23, 1983. I didn't tell you how. It was while replacing blown bulbs in a string of Christmas lights along the roofline of our house on Elm Street. (No, not that Elm Street, but you did ask for spookiness, so I couldn't resist pointing out the coincidence.)

I fell. The newspaper article said thirty feet. They got that wrong, but I admit it seemed that high on the way down. We were gearing up for Jimmy's first Christmas: baking, shopping, wrapping, decorating. Nothing was too much. Most parents will tell you excess is normal when you are reliving the magic of the holidays through the eyes of your own kids. That's my excuse and I'm sticking to it.

Close your eyes and I'll try to recreate the scene. Imagine Roseanne's house from the television series, only taller with a steeper pitch. Built in the 1930s. Possibly a Sears kit. White aluminum siding, with triangles of grey filling the peaks. A red brick porch runs the width of the front elevation, bordered on the left by a huge maple, just beyond the driveway. So close to it, lumpy roots nose their way through cracks in the concrete. That sucker had to be a hundred years old, maybe more; branches reaching skyward, twice the height of the house.

The porch roof is a squat inverted V pointing to a bank of three master-bedroom windows. I'd outlined the V with lengths of multi-colored lights.

Those great big fat ones, very old-school. Also strung them around the front door and picture window that looked out onto the porch. Then around the bank of upstairs windows. I covered the mammoth bushes that massed against the brick with twinkle-style lights. More than a thousand tiny bulbs there alone. Screwed a jolly light-up Santa head to the second story above our bedroom windows. (He came loose the first year and dangled upside down staring in at us while we watched TV in bed. Talk about scary.) We'd also inherited a pair of wooden candelabras made by Denise's Uncle John, each four-feet-tall, lacquered red, and topped with palm-sized flame bulbs. They flanked the front door.

By Christmas 1983, we'd owned the house for four years, and I'd put together an impressive decorating resume. I'd even drawn up a schematic so my design could be assembled efficiently year after year.

Hello? Electrician.

I admit, I could have stopped there, but why? Symmetry demanded I finish the job.

Above the porch looms the second story, capped by its own steeper inverted V. I outlined that highest peak, too, with even more fat bulbs in colors of red, green, blue and yellow. My brother-in-law, Len, who lived two doors down had been trying to out-light me since the day he moved in. An epic fail. That last year, I spotted him standing outside on the curb, staring up and shaking his head. Len is the male version of my wife: same fair hair, same Roman nose, and—from what I could see while I sat straddling the peak? Same scowl. It was an expression I'd come to recognize and love after four years of exposure to it from Denny, so it only made me grin and wave.

Len did not wave back, just kept shaking his head.

Finally he yelled.

"When do the sheep and camels arrive for the live nativity scene?"

That was the year he gave up trying to compete, bowing before my obvious superiority at Christmas pyrotechnics.

If I had known three lightbulbs grouped together next to my knee would flicker out in a curl of smoke two weeks later, I'd have replaced them before I climbed back down. Pardon the cliche, but they would be the death of me.

Quick side story. I know, I know, another one. But as Sir McCartney pointed out, if you don't fix the hole where the rain gets in, I'm going to traipse off any old place. Or something like that.

Denise was not happy with me the first year I put up those lights. We'd bought the place together before we were married—before I'd even proposed—and were still living in our respective apartments while we fixed it up. We're pretty handy, and her folks were, too, so we were having a merry old time painting and scrubbing and grouting. What we were not enjoying was the cost of every damn thing. Denise scoured high and low for the best deals, and I performed all the manly labor gratis. Nonetheless, our checkbooks were squealing in pain.

The balmy November day that I decided to surprise her with a display of my holiday expertise, she had been hiking from store to store trying to find affordable draperies that didn't look like bedsheets to cover the picture windows in our living room and dining room. When she pulled into the driveway, her feet were hurting, her head was hurting, and she was $100 lighter in the pocket than she'd intended to be. That doesn't seem like a lot now, but in 1979? When the average Toledo teacher made around $9,000 a year, and a newly minted electrical design technician with an associate's degree made less? It was a killer.

And what did the love of my life find when she returned home? The love of *her* life grinning like a loon, screwing small brass hooks into the aluminum siding, surrounded by bags and bags of Christmas lights. About $100 worth.

She climbed from the car while I gestured, arms spread, at my handiwork. "Surprise!"

She took the steps slower than a glacier makes its way across Greenland, clutching her too-damn-expensive bag of drapes to her chest. Looked around like she'd stumbled into an asylum—not the reaction I'd been hoping for—and burst into tears.

Ah ha! you're thinking. A psychic premonition that those merry lights would one day herald disaster for our young lovers. Nah. Just a case of two people who had yet to learn to ask what was in the kitty before emptying it. She eventually stopped crying. And being mad. And we ate a lot of Ramen that month. Just a side story, like I said.

The real foreshadowing came a year later.

It was late summer 1980 when Denny had the dream.

You know the kind. A nightmare so real, when you wake up, your ears still ring with screams and there's a sweet stink of sweat on your skin. The kind of dream, that even if you turn on a low light, get up to grab a drink of water, and splash some of it on your face? You can't shake the feeling it's happened.

My wife told her mother every scary detail. I had to die to hear about it.

Oh, right. You don't know. Eavesdropping on those we've dearly departed ought to have its own chapter in the afterlife manual. Hey, maybe it does—I wouldn't know since I pitched my copy. The thing is, those of us who choose to hang around can plunk ourselves in the middle of any action, at any time, in any place.

Think of it as cosmic cloud storage: a backup of everything you've ever done. Forty years after the fact, I can pull up a chair at my mother-in-law's kitchen table and listen in. You can, too—but be warned. Here come the goosebumps…

Denise lifts her palms. "It was… I don't know, Mom. Freaky." She flutters her fingers as if the right words can be caught and held. "I was wandering around outside our house, looking for a way in, but all the walls were blank. No doors. Like faces without mouths. Then…" She tries to snap her fingers but they are damp and only thump. "I was on the porch—the front door hanging open."

She stops to rub her arms. I'd like to help warm her but that's one of those skills we lose. Listening in on history: check. Touching and holding: uncheck.

I wait, as I always do when I revisit this moment. Listen, as I always do to the grandfather clock in my mother-in-law's living room as it fills the silence with ticks and tocks.

"I wanted to run in," Denise finally says. "But I couldn't. The air was too… something. Heavy, I guess. Or thick."

She sighs, and knots her hands together on the tabletop. "We'd been robbed, Mom. I couldn't tell what was missing, but I knew something important was gone. I had to find Jim. I couldn't move fast enough."

Such is the way of weird dreams, right? I've lived the spoiler, so I know how this story ends, but repetition has not dulled its impact. My wife's words still make me shudder.

"Mom?" Denny asks. "Is it bad luck to repeat a nightmare about someone out loud?"

Esther Tomanski was an expert on how not to tempt fate: "Don't sit on the table; you'll be married before you're able." "Never open an umbrella in the house; you'll have ten years of fires to douse." (Or you'll put your eye out.) "If you shudder, a ghost just walked across your grave."

Yeah. Got that one nailed.

But on the day Denise told her mother about the dream, our expert on karma failed me.

"Not that I know of," Esther says. "Is it about Jim?"

Denise nods.

Mom leans across the table and squeezes those clenched fingers. "It's just that you're newly married." (We'd exchanged vows a month before, our rings still shiny and new.) "You have something to lose now. That's what you're afraid of. That's all."

This was pretty tender stuff coming from my mother-in-law. Not that she couldn't be warm and comforting, but she was a Bea Arthur kind of woman (who she resembled to a scary degree, by the way). Usually, you could expect her to be more *Maude* than *Golden Girls*.

Denny chews off a layer of lipstick before defying the gods of superstition. "I couldn't climb the stairs, Mom—had to dig my fingers into the plaster to drag myself up. And when I got to the top? Jim was, um…" Her gaze falls to join her hands on the table. "He was just propped there, his back against the wall, legs stretched out. And his eyes…"

She swallows. I've learned to watch for that click in her throat, to steel myself against the pain it causes.

"They weren't open. Weren't closed either. Like… I don't know. Window shades that won't stay down," she says. "And, Mom?

"He was… naked."

What my wife wanted to say was "dead." It's what she wants to say every time I've listened in. But it was easier for her to admit I'd been wearing no clothes than I wouldn't be needing them anymore.

Denny didn't know how she knew I was dead, but the image had been so clear, she'd forced herself to wake up from that disturbing dream—do the light, water, splash thing—then had laid awake the rest of that night to watch me breathe. I have eavesdropped on those long hours, too. Watched that night pass over and over, wishing I could change the outcome. Dying to stay with her. Helpless to do so.

"Why would I dream something so horrible?" she asks her mother. "Do you think it means something?"

"No," Esther insists. "Of course not."

But Mom was wrong again.

The Big Guy doesn't dictate the course of our life. I think I said that already, but it bears repeating. What he does sometimes do is prepare us for the shadows in our future. Tries to cushion the blow that appears to be coming.

Denny's dream was our warning.

We're going to be spending the next few months inside the Elm Street house, so let me give you the fifty-cent tour. Over the years, the place evolved along with its residents, so I've seen the paint morph from one color to the next, the textures alter as fashions changed. But my favorite incarnation will always be what Denny and I created.

The original house, as I think I said, may have been a kit bought from a Sears and Roebuck catalogue—looked a lot like the Fullerton model but without the attic gable. It also had upgrades not shown on Fullerton blueprints, like brick on the porch, cove ceilings in the living and dining rooms, and a breakfast nook addition off the kitchen. Thick mahogany woodwork and a built-in linen hutch were highlights of the second floor, as well as narrow walk-in closets in all the bedrooms. These were extras we prized, and hinted that perhaps the hype about the place being a Sears kit was just that: hype so we wouldn't bicker over the asking price. Didn't matter to us. We fell in love the moment we walked through the door.

Sadly, the woodwork on the first floor had been replaced with narrow blonde trim before we became the owners, and the mahogany on the second floor had been painted—along with every switch plate, glass doorknob, and art deco ceiling fixture. Whatever bozo did that carries my curse into eternity. I couldn't get the paint off those ornate light fixtures, and had to replace them, along with the switch covers. But the glass knobs cleaned up like diamonds. And the woodwork! Using the same portion of his brain that allowed him to slap oil-based paint on pieces of history, the previous owner had painted the baseboards and doors *without* sanding them first. Denny and I had a blast picking at the edges until whole sheets of paint stripped off the varnish like contact paper. I hold the record for the longest strip: seven feet by eight inches, pulled off without tearing. I could have wrapped a small mummy in it.

In the kitchen, Denny painted everything white—ceilings, walls and cabinets—updated the cupboard hinges and handles to simple silver, and I replaced the funky linoleum with an embossed tile that resembled white farmhouse brick. We also tore out the dingy grey asbestos countertops and replaced them with sage-green penny tile, then hung ivy-print wallpaper in the nook. The appliances were white, as well, and top-of-the-line digital— bought with money we received as wedding gifts. They included a dishwasher that the place lacked when we moved in. We hadn't planned on that little luxury, but after weeks of fighting over whose turn it was to wash and whose to dry, we opted to cut out a small section of cabinetry to make room for a base-model turbo-wash from GE. Figured we might be tight on storage, but our marriage would be a good deal happier.

By summer 1983, I had begun updating the plumbing to copper in the basement, and was in the process of converting the old knob-and-tube wiring anywhere I could reach without tearing out the beautiful plaster walls. I would never see those projects to completion.

We didn't know that would be the case, of course—although the house did try to warn us.

Remember those videos shot in New York just after the Towers came down, the air thick with concrete dust and the wail of car alarms? For several minutes there are no people in sight. There's a lot of noise, but no one's listening.

That was us. During the two months leading up to my fall, there were plenty of signs hinting danger ahead. But by themselves, they didn't amount to much. Nothing that required a musical stinger. (That's the problem with real life: no ominous sound track to set the mood.) Ah, but when viewed altogether? After the fact? Well.

Denise celebrated her thirty-third birthday by moping around, frowning to herself. That alone should have raised my psychic hackles. Age has never mattered to my wife. She'd passed her thirtieth without a whimper, but this time, she told me she had an awful feeling she wasn't going to see her thirty-fourth. That something bad was going to happen. That—God, dare she say it?—she was going to die.

Close, babe, but no cigar.

As for me, I suddenly found myself cast in the role of a Marvel Comics superhero: *Static Man.* Waging war against the evils of technology one domestic appliance at a time. If I tried to brew up a pot of morning caffeine, Mr. Coffee would go toes up with a touch of my magic fingers and a sizzle of burnt out heating coil.

Flip on the upstairs hall light? I'd get my fingers rapped by a hard shot of voltage as a scorch mark the size of a dinner plate blossomed around the switch.

Attempt to fire up my little blue Mazda? Instead of the spritely hum of a rotary engine, there'd be a single click followed by a lengthy, you're-going-to-be-late silence.

It got so bad, I was thinking about wearing rubber gloves full time, and taking out a loan to finance replacement parts. But, hey, the house was old, so was the car, and Mr. Coffee was a hand-me-down.

Then.

We got robbed.

It happened around four in the morning, a time police told us is preferred by many burglars, the hour most people are deep in REM sleep and less likely to hear footsteps or creaking doors.

Our burglars hadn't factored in the possibility that they were dealing with fairly new parents. When you have a three-year-old daughter and an eleven-month-old son, REM is a rock group. We've long forgotten it has any other meaning.

Denise caught the sound first: the soft *rrrrp* of the loose floorboard in the hall outside our bedroom. Less than six feet away, I figure. Gutsy bastard. Denny gave me a pretty-please elbow to the ribs. "Rachel's up," she grumbled.

I think I said, "Hmm." Or some other single syllable that translated to "You deal with it. I've got work in a couple of hours."

Silence reigned.

Then the *rrrrp* came again.

Just in case you are not sufficiently weirded out, let me point out that all our bedrooms are on the second floor, each of us no more than a half-dozen strides from the other. If you put yourself in the doorway to our room, facing out—let's call it six on the clock face—to your left at twenty minutes-to is Rachel's room. Straight ahead about ten feet down the hall at high noon is Jimmy's nursery. He's still in a crib—something we wish Rachel still had because she's established herself as a night person who likes nothing better than to get up and gather her toys for a rave. I was already dreading her teen years. At five-after on the clock face is our tiny bathroom, followed at quarter-past by the stairway leading to the first floor.

Those stairs drop down a handful of steps to a small landing, take a hard right, and continue the rest of the way to a wide bottom landing and the coat closet. They open on the right into our combined living room/dining room el. The kitchen fills the remainder of the first floor, tucked into the corner created by the arms of those other two rooms.

There are three doors to the outside: one in the living room next to the coat closet. It takes you to the front porch. Another is located at the rear of the kitchen, leading to the back porch, garage, and yard; overhead are Jimmy's room, the airing deck, and bathroom. A third exterior door is located midway down the right side of the house, accessing the driveway. You get to it through an interior kitchen door that closes off a second set of stairs identical to the one above it, but ending in the basement. That third exterior door is off the basement stairs landing.

We hardly ever use it.

Neither of us checked it the night of the break-in (no breaking needed, as you are about to learn) because we'd both assumed whichever one of us had come through there last had flipped the deadbolt. Not only did someone not do that, the screen door had not caught properly, and a shot of Mother Nature had blown it open.

Along with the interior door.

Not a lot, mind you. Just enough to shout, "Welcome, all ye who would enter here."

So. Back upstairs we go, where Denise is now rustling around under the covers, trying to guilt me into chasing our party girl back into her cute little canopied bed.

With the third *rrrrrrp*—longer and farther away than the others—she abandons that futile tactic, choosing instead to jump up and stomp her feet a couple of times. A fair warning to Snow White that the wicked witch is about to descend and place her into an enchanted sleep.

I slit one eye, and watch Mom bam bam bam her way to Rachel's door.

A door that is closed.

Denise has already grasped the knob and thrust it open before realizing this should not be necessary. I am a few sleepy thoughts behind and I don't catch on right away.

Rachel's door is never closed at night. Nor is Jimmy's. (Sorry, Fireman Bob. The better to hear them, my dears.)

I watch groggily as my wife stands there a moment, gaze twitching from the glass doorknob in her hand to our daughter tucked up safe and warm in her bed. I see Denny turn her attention to the hall, eyes tracking to high noon, focusing there a moment as she takes in a second closed door.

I, still clueless, blink a couple of times as sleep tries to drag me under. Denise lets go of the handle, steps toward the stairs. I think maybe she is going to use the bathroom as long as she's up. But she lurches to a stop, hands at her sides, fists clenched, as motionless as a deer that's caught the scent of man.

I don't know how long she stood there, stationary between Rachel's room and the top of the stairs. I might have fallen back to sleep. It wasn't until the mattress moved beneath my hip, that I roused myself enough to ask, "Everything okay?"

Denise is sitting on the edge of the bed, her back to where I lay curled on my side, her face pointed toward the hall. Jimmy's door is still closed, and I wonder why she hasn't gone the rest of the way down, past those stairs, to open it. She doesn't speak, only sighs to me in answer. Or maybe she was shushing me. In the aftermath of the excitement, I forgot to ask.

I do notice that the house is *quiet* quiet. You know what I mean? The kind of silence that is unnatural. As though the pipes and rafters are holding their breath. Suddenly, I am not as sleepy as I was a moment before.

Still, nothing happens, and a few minutes later my wife mutters to herself, "Being silly. Imagining things." With that, she swivels my way, lifts the blankets, and slides in to cuddle.

We both hear it when the kitchen door to the basement stairs opens. You can't miss it. It's a noise halfway between the death shriek of a small animal and a bottle rocket misfiring. Neither of us moves.

"Did you hear that?" she whispers, in a voice I don't recognize. "Someone's in the house." My wife is anything but timid, occasionally bordering on harsh and sarcastic. She presents an appearance of strength and confidence, even when she's feeling anything but. More so then.

That night? She was terrified.

We wait.

I understand now why prey go stock-still when facing a predator. We are hoping it won't notice us.

For what seems like forever, we hear nothing more. I gotta tell ya, silence can do a lot to convince a person there was never anything to worry about in the first place. I even begin to nod off. Then Jimmy's soft fussing ensures that neither of his parents will close their eyes.

Our son has an inner alarm clock permanently set to "feed me." I figure it must be closing in on five A.M.

His complaints escalate.

I groan, conceding without speaking. *Yeah, my turn.*

"I've got him," I say, and slip out of bed. Denise sleeps nearest the door, so I have to skinny sideways between the bed and wall to get up without climbing over her. She jolts upright, and watches me. "Be careful," she says.

Well, damn, woman. What happened to silence is bliss? Ignorance is golden? Nothing to worry about here?

I make my way around the footboard and into the hall. The only sounds are the creaking floorboard as I pass it, and the baby curses coming from the nursery straight ahead. I open Jimmy's door and he stops bitching, greeting me with a toothless grin. Any concerns I might have had flee with his smile. That is my son's special gift. He loves unconditionally and lets you know it at every opportunity. Home intruder or no home intruder, all is well in my world.

Denial is more than a river in Egypt.

I pick Jimmy up, trundle him to the changing table and do the basics, tuck a pacifier in his mouth to hold off any additional demands for breakfast, and carry him with me into the hall.

Immediately, I know this is a mistake. From this angle, I can see a glow of light from the floor below, illuminating shadows near the top landing.

Damn, woman, I think again. She just had to be right. Someone is indeed in *my* house, and they've had the balls to switch on lights to help them ransack the place. In an instant, I bypass seeing red and leap straight to black with lightening bolts of purple.

I stalk to our bedroom, holding Jimmy outstretched for my wife's waiting arms. Denise doesn't ask me what's wrong. Takes him, and hands me a robe she's pulled from a hook in our closet. "Be careful," she repeats. But I am past careful.

I walk on silent feet to the top of the stairs, lean out over the short stack of steps.

"Jim," she hisses at me. "I'm calling the police." There was no 911 in our area back then, so she's going to have to punch 0 on the bedroom phone and report our emergency to an operator. Later, neither of us remembers making that call or what was said. I place one bare foot on the second step, and twist my torso to gain a view around the corner. "Jim," she hisses again. "Wait. Damn it, wait."

I don't step down to the small upper landing. I don't have to. Bending from the waist, I have a sliver-sized view of the bottom stairs. "Lights are on," I whisper back. "Coat closet is open." I take one last step, balancing on my toes. The sliver becomes a good-size crack. "And your purse is gone."

"Come back," Denise commands. I have no problem obeying.

The police are on their way.

The two officers who circle the outside of our house, flashlights bobbing, finally come to the door. They tell us to remain on the porch while they check the interior. We tell *them* our daughter is still asleep upstairs. They nod their understanding, and go in search of prowlers.

We marvel later that our precious little night owl never woke up despite the noise and confusion. Rachel would have thought the whole thing a great adventure. Even Jimmy studies the scene with froggy eyes, forgetting his need for immediate sustenance. For the first and last time ever.

Once our house is secure, the officers allow us back in so we can take stock.

Drawers and doors stand open in the kitchen cabinets, as well as in the dining room china hutch. The silverware we'd collected as wedding gifts is still in its wooden storage box, which now gapes open on the floor. The knifes and forks and spoons inside are jumbled together as though they've been fondled, then abandoned. Not pawnable, Cop Number One explains. I try not to be insulted.

A sealed and addressed birthday card for my niece, Shana, is missing from the outgoing-mail basket on a sideboard. "They probably figure it has money inside," cites Cop Number Two. Half of our portable intercom system is missing, as well. A dust-free square marks the spot where it previously sat on top of the console TV. We were using a set of them as baby monitors, so the mate is in Jimmy's room—where it sits still. Dumbass crook didn't spot it when he closed my son inside. Go, team stupid. We also had a kerosene heater (*had* being the operative word) stored for the night atop a cold air register near the front door. Utility costs had skyrocketed that year, and cheap kerosene made such heaters the decorating accessory of the season. No longer for us; it too is gone.

Denise's purse rests upside down on the sofa, contents spilled on the cushions and floor. Her wallet sprawls beside it, minus the grocery money, her credit cards, driver's license and Social Security card. We would find her keys in the gap between the sofa's arm and seat later that day.

Those keys would have explained something that bothered our two officers. They'd told us their department was tracking the activities of a two-man team working homes in North Toledo, and they knew a lot about how these crooks operated.

1) Hit when homeowners are snoring loudest. *Check.*

2) Identify an easy entry. They preferred houses with airing decks and tower antennas that could serve as handy ladders. We had both, but had opted to leave a door open so they could mosey on in. *Idiot Check.*

3) Turn on a light, so if neighbors look out they won't think anything of it… as opposed to their reaction should they spot a weaving flashlight beam. *Check.*

4) Split up, with one partner whipping through the main floor, and the

other tackling the top in search of wallets, jewelry and piggy banks. (Yeah, you heard that right.) *Double check.*

Side note: (Like you didn't know *that* was coming.) The police knew there were two men because a homeowner had awakened, confronted them, and been bludgeoned while attempting to protect his stuff. When he came to, he provided a sketchy description. "So," Cop Number One pointed out, "the smartest thing you did tonight, Missus Meyer, was step back from the stairs and wait for them to beat it out of Dodge." No, the smartest thing my wife did that night was to not give a rat's ass about stuff. Like me, she knew the only things of real value in our house were irreplaceable. "Take it all," we would have shouted if we'd found the courage. "Take it. Go. And leave our family alone."

Okay now, where was I? Oh, right. The thing that bothered our two coppers was number five on the burglary checklist: steal a car.

The thieving twosome had done so at all of their previous break-ins: loaded their ill-gotten gains inside another ill-gotten gain, and driven away. On first inspection, my wife's keys were missing, so why hadn't they taken the car? Our police officers mulled it over for a moment and decided that once the bastards knew *we* knew they were inside the house, stealing a car would damn near guarantee patrol units would be looking for it within minutes.

I could have told them, even if the creeps had tried, my battered blue Mazda needed a less vocal starter and Denise's flashy red Sebring needed a new muffler. Any attempt to ride off into the sunrise would have awakened the entire neighborhood and portions of the next county.

Before Toledo's Finest departed with the report of a crime that would never be solved, they hastened to point out how lucky we'd been. The haul had been skimpy: a small chunk of cash, a MasterCard and Visa I managed to cancel before the stores opened, half of a now useless intercom system, a birthday card filled with nothing more than good wishes, and a big-assed heater that I still wonder how they toted away, on foot(?), at a dead run(?), to God knows where.

Oh, yeah. They'd also snagged one of the six bottles of wine we had in a small rack in the dining room. The most expensive bottle, natch. We'd been saving the pricey French Bordeaux for a special occasion: our tenth wedding anniversary or midnight New Year's Eve 2000. To make matters worse? Cop Number Two said they probably had no idea of its value. Were probably guzzling it down as we stood there chatting.

I hope they choked on it.

The men in blue closed their goodbye speech to us with a warning: be especially careful in the months ahead. This same team was known to come back after the insurance claim has been paid and you've purchased all new goodies to steal.

Huh. And they called us lucky? Still, all in all, we hadn't lost much—only our sense of security. And my youthful belief in my immortality.

See, as I stood at the top of those stairs, adrenaline pumping, heart racing to its redline? I realized I could die. That this might be my last minutes on earth. And that nothing would stop me—not even that unknown beyond— from protecting my family.

It's probably a given to you by now that if the burglary was meant as a cosmic warning to us of direr things to come, we missed it. No surprise. Denise's dream about us being robbed and finding me dead had been four years in her past. And I'd never known about it at all. So, "Act One: The Burglary" ended up being just another unheard alarm wailing in a grey cloud of obscurity.

Except. Maybe not.

When Cop Number One first asked me to explain what happened, I'd started out by saying, "My wife heard a noise and thought it was one of her kids." Denise had given me a puzzled look, but said nothing to correct me. Probably chalked it up to nerves.

But, seriously, people. One of *her* kids?

Hers. Not ours.

Like my subconscious was beginning to suspect something I was not yet ready to admit.

It occurs to me I haven't explained the title of this chapter. I'm almost done with it and you have yet to find out what I mean by "Conversation Interrupted."

That has to be driving my lovely wife batshit crazy. Did I mention she's OCD? Makes Monica from *Friends* look like a candidate for *Hoarders*. Think I exaggerate? We had a repainted Goodwill dresser in our closet that had been repurposed for—wait for it—shoes. Not socks or sweaters or scarves or ties. (She bought a special hang-on-the-wall rack for both of mine.) Shoes. One drawer for me. One for her. A really deep one for boots. That drawer had a tattered towel in the bottom to catch drips. She'd drafted a list of features to look for when she went bargain hunting for that stupid dresser. An addendum to her shopping list.

I swear to God—who will back me up on this—my wife's lists have lists.

I know for a fact she still does this. Only now, instead of a long narrow strip of paper tacked to our fridge with a magnet, she has lists on her phone. Note the plural. Yes, thanks to the marvels of modern technology, Denny Lou has gone rabid. In fact, I'll bet she has more than five lists on her smartphone right now. Go ahead, dear. Punch them up. Be honest. How many lists are stored in your special "LISTS" folder?

Yowzah! We have a winner. I'll take the jumbo-size purple elephant on the top shelf, please.

Nineteen.

Nineteen lists. Do people really need a separate check sheet for the following? And I quote:

> *Groceries*
> *Doctor Notes*
> *Gift Ideas*
> *Stuff to Remember* (What? No "Stuff to Forget"?)
> *Community Theater Research*
> *Future Theater Marketing*
> *TV Shows to Catch Up On* (??!!!)
> *Movies To See* (ditto the ??!!!)
> *Books To Read*
> *Clothing Sizes*

> *IRA Info*
> *Passwords*

Plus an all-purpose *To Do* (in case she's discovered something that doesn't rate its own list), and last but not least, *Toppings for Curry Chicken.*

That's not including the five lists Denise has for her various novels in progress.

Come on, babe, delete one. Just one. I would bet you she can't do it but it's greedy to win more than one purple somethingorother.

Okay, okay, okay, honey, I'll stop snickering. Let's just say Denny is hell on lists.

We had one for Christmas 1983. It outlined every single detail we hoped to accomplish before the twenty-fifth of December. I say *we* because, over time, I had come to find my wife's obsession helpful. I was finishing more projects than I ever had in my life. And enough cannot be said about the high you get when you strike a big fat slash mark through the last item and two-point the bastard into the trash. (For Denise, the "slash" has always been a wavy squiggle, sort of a long series of lowercase cursive n's. Very distinctive. And a subtle way of pointing out which of us was ahead in the race to that two-pointer.) But I digress. Yeah, so what else is new.

Anyway, by December twenty-first, we'd already slashed and squiggled our way through Decorate Tree, Decorate House, Bake Cookies, Pick Up Kielbasa for Christmas Breakfast, Buy Jim's Gift, and Finish Assembling Strawberry Shortcake Dollhouse (more about that debacle later). The only items left were mine: Pick Up Denise's Gift and...

Yeah. Replace Bulbs.

I'd meant to do that earlier in the week. Toledo had been toasting under an unusual heatwave, with the previous day's temps in the seventies. So warm, Rachel had played in the backyard without a coat, and Denise had opened the windows. The weatherman was calling for a cold snap, followed by a touch of sleet and several inches of white stuff over the next thirty-six hours. If I'd remembered to pick up the replacement bulbs earlier, as planned, that lightless patch in the top string would have been dead no more.

Same goes for me.

But there it was, Replace Bulbs, still on the list when I left for work.

"Gonna do that," I muttered on my way out the door, "before the weather turns." I had hopes the mild temps would hold until I got home around four. Maybe the opal ring I'd picked out for Denise wouldn't be ready for pickup until the twenty-third, but those burned out bulbs? I could definitely scratch them off before bedtime.

Denise beat me to it. While whipping up breakfast for the kiddos, she decided replacing those lights really wasn't an earth-shattering need. Certainly wasn't worth the trouble at this late date, especially since she didn't want me to shinny up on the housetop once the snow fell. A line of cursive n's was banishing the item from "Christmas 1983" about the same time I was settling down at my drafting table with a first cup of coffee.

I know. Rather uncharacteristic of Mrs. Get It Done, wasn't it? It would seem her subconscious was trying for a last-ditch save. Still, she blames herself. Beats herself up over the fact those damn bulbs were on our list in the first place. Figures, since I'd never had any list-making tendencies before I married her, it had to be her fault.

Survivor's guilt. When shattered by the loss of someone we love—someone who has no reason to be gone so suddenly and so soon—every single one of us will punish ourselves with shoulda and coulda and why didn't I.

How many times must I say this, babe? It was not your fault. I was an adult and I made my own decisions. It. Was. An. Accident.

Damn, she's tearing up again. Almost forty years gone, and the loss continues to hurt. Hurts me, too.

Hey, dying doesn't mean we don't feel anymore.

Even you guys who are thinking, "This is warm and fuzzy and all that, but really, this book is no more than a grieving woman's wishful thinking"? You may be right. But this is true, as well: we exist because you exist. We live because you remember us. We breathe and laugh and cry with every retelling of every story you hold in your heart and pass on to others to retell in their own way. If that isn't pain. And joy. And love everlasting.

Then I don't know what is.

I will share your emotions, woman, for as long as you live. Probably for a generation or two beyond.

So, stop typing for a minute. Go get a drink of water. You guys? The ones reading? Go do whatever it is you can do for—say—ten minutes. We'll pick up here, in a better frame of mind, when you get back.

Okay. All cried out. But it's probably best if I cut to the chase.

I remembered to buy the bulbs.

I came through the door at four o'clock, all smiles, waving a four-pack of varicolored replacement lights and chanting in a sing-song, "Guess what I got?" If you've never heard "whaaat" pronounced with two syllables you've missed a treat.

Denise was pulling her mom's best-recipe-ever Mac and Cheese out of the oven. Topped with bacon. I'm a simple culinary soul and it's one of my favorites. Smelled like crispy slices of heaven.

Jimmy and Rachel were playing in the living room. By that, I mean Jimmy was wondering what to do with a dishrag Rachel had traded to him for his toy xylophone. My daughter's blonde bob was dipped low, nearly touching my son's darker curls. She was wearing bright red overalls; Jimmy was clad in a kid-size UT sweatshirt and Huggies. I don't know why I noticed. Couldn't imagine why the image of my kiddos huddled together would bring a sudden lump to my throat. Maybe it was because they weren't fighting for a change. Sure. That had to be it.

My wife looked up as she hefted the casserole onto the stovetop. "Seriously?" she said. "*Now* you remember? I thought it was going to snow."

I moved into the kitchen, eyeballed the refrigerator list, and gave it a grin. "Not yet. Getting colder though." To prove it, I wrapped my arms around her from behind.

"Yikes! Stop that!" she complained. But not really.

I didn't bother to take off my jacket. I loved the damn thing. It was one of the gifts Denise had opted to give me early, in anticipation of the shift in temps. It was light grey and stylish with these neat zippers on the pockets and sleeves, a complete upgrade from the gaudy So-Seventies thing I'd been living in for six years. Despite the morning being mild, I'd worn it to work. My friend Ken had made a few disparaging remarks, proving to my satisfaction that it was indeed cool. I planned to wear it indefinitely. Meant to tell my wife that, but got distracted. "Gonna change into my work boots," I said instead. "These tennis shoes will be too slippery."

She shot me a look over her shoulder as I headed for the stairs and the boot drawer. "You're going to do it now? I'm about to set the table."

"It will only take me a sec."

Those were the last words we spoke to each other in this life. I didn't get to tell her how much I liked my new coat. Didn't get to share what I'd decided about school—that I was going to go back to complete my bachelor's, and was hoping she'd make good on her vow to help me ace English.

Didn't get to say, "I love you."

I mean, come *on*. In the movies, the leading man always gets to say "I love you" before he steps into the path of that speeding car, speeding bullet, or other fast-track disaster. But for us? No crescendo of dramatic music. No duh-duh-duh duhhh. Damn those missing sound cues.

Just a promise to be right back that I would not get to keep.

A conversation interrupted.

Chapter Four: Prologues

You know those things at the beginning of a novel? The shortish bits that explain something that occurred in a different time or place? You know. They're like... uh... background stories. Details that are important for you to know if the rest of the plot is going to make sense. Come on. You know what I mean. What are they called?

I know my wife knows, but she's sitting there grinning, letting me fumble around looking like a dork.

What's that, sweetheart? (There's never a sarcasm font when you need one.)

Hmm. She says it's part of my character not to know.

Double hmm. So, what you're saying, sugar britches, is that what I think of as *dorkiness* you claim is *characterization*? Let's call it for what it really is, shall we? Revenge for dissing your boot drawer.

Prologues! Right.

I need to give you a prologue. Yes, we are no longer at the start of this book. But if you were expecting me to continue straight ahead, not passing go and not collecting two hundred dollars... where have you been the last thirty-some pages?

Besides.

I'm not ready to talk about the fall.

So, while I gear myself up for that, why don't we strap in to the Wayback Machine and clear up a few details. Prologue One (as in "Yes, there will be more than") is titled "Honeymoon."

I proposed to Denise the same day we closed on that big old Elm Street house. We'd just returned from spray-painting SOLD on the For Sale sign, and were in my apartment, high on the fumes of sacrificing our yet-to-be first-born child to the gods of mortgage. Hell, did I need a beer. I'd never bought anything that expensive in my life. A major first. Raising a Bud seemed like the least I could do.

I yanked on the knot of my tie, wiggled it until it felt less like a noose, then shrugged out of my seldom-worn sport coat and dropped it over the back of a kitchen chair. Where it would likely stay until the next time I signed away my future life savings.

It was while standing in front of the open fridge, hand extended—that it hit me. I was feeling pretty damn happy about the whole thing. Shouldn't I be shaking in my size ten Adidas? I mean, I'd just locked myself into a thirty-year-fixed at twelve percent interest with a woman I wasn't even married to.

Nope, I decided. Not one bit scared. And the reason was obvious: if Denise Louise Tomanski owed buckets of money that she couldn't repay without the help of James Patrick Meyer, then it followed she would have to stay with said co-signer for at least the life of the loan.

It also followed that if *that* was cool with me—beyond cool, even—then why should she stay Denise Louise Tomanski? Why not shorten her name so it was easier to sign at the bottom of all those checks to First Federal?

I passed on the Bud, closed the fridge, and caught her as she was moving down the hallway toward the bathroom. Damn, the woman could fill out a skirt. "Come sit with me," I said, tugging her through the archway to the living room.

"Can it wait?" she countered, tugging equally hard, back the way she'd come.

"Nope," I said. "Now." I think I giggled. (God, I hope someone edits that out before this goes to print.) I was feeling nervous all of a sudden. This would be the second major thing I had never done before in my life. A real whopper. That's a lot of firsts for one day. A manly chuckle could be excused.

Denise wasn't having it, though. She twisted free of my hand, and turned. Her skirt looked even better walking away.

But what the? I figured she didn't realize how serious this was, and would have to be shown. I'd have swept her up into my arms, but we're the same height and weight—that we both admit to. What's ten pounds one way or the other, hmm? (Trade you the manly giggle for the weight reference, sweetheart.) It wouldn't make a positive impression if I dumped us both on our derrieres. Instead I stepped behind her, wrapped my arms around her waist and hoisted her off the floor. Then I carted her into the living room, where I sat us both down in a beat-up armchair that had come with the rental. She struggled, really put some effort into it, but I managed to keep her pinned on my lap.

"Jim!"

"Denise!" I countered. Clever repartee, eh?

"Is this going to take long," she muttered, squirming. "Seriously, Meyer. I have to…"

"Only as long as it takes you to say 'yes'."

Yeah, that shut her up. No further explanations were required. She simply pivoted at the waist and stared. "Yes?"

"Yes. As in…"

"Will I marry you?"

"Did you have to step on my line? I was about to say, 'I love you, and you love me. We've just bought a house together that I presume you know was not intended for investment purposes. That I mean for you to live in it. With me.' " I grinned. Probably looked stupid doing it, but a lopsided grin was better than another cute but masculine giggle. "Then I would have said, 'Why not marry me, while we're at it?' We'll save on taxes."

Denise laughed. Then cried. Then kissed me. And finally closed the deal with a heartfelt "I swore you would never get around to it. Of course, *yes*. You big dumb."

I was considering turning my successful proposal into a pre-honeymoon moment, when Denise wriggled out of my lap and stood up.

"Hey, where you going?"

She lifted one shoulder in apology. "I have to pee," she said. "Your timing was atrocious."

True. But it's a great story to tell our grandkids.

To speed things up, we can segue through the wedding planning in a single paragraph. Denise did the bulk of it, and I did a lot of nodding. Live polka band? Sure. Tailcoats and cummerbunds? Why not, I'm skinny. A wedding cake designed to look like a cathedral? Made by the bride's mother and sister? You bet. I'd seen their work and it was awesome. Not to mention, free. Include *all* of our siblings in the wedding party? The more the merrier. With Danny and Brooke as ring bearer and flower girl, the total lined up at the altar in Holy Rosary Cathedral would be sixteen. I do admit I would have balked at the salmon-colored shirts that matched the bridesmaids' dresses, but my fiancee pointed out that only my groomsmen would wear them. My shirt would be ivory to match her gown. Now, *that* I could get behind. Sorry, boys. Get your own wife if you want to dodge that bullet.

The only bone of contention was the honeymoon destination. Denise wanted to go to New York. I agreed it would be fun and a nostalgic choice, seeing as how we both loved live theater and we *had* met during an audition. But I futzed around, complaining it would be an expensive trip. Not to mention, neither of us had ever been to New York. The place was massive. Dangerous. We could get lost. Mugged. Something.

None of those were my real reason, but Denise bought into the package.

Then she suggested we be crazy traditional and go to Niagara Falls. After all, it was newlywed approved, steeped in romance, and smaller, more manageable. Less chance of getting lost. Plus, it had the money-saving advantage of being relatively close. We could drive to it in around seven hours. Again, I had objections. Niagara was a cliche. Ridiculously touristy. And after you've seen water spill in mega-tons over a cliff, what else was there to do? Besides sex, of course. Which would be excellent, but didn't she want a few extras? What were the restaurants like? We'd have to exchange American dollars for Canadian. Wouldn't we need passports?

She gave me a piercing stare. I swear I could feel it penetrate my brain pan and melt chunks of grey matter on its way out the other side. "All right, Jim," she said. "Where do *you* want to go?"

St. Louis.

My older sister, Jan, had honeymooned in St. Louis and they'd had a grand time. They'd even seen a semi-tractor trailer with a camel painted on the side declaring *Humpin' to Please.* Had photos of it in their wedding album. "I mean, how funny is that?" I coaxed. "Like a cosmic sign or something. Come to St. Louis. It's *the* place for honeymooners."

Denise said nothing.

"Humping? Honeymoon?"

More nothing.

Maybe she didn't get it.

"And there's the Arch," I pointed out, putting the pedal to the metal as I surged ahead, a tireless advocate for the St. Louis Board of Tourism. (Maybe the only.) I began to tick off the high points on my fingers. "Midwest affordability. Lots of restaurants of all kinds. Indian burial mounds. Mountains. Caves. Woods. Picturesque farmland. An old paddlewheel boat docked on the Mississippi." I gave her my winningest smile. "Plus, I know my way around."

Here's the thing. My mother's family lives in and around St. Louis, and I'd been to many a sprawling family reunion. Hanging out with all those uncles, aunts, and cousins—more than a hundred of them—was a highlight of my childhood. My mom's mother, Grandma Daugherty, (eighty-six years old at the time and counting) lived there. All Mom's brothers and sisters did, too. The house she'd been born in still stood, though now abandoned. I'd run around it inside and out since the day I could toddle. Everyone called it The Old House—capital T, capital O, capital H. For huge. It was rumored to have been a stop on the underground railroad. Tin roof. Root cellar dug into the ground out back. Didn't even have indoor plumbing. I couldn't wait to show it off to my soon-to-be wife.

Couldn't wait to show *her* off to the Daugherty clan.

Now, I know St. Louis was not Denise's idea of a dream honeymoon, but I can be damn adorable when I try. "Humping to please?" I whispered into her delicate shell-like ear.

She sighed.

We went to St. Louis.

Did you know Missouri is pronounced Missouruh, *not* Missouree? That's according to my mother, Patricia Daugherty Meyer, a native, so she ought to know. Please respect her wishes from here on out.

Any way you say it, I had plenty of other names for the state before the honeymoon ended.

How was I to know that the week we'd booked would fall smack in the middle of a killer heatwave? Killer being the operative word. It was ninety-nine in Toledo the day we wed, with a hundred percent humidity. Quite a trick when you add in the fact that it didn't rain. All that water just hung in the air, soaking into every conceivable bit of wedding lace and tuxedo gaberdine. We sweltered. But St. Louis? Over one hundred and fifty citizens of Missouri died while temperatures hovered at historic highs topping one hundred and ten. That's actual degrees. Fahrenheit. The heat index was considerably higher. I know this because the death count was the first thing we picked up on the radio as we passed the Welcome to St. Louis billboard. We'd been twisting the dial back and forth, looking for a strong signal and music other than country-western. What we got was a running tally of just how bad a mistake we'd made coming here in the middle of July.

Okay, *I'd* made.

My dad had loaned us his car for the trip, knowing my Mazda was unreliable and Denise's Sebring had no AC. Smart man, my dad. Nonetheless, once we'd crossed the bridge over Ol' Miss, the heat gauge began to redline and the engine muttered in protest all the way to the Holiday Inn.

Okay, not the Niagara Hilton, but it *was* one of the chain's newest deluxe models: indoor pool, sauna, surprisingly upscale restaurant, and an indoor courtyard boasting leafy trees and flowering foliage—foliage that wasn't wilted or dried to a crisp from the heat, like the poor relations outside the windows. A pretty place, romantic even. Denise had no complaints. Neither did our now-joint checking account.

From the moment we arrived, avoiding the heat became a way of life. The newly minted Mr. and Mrs. Meyer found themselves hustling between one air-conditioned space and another, one Big Gulp and the next, wiping sweat out of their eyes, and trying to pretend they'd packed the perfect lightweight clothes to make the whole experience bearable. We had not. It was not.

It didn't stop us from doing and seeing everything I'd promised, though. On day two, we went up inside the Gateway Arch, cozied together in an elevator car the size and shape of a commercial clothes dryer. Day three: we cruised the rolling foothills on the outer reaches of town, admiring the rustic beauty and testing the car's endurance. Then, despite my professed knowledge of the area, managed to get ourselves turned around in the woods at nightfall—which, when you are waaaay out past the city lights, doesn't so much fall as slam.

Day four saw us touring Meramec Caverns where Jesse James and his brother once hid out from the law. Truth? The caverns were the coolest place we visited. Literally. It's a steady fifty-eight degrees underground at all times, as opposed to the one hundred and fifty-eight degrees it felt like above.

We even found a romantic seafood place and had crab legs for the first time. I would reorder them on numerous occasions at other restaurants, but they were never quite as succulent as the ones we shared together that evening of day five.

We also took in the picturesque farmland around Grandma Daugherty's tiny ranch house where we stopped so the matriarch could welcome the newest female into the fold. After that, we moved on to more spectacular vistas around Grandma's original home, The Old House.

It was day six and Denise was being a sport, running up and down the hill beside the hundred-year-old farmhouse, joining me as I relived my childhood. She even ducked under the humming combs of mud dauber wasps on the porch ceiling to peek in the windows. Sadly, the doors of The Old House were locked. My Uncle Glennon and Aunt Kate who lived across the dirt road from the place told us the mining company that owned the land had taken security precautions. We whiled away the hot afternoon in Glennon and Kate's kitchen, draining tall sweaty glasses of lemonade over talk of the tornadoes that had hammered the area the week before and toppled a giant oak across the only road in and out of the property. Uncle Glennon had been forced to take a chainsaw to it, bit by bit, to clear a path so they could go out for groceries. The lopped off hunks of thick trunk probably still line the double-tracks of dirt that direct visitors through a shallow creek to the site of The Old House.

In the end, Denny had to agree: the trip had been the time of our life.

As we repacked our luggage on day last, the only highlights we'd not enjoyed were the paddle-wheeler docked on the Mississippi in downtown St. Louis, and the Indian burial mounds. With no more than a morning left for sightseeing, we decided on a quick trip to the mounds on our way out of town.

It wasn't quick enough.

Temperatures had begun to abate in Greater St. Louis but were still plenty hot on top of those ancient grave sites. The sun battered us from all directions, stinging the eyes and softening the soles of our tennis shoes. There were no trees. Not even tall bushes. Nowhere to sit, unless it was on our asses on the ground. I don't think we stayed longer than half an hour before trotting back to the car—at a dead heat (hardy har har)—where we yanked open the doors and cranked down the windows to release the superheated air trapped inside. The upholstery left char marks on the backs of our thighs, like chicken on a Coleman. Finally, with the AC set on Arctic, we pointed the grill toward Toledo and home.

"Well," I said. "What do you think?"

"About the mounds? Not so impressed. But worth a look-see."

"No. About the trip. Was it everything I promised?" Now that it was over, I was feeling a mite insecure.

A grin formed beneath her oversized sunglasses. "Almost."

"Almost?"

"Well."

"Yeah? Spit it out."

She cranked that grin on full and shifted to face me, pulling one knee up on the seat (risking additional second-degree burns). "As I recall, you promised me some humping to please, Meyer. And on that, you did *not* deliver."

Turned the way she was, away from the passenger-side window, she nearly missed it.

A tractor-trailer whizzed by in the opposite lane heading west as we streaked away going east. A leggy cartoon camel stretched out along its side like a thoroughbred racing for the finish at the Kentucky Derby. Bracketing that laughing, steam-snorting dromedary was a three-word slogan.

Yep. All together, now… *Humpin' to Please.*

We would learn later that the spokes-camel had a name, Snortin' Norton, and the trucking company that bore his image was Campbell 66. It had been a good-sized firm in its heyday, around 1950-1970, with hundreds of trailers working stops along Route 66 from St. Louis to Springfield. By the time we saw Norton's foolish face in person, deregulation had been steadily whittling away at the company. Only a fraction of its fleet still worked the roads of Missouri during that July of 1980. Campbell 66 would go bankrupt six years later.

"There! There! There!" I screamed. Denise spun around just in time. I was thinking about slamming on the brakes and cutting across the median to give chase. "Do you have the camera?" I hollered. "Where's the camera?"

Denise couldn't even answer me. Both of us were dissolving into fits of laughter, snorting along with Norton, as he sped out of sight.

"Damn. We should have had the camera."

Denise patted my knee, and sucked snot back into her nose. Such a sexy thing, my new wife. "It's okay," she hiccuped. "I wouldn't have." Another snort. "Let you." A fast swipe of her palms across tearing eyes. "Put it."

She couldn't spit the last of it out until she'd hiccuped one final time. "In the wedding album."

I don't think we stopped snickering and giggling until we hit the Illinois border.

Postscript: We'd planned to drive ten or so hours straight that day, figuring we'd pull into our home-sweet-home driveway by midnight.

Didn't happen. My stomach began its revolt an hour after waving goodbye to Snortin' Norton. My head added a steady bing-bang-boom during hour two. Denise feared I'd become dehydrated following our desert assault on the Indian burial mounds. She insisted we pull off for fluids at the next Fork and Spoon icon. I think that exit offered our choice of Mickey Dees or BK. We opted for Coke, and supersized it.

It didn't help. It was like my body was sucking up the moisture and sweating it back out—but without the sweat. We continued to stop every hour thereafter, but switched to water. My gut was not amused and kept trying to send anything I swallowed back the way it had come.

We surrendered somewhere west of Indianapolis, picking the first motel we came to. Didn't even unload luggage. Just asked for a room and staggered inside. Correction. I staggered. Denise worried her lower lip.

You know how cheap-to-moderate motels can be, right? No matter where you set the thermostat it's either too hot or too cold. I would have thrown a party for too cold, but only lukewarm accepted our invitation.

By this time, Denise was borderline panicky. Kept checking my forehead, an action that was annoying the hell out of me. Which did *its* part by annoying the hell out of her. We'd not eaten lunch or dinner, my stomach being on strike, but I did tell her to go grab something. Okay, yes, sorta Walter Matthau in *Grumpy Old Men*. But in my defense: I was wishing I felt well enough to join her and hating her the tiniest bit for even considering going without me. Flip side: Denise was starving, but felt obligated not to leave me alone. The result: we grumbled under our breaths at each other, went foodless, and swallowed our mutual irritation. Not so tasty.

When I complained my head was spinning, Denise checked it again —"What? Like you think it's going somewhere?" I bitched.

It's true. Men are not good patients. I, at least, do not do sick gracefully.

Denise growled something I didn't catch but I assumed would have made a Marine blush. Then she said, louder this time, "You are burning up."

Thank you, Mrs. Obvious.

"Get your clothes off."

It tells you something about my state of mind that I did not think she meant that in a provocative, come-to-mama way.

I stripped and nearly stumbled to my knees doing it. She in the meantime filled the bathtub with the coldest water she could strangle from the tap.

I climbed in, slid down until my chin touched wet, and dropped into a coma. Or so I was told later. Denise wandered in and out over the next hour, making sure I didn't drown, draining the water when it grew too warm, and adding more cold as needed. Finally, she was able to rouse me, drag my limp self over the side of the tub, and maneuver me to the room's sole double bed.

The second coma grabbed me before my head met pillow.

Denise left me there, naked, sprawled motionless atop the spread, and went in search of a protein boost. She settled for a bag of pretzels and a can of Faygo Orange from a vending machine outside our door. With my body still pumping out heat, though probably only slightly above 100 now, she absconded with the spare pillows and spread them on the floor next to the bed. From there she could lie down, watch television, and reach up periodically to make sure my body temps were continuing to fall.

As reassured as she could be, she settled in to hear former actor Ronald Reagan accept the Republican Party nomination for president.

By around three in the morning, Denise decided I was teasing 98.6 again. She climbed under the covers on the other side of the bed, leaving me to finish cooling off on top. By morning, I was fine, ready to tuck into a huge breakfast. Crisis averted.

The event would become legend in our family. Newlywed Denise Meyer shared the final twenty-four hours of her honeymoon with Snortin' Norton, a comatose heatstroke patient, and the 40th President of the United States. How many new wives can say that, I want to know?

And she wanted to go to New York. *Pffft.*

Chapter Void: Pieces

I'm not hot anymore. Actually, I'm shivering. Cold water must be working. Not doing anything for my head, though. It's banging like old plumbing. Worse than ever.

Where are we again?

Indianapolis. That's right.

Isn't it?

Can't tell for sure because nothing is clear. My eyes are open, but the air is full of steam. Maybe static. A red mist.

"Hey, buddy? You all right?"

It's a male voice. One I don't recognize. The desk clerk? Did Denise call for an ambulance? I've been worrying about that. Let's not go overboard, babe. It's not that bad. Stop fussing. I just need to rest and cool off.

But I am so damned cold.

Something wet and warm trickles out of my ears. My nose, too. Must have dozed off and slipped down inside the tub, sucked in a little water.

"Guy? Do you live here? Is this your house?"

I try to tell him, *No. This is a motel, you idiot. Your motel.* But I think I insulted him because he groans.

Wait. Was that me? Did I just do that?

"Hold on, okay? Lie still. Let me go get somebody."

I call to him as he moves away. *Don't need help. Just give me a minute.* I think to myself, *Sit up.* My knees are bent, my feet already flat on the floor of the tub, so I stretch my arms out at my sides, palms down, prepared to push.

It's as far as I can go. Maybe I need that ambulance after all. Damn. Not looking too macho, James. What a bad impression to make on your wife on the last night of your honeymoon.

A rope of fear tightens around my throat. My wife. Where is she? *Hey, man! Wait. Find Denise, will you?*

Don't leave me here alone. I need my wife.

Denise.

Honey?

I think she should come feel my head.

Hurry.

I think it has gone somewhere after all.

Chapter Five: Click

If you think you've avoided one of my backstory prologues, think again.

I need to point out that when Denise and I got engaged in November 1979, it was for the second time. The first engagement was in February '78, and I blame Oscar the ghost entirely.

While you ponder all the ways those sentences are disturbing, I will flip a coin to decide where to start my explanation.

Heads.

Oscar it is.

After my stunning debut as an undertaker in *Send Me No Flowers,* the Washington Local School District, of which Whitmer High School is a part, discontinued class plays.

I swear, it was not my fault.

The productions had become a financial drain on class treasuries, so the powers-that-be opted instead to offer a winter play, funded by a one-time stipend. Auditions would be open to the entire school, and any future winter productions would hinge on the success of the one that came before. Make money? On with the show. Lose money? The curtain falls.

Denise Tomanski would direct.

Having wowed her once with my skills, I was confident I would score a role in that year's pick, *Mousetrap* by Dame Agatha Christie. The choice would turn out to be good news for the new financial format. Not so much for Dame Christie or myself.

The mistress of who-done-its died weeks prior to our show's opening, and every magazine, newspaper, TV report, and radio talkshow in the country mentioned how *Mousetrap* held the record for longest running stage show in history. As a result, tickets for our production sold out overnight. Sorry you passed away, Dame Aggie, but thank you very much for the free publicity.

As for me? I did not get a role. *Mousetrap* features a small ensemble cast, where every player must deliver long involved important speeches—something I had already proven I sucked at. Through a straw. Hard enough to flatten it. Miss Tomanski did, however, recognize young Meyer's budding skills at electronics and asked (begged?) him to take on the role of Stage Manager. Which he graciously did.

She was never going to be rid of me again. So thanks again, dear Agatha, from the bottom of my heart.

From that point on, I and two other Whitmer grads, my friend Jeff and my then-girlfriend Debbie, would make an annual trek back to those hallowed halls to volunteer our services for the winter show: hanging lights, manning the tech board, building sets, and slapping greasepaint on the next generation of high school thespians.

We three were also instrumental in spreading—and enhancing—the myth of Oscar.

Every good theater is haunted. Whitmer was no exception. Over the years, scads of students had sworn they saw a male figure, dressed in black pants, white shirt and black vest, sitting in the upper right corner of the auditorium. Never when you looked straight at him, mind you. Only as a blur out of the corner of your eye when he appeared to rise or sit.

Our generation had nicknamed him Oscar for his unfailing ability to turn even an ordinary performance into an award winner. Example? In the play *The Impossible Years,* a painter wannabe with visions of becoming the next Jackson Pollock points with a flourish at a framed monstrosity hanging on the back wall. "That, sir," he proclaims, "is not a *mess.* It is Vincent

Schmedlapp's *View of the Bronx*." The line always earned a chuckle from the audience—until the night the painting "slipped" off its nail and slid down the wall with a crash. Right on cue. Like an exclamation point at the end of *Bronx*. That night? The line got a howl and its own round of applause.

Oscar. With a little help from his friends.

Stuff like that happened so often, in fact, casts began anticipating Oscar's tricks. And I and my cohorts were happy to oblige.

In 1978, Miss Tomanski—now Denise or Denny Lou to us old-timers in the inner circle—selected *Wait Until Dark* for the winter show. It's a thriller about a blind woman who accidentally acquires a doll filled with heroin. A trio of bad guys pretend to be a trio of good guys to con her into handing it over.

Jeff, Debbie, Denise and I were enjoying a pizza after rehearsal one night when the discussion about The Gag first came up.

"So, what's it going to be this year, guys?" Denise asked.

I shrugged, mouth full of pepperoni.

"I'm thinking it ought to be a con of some kind," Jeff put in between swigs of beer.

"Oscar's going to con the cast?" queried Debbie.

Denise dabbed tomato sauce off her chin. "Oscar isn't capable of anything that subtle."

"He is if we help him." That was from me.

"Help how?"

"We set up our own con. Everyone knows it's us anyway."

There were nods from around the table as the pizza slowly disappeared. Oscar would do what Oscar would do. Team Tomanski would add flourishes. Every cast had found us out eventually.

"So?" said Jeff. "What's the con?"

Denise thought a minute, grinned wickedly, then nodded at Debbie and me. "You guys should pretend you got married." Her expression said this was a wonderful idea. I was cool to it. Things were up and down between me and Deb. Married seemed a bit of a stretch.

"Nah," Jeff intervened, to my relief. "Too easy. No conning required. It's got to be fantastically impossible. Ridiculous, even. Like… I don't know. Like *you and Jim* ran off and got married. Now *that* would be ridiculous."

Maybe I was being thin-skinned. Or perhaps I was eager to prove my acting chops once and for all. "I could pull that off."

Denise snorted beer into her sinuses. When she was done choking, she laughed. "No way, Meyer. I would never run off to tie the knot. It's a full-on white wedding extravaganza for *moi*."

"Okay," I countered. "So we'll pretend we got engaged."

From there, The Gag developed into The Con. We all agreed we would do nothing to spread the rumor ourselves. We would leave it up to the cast to stick their own heads in the noose. I would simply start picking Denise up for rehearsals and dropping her at home afterwards. Debbie would refuse to talk to me any time cast members were around. Jeff would pretend to be caught in the middle. Denise drew a line at painting our initials inside a heart on the back of one of the flats. She did agree to let me pop in between classes now and then for lunch. No close encounters. Just soup, sandwiches and something for students to gossip about.

By the way, there's a sidebar to this story. Second by-the-way: isn't sidebar nicer than saying Jim's gotten off track again and is heading for Katmandu?

So. Sidebar: Denise and I had been arguing a lot that year during rehearsals. Over the damnedest things, too. Like why hadn't I finished bracing that back wall yet? And why didn't she recognize I was doing this for free? And why the hell couldn't I get to the theater on time? And why did it always escape her attention I had a nine-to-five job?

I threatened to quit. Figured maybe this partnership had run its course. She considered firing me (quite a trick since I was a volunteer). Wondered what had happened to that sweet agreeable kid.

And therein lay the problem. I wasn't a kid anymore and she wasn't Miss Tomanski. Our relationship had changed and we both were struggling to get comfortable with the new fit. Turned out, those impromptu lunches helped. Just two people sharing an inside joke and a laugh.

During one such lunch, she brought me flowers, and apologized. Yeah. Pretty cool. Told me she would make a greater effort to ask my opinion and not spout orders like I was slave labor. I tried not to gloat and withdrew my resignation.

After the apology we stopped arguing.

And I decided to buy her a ring.

For The Con, guys, The Con. Stop trying to read ahead.

Now, to call what I bought a zirconium would be blatant flattery. The plastic bag it came in was emblazoned with a big red K. And to be honest? It was a doorknob masquerading as a ring: a hunk of glass (perhaps plastic) set in a circle of sterling (perhaps plastic). Totally unbelievable.

The silly thing fit.

We laughed ourselves hoarse. I suspect someone upstairs was laughing, too. But I'm only guessing.

As for the rest of The Con, everything went according to plan. Oscar's partners in crime kept their lips zipped. None of us talked about rings or engagements. But it didn't matter. Cast member mouths were flapping within days. Had we called it, or what?

What we had *not* anticipated was that the entire school would join in. A male teacher Denise hung out with even cornered her to ask if there was something she wanted to tell him before he shelled out for a movie that weekend.

Too late to back out now.

We revealed The Con at the cast party on closing night, and I did the honors. As actors and crew members gathered round, I held up Denise's hand to display Fake Diamond. "You've probably all noticed this by now," I began, my voice dripping with emotion. (Eat your heart out, Brad Pitt.)

"Can't keep a secret from you guys. But I don't think you recognize its true value to me."

Eyes were brimming, girls were sighing.

I slipped the ring from Denny Lou's finger, held it up alongside my open can of Bud Lite. "Six dollars and ninety-five cents," I said. Then I dropped it inside the can, sloshed it around a little. "It was a Blue Light special, you goons. You've been conned."

I don't remember much after that. The four of us were hoisted into the air and whisked outside to be deposited in snow drifts up to our elbows. All around us outraged teenagers laughed, screeched, and protested.

Complete success. A masterpiece of trickery. Two thumbs up from the critics.

So why was Denise sitting so quietly beside me on the ride back home? Why was I feeling so low? I mean, we'd pulled it off. Best gag on a cast ever. They'd talk about it for years. We should have been celebrating.

It was over.

I pulled up in front of the entrance to her apartment, put the car into park, and made an effort to laugh. "You were a sport, Tomanski. Thanks."

She chuckled. Sort of. "It was the ring. Your idea for that, Meyer. Did you get it back?"

Was that the tiniest bit plaintive?

"Yep." I pulled it out of my jacket pocket and held it up. It caught the light from a parking lot security pole, and twinkled. Ah, the power of halogens. "Want it?"

"May I?"

"No problem. Doesn't fit me."

Neither of us spoke as she placed it back on her finger and wiggled her hand. "Not one bit real."

"Nope."

"Worked."

"Yep."

"Well."

We were running out of monosyllable dialogue.

"I don't know what I'm going to do with all my extra time, now that the show is over," she confessed.

"Start planning for next year?"

"Probably." She paused, gave me a look. "Are you going to come back?"

Not: "Are you *guys* going to come back?" You. Singular.

"Wouldn't miss it."

She grinned and it lit up the car. "Great! Same time next year then."

When she stopped grinning, I felt the loss like a punch in the gut.

"Well."

"Right."

I was afraid we were going to start over from the top so I ad libbed. "Don't forget the cashbox."

It was resting in the middle of the backseat.

She inhaled, startled. "Oh wow, yeah."

She turned to her left and reached for it at the same moment I twisted to the right aiming for the same destination.

Our faces ended up inches apart. Like a grade B chick flick. There might have been music swelling. On the lowest setting. In the background. Maybe.

I kissed her, wondering if I'd lost my mind.

She kissed me back.

It spun out longer than friendship, just shy of Holy Hell.

She broke away first.

"Oh geez. I'm sorry." She pushed hair out of her eyes. "Chalk that up to method acting or something, okay? Still caught up in the role, I guess." She grinned at me—but nothing like the first grin. This was a silent pat on the head. "We'll laugh about this tomorrow. Promise."

I studied her eyes. And smiled in return. I felt the difference and so did she. This was not the smile of a kid who would be patted on his way. A foot was in the door, and the man studying her carefully was prepared to kick it wide open.

That's when it hit me. *So this was what all the arguing was about.*

Click.

Chapter Void: Sounds

I'm not in the bathtub.

Not in Indianapolis.

My vision is still offline, so where I am is a murky question mark.

Denise has come and gone and come again, a pale oval haloed in sunshine against grey gauze. I can't actually see it's her, but I know her scent. Would recognize her voice in a crowded concert hall. "Jim!" she cries the first time she hovers above me. "Jim! Oh, Jesus. Jim."

I've heard that fearful timbre once before—can't quite get a handle on when that was or why. It makes me shiver.

"Don't move."

She's leaving me, the grey gauze rushing in to fill the space. "Don't let him move," she orders. It comes out as a squeak.

Wait, I holler. *Where are you going?*

I start to panic, but she comes back fast.

Suddenly I don't feel so freaking crazy miserably cold.

The afghan, I think. The one we got as a wedding gift from her aunt. My wife is wrapping it gently around me. My wife? So she said yes, eh? Good. Very good.

"What happened?" she asks.

I was hoping you'd tell me, I wisecrack. She doesn't seem to hear me, so I try again.

And hear myself answering in someone else's voice. "There was a noise," NotMe says. "I turned around and saw this guy. In your driveway. Not moving."

Denise's driveway. That's where I am. But her apartment complex doesn't have a driveway. Just a parking lot. Maybe that's what NotMe is talking about.

I do remember that parking lot.

Finally. Something I know for sure. A plastic ring. A kiss. A promise to myself not to let her put things back the way they were.

NotMe continues talking without my consent. "Saw a light on in your kitchen. Ran to your back porch."

Back porch? Kitchen? Denise's apartment kitchen doesn't have a window. Or a porch. A small deck. Is that what I mean? And that doesn't clear up the mystery of what we are doing in the parking lot.

I want to ask her, but she is rushing away again. This time, I hear her bare feet slapping against concrete.

You're gonna catch your death, I holler.

Sounds of silence. Then a quick intake of breath. The yelp of a rubber sole scuffing a smooth surface. The noises are soft but my head ricochets with them. The pain is awesome. *Denny,* I call out. *Got any Tylenol?* Damn, this hurts. All in the base of my skull.

It's the hard ground. That's what it is. Pressing up and up and up through bone, a spike of torment digging for a target it has yet to reach. I groan. *Yes, that's really me.* I roll onto my side to escape that pillow of concrete.

"Hey! Don't do that."

A hand grips my shoulder and I slug it away. *Don't touch me, asshole.*

Two quick shoe yelps and the hand jerks back. *Get lost,* I tell NotMe. *This is not your driveway.*

Not your story. Not your wife. Not your pain.

Mine.

Something is not right.

The sounds around me are ratcheting up. I hear a sharp whistle. It's the wind rising to rattle a skeleton above my head, bare bones clicking and clacking like castanets. There's another softer rattle, too: a pellet-like noise that matches the icy shrapnel tickling the side of my face. I bat at it, just as angrily as I did NotMe. I'm more furious than I ought to be, but I just don't want anyone or anything to touch me.

Except Denny. Who isn't here. Has not returned. *Hey, hon. What's the hold up?*

Her voice comes to me from far away. Like all the sounds left to me, it is an anchor. I hold on tight. Pull it close. "…he fell. I need an ambulance…"

Ambulance? Yes. Definitely. Not sure why, but yes. Come help her, somebody. Hurry.

"…stay on the line. I'm going to talk to emergency services. What's your name?"

"I already told…"

"Your first name."

"Denise."

"Okay, Denise, I'm with you now. I'm going to go away for a bit to get you some help. Denise? Stay calm. I'll be right back."

Okay then. She won't be alone. I can wait. Help is coming.

I listen in as a kind voice relays instructions. "…keep him immobile and warm…"

"Doing that…"

"Is there someone close by you can call to come be with you?"

"Oh geez, yeah. My brother…"

"Do that, Denise. An ambulance is on the way. God be with you."

There's a pause in the conversation. A long tone, a series of beeps too pleasant and musical for the occasion. The ring of a phone. My hyper hearing picks it up like stereo: one ring heard through a telephone receiver in Denise's kitchen. *My kitchen? Yes. Mine.* Another from inside a house two doors down.

It rings and rings and rings.

Then a disconnect. A second tone. More musical beeps and bloops. More ringing. This time, though, one of the stereo speakers is one street over—I think. But it might as well be miles. It, too, goes forever unanswered.

No one's home, I realize with absolute clarity.

This will be the last time in my present life that I muster my thoughts so clearly. A last chance at coherence before the fog of pain drags me under. *Christmas shopping. Everyone's doing last minute shopping.* My brother-in-law and his family. My mother- and father-in-law who live a street behind our house. *Our house. Not Denise's apartment.* My driveway.

My house. Lit up like Christmas. Because it is.

I fell.

That hurts too much to think about. I shove it into our coat closet and slam the door. *Call my dad,* I holler. It comes out as a gargle, but I keep trying. *Dad will come. Dad will know what to do.* He lives farther away than anyone in Denise's family, but that won't stop him. He'll fly to us. *Smartest man I know, my dad. A doctor, too.* I know now I need one. Bad.

"Hello?"

Mom! Thank God. Mom, get Dad.

"Jim fell," Denise says without preamble. "He's hurt. Really hurt. An ambulance is coming…"

Mom takes over, like only she can do. Cool, calm—but I feel the touch of her stress like a kiss on a bruised knee. She is sensing what I already know: Denise is scared. "You called for help. Just as you should have. Smart. Now, stay with him. Your father is coming. He'll meet you at the hospital. Everything is going to be all right." Mom believes this. We all will believe it for several more hours.

"And, Denise," she adds before she hangs up. "Tell them to take him to Saint V's. You hear me? Tell them who Jim is. Who his father is. Don't let them take you anywhere else."

"I won't. Thank you. I'll tell them. I'll drive the thing myself if I have to." Denise is trying to defuse the dread that swamps them both. It almost works.

There's a click as the phone call ends. More sounds of silence. Even NotMe has stuffed a sock in it.

Then it reaches my ear. Over the wind. Over the wild lub-dub of my scrambling heart. Over Denise's sobbing breaths as she runs, again barefoot, outside and to my side.

It's the scrabble of tiny fingers against glass. The thump whump thump of tiny fists on a storm door. "Dada. Out. Out." It's a cheerful sound, and I welcome it. So much better than rattling bones and empty phone calls.

Just a kiddo wanting to go outside and join in the play.

Oh, Jesus. We have kids.

Chapter Six: Oscar Meyer

Turned out, we brought an extra souvenir back from St. Louis. It wouldn't arrive for nine months and three days from the date of our wedding, but Denise had a hunch it was coming. She had a funky dizzy spell in the middle of the afternoon less than two weeks after we settled into the lull between "Here comes the bride" and "What do you mean I don't fold your jockeys right?"

At the time, she was babysitting for her sister Daria's two-year-old daughter, Jennifer. Denny met me at the door when I got home from work, her hand thrust down to catch little Houdini before she could escape to the porch. My shiny new wife had a gleam in her eye that made me wonder how fast I could get out of my clothes. And what to do with the potential witness.

Whoops. Wrong gleam altogether.

"Meyer," she said. "I think we're pregnant."

We'd had the Do We or Don't We talk before we'd exchanged vows, and had decided we did, we really did. We wanted to start a family as soon as possible. But, holy cow, if she was right? My boys had worked fast. On behalf of feminists everywhere, I will add that Denise's girls hadn't been slouches either. (When two years later Jimmy came along at the same record pace, we decided all we had to do was say the word sex in unison and we could add Huggies to our grocery list.)

"Are you sure?" While still my fiancee, Denise had been taking the pill, but as W Day grew closer, she'd tossed the refills. "Didn't Dad say it could take six months or longer for your system to adjust?"

Oh, didn't I mention that? Yeah, my father was Denise's gynecologist. Dad offered his services to all the women in the family, my sisters included. Denise had been thrilled. Doc Meyer had the largest practice in the city, and was highly respected in the field. His fellow physicians would vote him Chief of Staff at St. Vincent Medical Center a few years down the line. In my wife's opinion, we and our babies-to-come couldn't do better than William J. Meyer, M.D.

"He said it *could* take that long." Denise hoisted Jenny to her hip, giving her niece a fond kiss on the head. It was a glimpse of the mother she would be —and it looked damn good on her. "He was wrong."

"You've missed a period?"

"Not yet. But I will." Denise went on to explain the weird dizzy spell and how it just felt... *different*. Like nothing she had ever experienced before.

Huh. I hadn't realized dizziness had levels of subtext. But, hey, her body. If Denny Lou said we were knocked up, I was willing to bet the hammer had swung.

There was considerable scoffing when she called the office of Diethelm, Meyer, Rost and Sharma to discuss an appointment. And it didn't let up the following Sunday during a visit to my old homestead.

"No one gets pregnant on their honeymoon," my father said, the voice of authority backed by years of experience and a medical degree. "It's a myth." He was planted, legs spread, in front of the fireplace, arms crossed, speaking around the stem of a pipe he held tight in his teeth. Dad is a taller, older version of me, with bushy hair just beginning to whiten. He hadn't completed his metamorphosis into Santa yet, but the belly was getting there, and he'd nailed the laugh and twinkle.

My mom was knitting something—I can't remember a time when she wasn't—eyes on her flying needles, a cup of coffee cooling at her side. Imagine Judi Dench with salt-and-pepper hair, wearing a red plaid shirt, and minus the snooty Dame thing in front of her name. That's my mom. Has the same dry tone, too. She didn't look up from her knitting, simply spoke. "Of course they do. Just because *we* didn't, Bill, doesn't mean..."

"Humph," my father interrupted, puffing on his pipe. Was that a you're-right humph, or a no-way humph? Hard to tell. "Now, when she misses…"

"She doesn't have to," Mom put in. She wrapped a curl of yarn around a needle, flicked it right then left, and added another curl. "They're pretty accurate, right…?"

Dad's pipe was sending smoke signals that I suspected spelled, "Yes. Yes they are." But he was hedging his bet. "Not always."

Denise and I exchanged smiles. It was always a treat to watch my folks communicate in couples-speak. I wanted to be like them when we grew up.

Mom's turn: "Of course, not always. They know that. You can always do another."

That one threw me. Maybe too many dangling whatchamacallits. "Another what?"

Mom halted at the end of a chain of stitches, slipped a needle through the last one to hold it in place. She gave my dad a quick smile, then picked up her coffee for a sip. Spoke over the rim: "Stop teasing them, Bill."

About that coffee. (Yep, another zig and zag, but I'll be fast.) Everyone knew the coffee in my mother's mug was usually cold, but she never seemed to mind. She would stay on task for hours, not stopping for top-offs until she hit a convenient endpoint. The results were gallons of Maxwell House consumed cold, and closets bulging with handmade treasures. Eventually an entire bedroom would be set aside to hold the hundreds of crocheted, knitted, sewn and quilted items Patrica Meyer crafted with exquisite detail. Every family member for a couple of generations would own at least one of her prized quilts. Brooke's flower girl dress for our wedding had been designed by my mom to match Denise's gown down to the last stitch.

So, Mom's coffee was always cold, in contrast to the warmth of her heart. A day would come when my daughter would beg to share both every time we came to visit: a sip of Grandma's cold coffee and a "noisy hug." At the time, however, Denise and I didn't know for sure we had a daughter, or any other flavor of bun, in the oven.

We would soon enough.

Dad chortled, rubbed his hands together like a giddy mad scientist, and dashed off to the master bedroom. When he returned, he was holding a plastic medical cup.

"Okay, let's do this thing."

The decade had not yet arrived when couples could saunter off to the drugstore for a pee stick. But they no longer had to wait weeks after giving a shot of blood to see if the rabbit died either. So when Dad pulled my wife out from under my arm and pointed her toward the bathroom, I had an inkling of what was afoot. He handed my wife the cup, and instructed her, not-so-discreetly, to "give me a sample, dear. It would be best if we did this first thing in the morning, but it might show up anyway."

He gave me a wink over her shoulder. "Don't worry if it comes back negative. Doesn't mean you're not carrying, only that it's too soon for the test to read."

Denise's expression as she rolled the cup between the palms of her hands told me she was wondering if she could produce on command. My brave soldier squared her shoulders, and vanished behind the bathroom door.

Dad took up a position outside, swaying and puffing. Then for no rhyme nor reason, he removed the pipe from his mouth and sang, "I love a parade!" Off key, but with considerable enthusiasm. Dad was always belting out tunes with little warning. For him silence wasn't golden; it was a signal to cue the orchestra. This was still new territory for my wife, however; so I could imagine her behind that closed door, jumping in surprise and fumbling the plastic cup. *Cripes, Dad,* I thought. *Have a heart.*

(For those of you who knew my father in this life, you may be pleased to know he's found a way to continue singing in the next one, too. Gets requests for *The Old Lady Who Swallowed a Fly* on a regular basis. Go figure.)

Time passed, along with a couple more verses, while Mom purled away at her knitting, and I stared out the window trying to look like a man who was used to waiting around while his wife peed in a cup.

When the chorus came back around, Dad paused to call out: "Just leave it on the sink."

There was a soft swish of running water from the bathroom, and Denise stuck her head out. "Okay. What's next?"

My father curled his fingers like a tiny audience doing a wave at a flea circus —a gesture that said *right this way*. "You come out. I go in. And everybody waits." He pulled something out of his pocket and did the side-step tango with my wife as they switched places.

Denise gave me a half-priced smile and joined me on the sofa. "I don't suppose we could have done this at his office," she murmured under her breath.

Mom's eyes sparkled, her fingers flying over the whatnot taking shape in her lap. "But that wouldn't have been nearly as much fun for him, now would it?"

I was starting to get a little excited, sitting there, kneading my wife's fingers. I told myself not to expect too much. Not yet. And that even if we were not pregnant, it would be no hardship to practice, practice, practice.

Finally the door opened, and Dad rejoined us. He was frowning: a furrow in his forehead deep enough to plant corn. *Damn. That can't be good.*

He shook his head, sorrowfully at Denise, then with obvious disappointment at me. *Hey. I'm doing my best here. Give us time, already. I've got this. I'm good at assembling stuff. Don't need an instructions manual either.*

My inner monologue would have gone into overtime if my wife's gynecologist-turned-obstetrician hadn't broken his silence.

"Well."

Pause followed pregnant pause. (Sorry. Couldn't resist.) Then he fired up his Saint Nicholas grin. "Congratulations, you two! You're going to have a little baby human."

My dad loved a good joke. So much so, he collected them. Kept files of them he would eagerly show you if you doubted the rumors. So it served him right if Denise and I decided to make him the butt of one for a change.

A few Sundays after learning we were pregnant, we again found ourselves at Mom and Dad's, this time lounging on the screened patio out back.

My folks' house had started life as a small three-bedroom, one-bath bungalow, and had evolved into a five bedroom, two-bath sprawling ranch, boasting a den with fireplace, small California basement, humongous family room, screened-in patio, and a dining room that could host a state dinner.

The place had grown out of necessity. I am one of eight brothers and sisters. In descending order, we are: Jan, Bill, Tom, Kay, me, Mike, Beth, and Joe.

Relax. There won't be a test. If you need to know anyone personally, I'll make the introductions.

So, okay, back to the porch. Mom had brought out glasses of something cold to counter the Indian summer that had landed on Toledo's doorstep. She'd left her current knitting project inside and was happily discussing nursery decor with Denise. Dad was mulling over the idea of firing up the grill.

Denise had confessed to thinning out our wardrobes and was wondering how to recycle my old jeans and her old knit dresses into something useful.

"Yes, I do think you could make your own rag rug," Mom said. "I could show you."

Old jeans? I don't have any old jeans.

Before I could ask Denny what she was talking about, she elbowed me in the ribs.

My father had been shuttling in and out of the house, and had finally emerged juggling a plate of burgers and a clutch of cooking utensils.

What's with the nudge? I wondered. *Does she want me to help him?* The grill was sacred territory. Trying to usurp it from my father was grounds for disinheritance.

Apparently I had yet to master the wife-to-husband handoff.

When I looked puzzled, Denny Lou lifted one eyebrow in classic Spock fashion, and nodded at my father.

Oh, right. I had a cue. Damn near fumbled it.

"By the way, Dad," I jumped in. "We've been thinking about baby names."

"Already?" He stopped juggling and set the plate on the small counter that jutted out from the grill.

"Never too soon," I assured him, trying to maintain a straight face. "We're still debating what to call it if it's a girl."

Dad nodded, only partially engaged in the discussion. It was more important to him at the moment to get his various master-of-the-flame implements lined up on their proper hooks.

Denise delivered her portion of the script like a seasoned pro. "What do you think of Rachel Louise?" she asked my mother. "Jim sort of likes Gina Louise, but I'm afraid that sounds like a stripper."

Mom could have chuckled, but would never dare. She would be diplomatic, even if it meant chewing off her own tongue. "They're both pretty. Though I lean toward Rachel. Why Louise?"

"It's my mom's middle name, and she was the first female child in her family. She passed it on to me, since I was their first female."

Dad had stepped back from the grill and was studying his arrangement.

"Jim and I thought we'd continue the tradition." (Note: I now have a granddaughter named Ariel Louise. May the gods of wrath descend upon her if her first female child doesn't carry the torch into a new generation. Got that, kid?)

A second shot to the ribs reminded me the followup line was mine. "But, Dad," I chimed in. "We're pretty set on what we want if it's a boy."

"Yeah?" He could just as easily have said "Snowball?" My father was far more interested in switching the tongs with the fork, and was reaching for the spatula, perhaps preparing to execute a triple play.

A snare drum flourish and cymbal crash would have been appropriate, but you can't always get what you want.

"Oscar," I said.

I'd never delivered a line with more Tony Award-winning panache. So I said it again for anyone in the last row who missed it.

"Definitely Oscar."

Dad didn't drop the tongs, or flip the fork into the air in a half gainer. He did, however, do a passable imitation of that cymbal crash.

My mom? I swear, she never even flinched.

Dad choked out an "um," followed by a swallow they probably heard next door. "Oscar, eh?"

Mom picked up her drink and was hiding behind it, pretending to sip. I caught Dad shooting her The Look. (It seemed I wasn't the only husband who relied on cues from his wife.) He watched her without blinking as she seemed to consider.

When she nodded, my father relaxed, smiled like a rising sun, and turned to place his tools in their correct order. He did place two of them on the same peg, but that was the only sign Denise and I had that our joke had scored.

Whatever we'd expected? It was not this. My parents were willing to accept any name we came up with. And love it. Abner. Cosmo. Hershel. It wouldn't have mattered. Yes, even Oscar.

"Guys?" I sputtered. "It's a joke. You know? Oscar as in Oscar *Meyer?*"

Dad's shoulders slumped in relief; his head tipped back, eyes closed, as though he'd escaped a car crash unscathed. Mom put down her glass and said something I had never heard leave her lips before—or ever would again. "Oh, thank you, dear God."

Like I said, my dad loved a good joke. But as I now know, the Big Guy enjoys one even more. And *he* always gets the last laugh.

Rachel Louise was born two days before my birthday on April 14, 1981, so we would have to tuck the Oscar idea away for baby number two. Sorry, Jim Junior; I did briefly consider hanging that name on you for sentimental reasons, a la Oscar, the Whitmer theater ghost. Then your mom pointed out the unfortunate jingle that would dog your every step once you started school: *"Oh, I'd love to be an Oscar Mayer wiener..."* You should thank her for that some time.

Jimmy, however, was twenty-one months in the future; so at seven pounds, eleven ounces, Rachel was the best present I had yet received.

She was also the only baby I knew who would enter the world to her own theme song.

Sorry, but I'm gonna have to hit the rewind button, people. Stop groaning. You should be used to it by now.

Back before Denise and I were married, during those cautious early days when we were both getting used to new sets of parents, we were invited to my folks' house for a get-to-know-you dinner. The dishes had been cleared and we'd retired to the den where the television was playing, as it typically was, with no one paying it much mind. I could tell Denny Lou was nervous, so I was joshing and wisecracking to help her relax. I wanted her to know that these two people she hardly knew would welcome her if for no other reason than I loved her.

On that night, however, I turned the joke meter up too high, helping her relax flat on her rear in a faux pas. Or is that faux p-a-*x*? Maybe foe pah? Isn't spelling tough enough, honey, without throwing another language at me? Sheesh.

Let me set the scene for you—in English, babe, if you don't mind.

Mom was crocheting a lace tablecloth and Denise was watching, rapt. Dad was standing to the side, in front of the TV, tamping tobacco into one of his many ornate pipes. "You look like a leprechaun, Dad," I said, waving my hand at the elf face carved into the meerschaum bowl. "*Some* might say, 'ridiculous.' But not me."

I let the pause grow old before I delivered the punchline. "Not out loud, anyway."

He removed the pipe from his mouth, turned it to study the image. "Ridiculous? Nah? You give it too much credit." There was a snicker in his eyes that warned me he might be about to break into a chorus of *Oh, Danny Boy*. But on the screen behind him, an announcer was cranking up to steal his thunder.

The commercial was for a watch that could—wonder of wonders—sing.

Yes, young ones, the world once functioned quite well with timepieces that did nothing more than tell time. In 1979, when this incident took place, Dick Tracy was still considered science fiction. Don't know who Dick Tracy is? Google it.

All conversation halted as we were drawn under the spell of the silver-plated marvel turning and sparkling under the hot lights of commercialism... "a masterpiece of Swiss ingenuity and a must for any style-conscious man.

"But wait! That's not all." The background music faded away, to be replaced by a spritely electronic tune.

The Yellow Rose of Texas.

"Yes, this incredible timepiece sings! Amaze your friends. Set your alarm by it. It's the best and only watch of its kind you will ever need!"

Need? Seriously?

"So, what would you pay for this high-quality timepiece? Two hundred dollars? One hundred and fifty? Well, hold on to your hats. The AMAZING Yellow Rose of Texas watch can be yours for the unbelievably low price of just fifty-nine ninety-five!"

Plus shipping and handling.

The silly thing was addicting—ludicrous, but appealing in a what-the-hell kind of way.

My mother and I were thinking it, but Denise would be the only one to say it out loud: "Talk about ridiculous. What *idiot* would spend good money on something like *that*?"

Dum-dum-dum dummmm.

My father turned in time to see a toll-free number flash behind him.

"I did," he said.

Casual as can be.

A shot to my woman's self confidence.

Direct hit.

Mom's fingers actually stopped flying. Her head came up, her eyes wide. "Bill, you didn't." I wasn't sure if she meant the purchase or the fact that he was confessing to it.

Dad didn't mean to embarrass anyone, of course. We all knew my father's penchant for the ridiculous. All except Denise. Late night infomercials loved William J. Meyer and his credit card. It would never have crossed his mind that the young woman presently turning pink in his den would be out of line for calling him on it.

He turned back to my mom, and puffed contentedly. "You get one, too," he assured her.

Yep, another "but wait!" My mother would soon be the proud owner of her own AMAZING Yellow Rose of Texas watch, sized to her dainty wrist but lacking the special sound effect.

Dad would complain she'd been gypped.

I'm pretty sure Denise's face was still red when a week later she got a call at her parents' house. "It's Jim's dad," her mother said, holding out the receiver.

Forehead furrowed, she put the phone to her ear and gave a tentative "Hello?"

The tinny electronic notes of *The Yellow Rose of Texas* played merrily down the line.

Denise's laugh joined my father's as the song trailed off.

Dad had defused the situation in his own patented way, but he was far from finished. William Meyer? Abandon a good joke when he saw one? Not in this lifetime. Or the next, if given the chance.

In the early morning hours of April 14, 1981, my wife's water broke and we awoke to a bloody mess. A quick call to dad sent us scurrying to the hospital—right after Denise insisted I pull the new comforter off the bed and place it to soak in cold water in the bathtub. Living with a perfectionist is not a bed of roses, but it will always be one unstained by life's little emergencies.

Dad met us there and quickly determined Denise had suffered a partial abruptio placentae and would require an emergency C-section.

It was only after the fact that we would learn how precarious the situation had been. Dad remained cool, calm and jocular; in other words, his usual self—something that hid the danger from us.

While we were being prepped for surgery, at a pace that should have raised warning flags, my father commented he had to run to his office for a minute. "I'll be right back," he said. Then grinned. "Don't start without me."

The office of Deithelm, Meyer, Rost and Sharma was located within the St. Vincent Medical Center, a few floors away. I did briefly wonder why my father was deserting us for even a short while when his third grandchild was about to make an appearance. It might even be the boy he'd been hoping for, to balance the two girls my sister Jan had presented him.

I didn't wonder for long, though. I was too busy slipping into a blue smock, and donning a matching hair bonnet and booties. Always stylin', that's me.

Dad was back in a flash and we were wheeled in under the hot lights of a surgical suite. The nurses raised a curtain across Denise's chest, blocking her view of the incision site. I stood on tiptoe to watch over the top as Dad made the first cut.

He whistled merrily. So at ease, I would not have been surprised to see him break into a soft-shoe routine.

"You're making the incision too small," a nurse warned him.

My father gave her a *pfft*. "Watch and learn, grasshopper."

More sniping followed, all good-natured and so casual it could only have evolved over years of camaraderie between my dad and the nursing staff. They called him Wild Bill with great affection—and now I knew why. My father was a marriage of contradictions: competent and comic, dedicated and delightful.

It took so little time getting Rachel out into the world that when he performed a repeat C-section for my son Jim's birth two years later I would ask him what was taking so long. "This one," he would answer, "isn't strangling for air."

For the record, there isn't a lot of blood and gore during a C-section. Dad made his various cuts to get down to the uterus, handed off the scalpel, and placed his palms on each side of the incision. I twitched in surprise. *What the hell?!* Lifting himself onto the balls of his feet, he pressed down on my wife's stomach. I had just enough time to think, *Sure glad she can't feel that,* before I stopped thinking altogether.

A tiny head popped out between my father's hands.

"Uh-oh," Dad said under his breath.

Denise gasped. "Jim? What's wrong?"

Without missing a beat, my father chuckled. "Nothing," he assured us. "Too cute to be a boy."

"A girl?" I asked, groping under the sheet for my wife's hand.

"Give me a second," he replied. Then returned to his whistling.

A moment later, a tiny slippery body slid out to join the tiny head. "A girl," he confirmed.

For the first and probably only time in her life, the baby herself had little to say. No wail. Only a single bleat.

"Jim? Jim. I can't see. What does she look like?"

I responded honestly, not knowing that what was on display was anything but normal. It was, after all, my first time in a delivery room. "Purple."

Denise was quicker on the uptake and suspected that was not good. "Purple?"

Rachel Louise Meyer was being handed off to the pediatrician, who suctioned her with quick but practiced ease. A moment passed in silence. Then two. And three.

An eternity later, my daughter made up for lost time with a loud, long, and bitchy cry.

I squeezed Denny's hand hard enough to leave bruises.

The Yellow Rose of Texas rang out in the white room, echoing off chrome surfaces and circling around to begin again.

Dad had been keeping the watch in his office so he wouldn't forget it on B Day, and the merry tune could not have come at a better time. Rachel's first APGAR test had scored a three. The potential for medical issues and cognitive damage was high. But as the music began to fade in the air, the pediatrician made a pronouncement. "Second APGAR's a nine. I think we're good."

Despite a rocky opening act, my daughter would grow up to boast an IQ of 138, be outspoken—often to the extreme, and would face down any obstacle that dared to step into her path.

She is also a lover of all things theatrical.

I blame the watch.

Chapter Void: Escape Clause

It's the most important day of my life. The happiest. The most hopeful. I've been up for hours, fidgeting, pacing, dressing, studying myself in the mirror and then redressing. In my opinion, bow ties and cummerbunds never look normal on a guy—and I want everything to be perfect.

A vehicle is coming soon.

It will take me to the church, where Denise is going to make a long walk down an endless marble aisle on the arm of her father Leonard.

To me. To become my wife.

She's carefully planned every detail, from the choice of an ivory dress and picture hat teased with lace—which I will confess later I barely noticed, my eyes devoted to her face alone—to a pair of white roses we will detach from her bouquet to present to our mothers.

She's chosen the music: *Ave Marie* before the start of Mass, sung by our dear friend Tina; *Sunrise Sunset* for the wedding party processional; Pachelbel's *Canon in D* for the bride's entrance. Her dad has lobbied hard for *If I Were a Rich Man,* insisting it should be a mandatory part of the ceremony for all Fathers of the Bride, but it doesn't make the cut.

Denise has asked me not to do anything different with my hair. To not get it trimmed for at least two weeks prior to the big day. To not shave my mustache. It's summer, so my beard is already gone, awaiting the return of cold weather to make its reappearance. But the rest she wants kept the same as always. She will not alter her own hair or makeup. Wants us to go to each other looking the way we did the day we "clicked." The same as we will always appear in our hearts, no matter how old we may grow together. So my hair is its usual dark curly mane; hers, a soft golden shag. She will wear the same perfume—which I have always loved. (So much so, that when she gives our daughter a spritz one day in the future, I will beg her not to do it again. It is the scent of my mate, and belongs to no one else.)

Denise's sister Daria will be her Matron of Honor. She will make my Denny Lou cry just moments before she steps out on that journey to the altar—and she will do it with a flick of a smile over her shoulder and just three parting words: "Goodbye, Miss Tomanski."

Jeff, my friend and partner in crime in The Con, will deliver one of the readings. Denise and I will recite a joint prayer we wrote ourselves.

The Catholic rite of Holy Matrimony will be performed by Father Kenneth Mormon, who will one day be summoned to the Vatican to serve as an assistant to the Holy See. Holy Rosary—a magnificent historic cathedral—will be our parish from now on. Not long after our wedding, Father will ask us to become Lay Speakers and Communion Distributors.

Today, when we exchange vows, Daria will be the only one to have remembered to bring a handkerchief. Having no pockets in her dress, she will give it to Denny's brother Chris to tuck away. The four of us—Bride, Groom, Matron and Best Man—will pass it back and forth, mopping away joyful tears.

So many tears. So many smiles. So much future ahead of us.

It is the most important day of my life. The happiest. The most hopeful.

And it will go exactly as my Denny planned, except for one small detail.

We'd decided to use the old vows, full of thees and thous, instead of the more modern promises currently in vogue. I had practiced them over and over because, though it is not a long speech—which as you recall is not my forte—it is a sizable block of words. Denise asked me weeks ago if I wanted a cheat sheet.

Hell, no, I told her. I can do this. Will do it without an instructions manual, if you please.

Probably should have penned them inside my shirt cuff or something, because I did forget one small promise. Nothing too significant. Just a little slip.

"I, Jim, take thee, Denise, to be my lawfully wedded wife, to have and to hold, from this day forward, for better or for worse, for richer or for poorer... to love and to honor, all the days of our life."

Denise will be unfazed by my omission, will reassure me no one noticed. Will call it my "escape clause"—a loophole I can slip through should I ever decide I want out.

Not in this lifetime, sweetheart. Not in the next either.

It's the most important day of my life. The happiest. The most hopeful.

Red lights flash. A siren wails. The vehicle is here.

I'm getting married today.

Aren't I?

Chapter Seven: 1-800-BERRY

I wanted Rachel to have the Strawberry Shortcake Berry
Happy House for Christmas.

Denise wanted Rachel to have the Strawberry Shortcake Berry Happy House.

Rachel wanted Rachel to have the freaking Strawberry Shortcake Berry Happy House.

Not that Rachel actually said freaking, or the rest of it. She was an amazingly articulate three-year-old, but she'd not yet gotten to the stage where she could tell us, "Mother? Father? See that beautiful concoction of red, pink and green plastic magnificence on the television screen? I would truly appreciate finding it tucked under the tree this coming holiday. Thank you for your attention. I will now retire to my room to pick up my toys, don my pajamas, and read myself to sleep with a selection from *The Pokey Little Puppy*. That will be all. You are dismissed."

But close.

My daughter already had the doll and its pet cat, both steeped in the chemical sweetness of polymer-fabricated strawberries. (She gave Berry and Custard a sniff every night before falling asleep—which made me wonder if they were habit-forming.) The poor things were homeless, however, and Kenner commercials were blasting day and night about the benefits of owning versus renting.

The problem was, based on its price tag, the dollhouse was located in an upscale neighborhood. The kit topped $125, and ran upwards to $225 assembled. In Shortcake dollars, that made the place a McMansion—and more expensive than the four walls we called home.

It wasn't looking good for the elves.

Then, while out picking up a few extras to pad Santa's sack, I stumbled upon The Sale.

As Denise would discover on Christmas Eve when she began unloading our purchases from the gift closet to the tree, we'd each been adding to the kids' haul behind one another's back. I'm pretty sure Toys R Us credited us for its increased price-per-share on Nasdaq that year. Still, I have no apologies. It was Jimmy's first Christmas, so man the toy torpedoes, full speed ahead.

What? Oh, right. The Sale. I was scoping out My Little Tonkas when I encountered that season's Holy Grail: short stuff's Berry Happy Home, including the deluxe furniture pack—*plus* a variety of add-ons we would normally have been unable to afford—priced at a scant $89.99.

If we'd had cellphones back then I would have speed-dialed my wife to shout the good news. Unfortunately, we didn't, so I would have to make a shoot-from-the-hip decision all by my lonesome. Probably a good thing. Not-quite-ninety dollars was still a hefty chunk of change. The Sale wasn't likely to stand up against Denise's financial good sense, no matter how low the price.

I stopped to do the math: Dimples popping out on apple cheeks versus $89.99? Dancing twinkles in cute little hazel eyes versus $89.99? The screech of pure joy that would shatter windows a block away versus $89.99?

I bought it.

Sure, it was the kit—totally unassembled, including every itsy-bitsy accessory. But, hey, I'm an engineer and a master of assembly, right? How hard could it be to put together a kid's toy?

The thing came in a box the size of Rhode Island, filled with a dozen additional smaller boxes, like one of those Russian nesting dolls on steroids: hundreds of pieces and parts, decals, foundations, walls, floors, a staircase, strawberry-shaped roofs (yes, plural), a working door, shuttered windows with matching window boxes, a porch swing, a trellis, and a ridiculously cute berry-shaped skylight.

Strawberry's home came with everything but a building permit, and I'm not sure I wasn't violating at least one zoning law by starting without one.

When completed, the Berry Happy House would stand three-stories tall and measure 26" x 19" x 26". Unassembled and unboxed, it littered the entirety of our living room floor, with spillover into the dining room. Our coffee table became command central.

Rachel was already in bed asleep the night we started. Jimmy was not— probably heard a refrigerator door open and was prepared to dispose of anything approaching its expiration date. I was sitting yoga fashion on the floor with him nestled in my lap: a general and his adjutant. Denise sat crosslegged next to me: Radar O'Reilly, the voice of reason.

I was reaching for the instructions manual when she beat me to it, slipping it out from under my fingers before I could toss it into the scrap box. "Uh-uh, honey. Not this time."

"What do you mean? I've got this. Common sense: start with the foundation, snap up the walls…"

"Jim, we've only got two weeks to do this."

"Weeks? This won't take weeks. Tonight. I'll have this baby standing before bedtime." I eyed the myriad pieces laid out before me. "Maybe a little overtime. Midnight. Latest."

"Jim."

She didn't have to say more. When she riffled the pages of the manual— which had been packed prominently on top—it resembled a telephone directory for a small township. Eighty-nine pages long. Had a cross-indexed table of contents. Diagrams. Blueprints. Front elevation. Back elevation. Side elevations. Denise flipped the book over and held it under my nose so I could see what was printed in large black letters against a banner of highlighter-yellow, outlined in screaming red. Jimmy tried to chew off a corner.

She said: "Honey? It's got a twenty-four hour, toll-free, one-eight-hundred crisis hotline."

I had to admit. That banner looked ominous. Like one of those vinyl tapes they string up around a crime scene.

"So? That's for the amateurs."

Denise sighed, but it was not a sound of surrender. I'd learned a lot about my wife's sighs over the course of our married life. This one was set in concrete.

"What if...?" She flipped open the cover, slid a finger down the index. "What if I act as your humble assistant? Just as backup." She smiled winningly. "You won't even have to touch this nasty old thing."

So, okay, she'd learned a lot about me over the last few years, too. "If you want," I allowed. "But you'll get bored." Let her play, I thought. It will give her something to do while I get down to the serious building.

How could I have forgotten the lesson of the TripTik?

It would take less than an hour for us to realize we'd embarked on an adventure worthy of a SEAL team: How to Build a Dollhouse in Eleven Days without Killing Each Other.

Yeah, I hate to admit it, but it took every one of eleven days—and that was with Denise reading each step out loud, sorting through boxes imprinted with Chinese subtitles, and snapping together the little leaf-shaped chairs, tables, and other garden-themed necessities of a Berry Happy life. As designated Designer, she was also the one to peel and stick one-hundred-and-one cutesy decals everywhichwhere. I named her General Contractor, too, so she would help repack everything at night's end while I stashed partially assembled walls and floors in various hiding places to await the next evening's festivities.

So okay, you are thinking, if Denise was the General Contractor, what did that make you?

Non-union labor—a position that demanded an expert in profanity. Sorry, Jimmy. Your tender ears are probably still ringing.

In my defense, I think any foul language that escaped my head and exited my mouth during this ordeal was completely justified. I mean, seriously? What kind of sadistic technical writer creates a list of instructions that ends on one page with the statement: "At this point you are ready to snap the component into place"?

Then begins a new list at the top of the next page—which you had to turn to get to—with the bolded statement **"But FIRST you MUST…"**

I think there was a half-second of lead time between Denise's shouted "Stop!" and disaster. Followup instructions indicated that once I'd snapped the component—in this case, the roof—in place, it was permanent, and those darling little shuttered windows would not fit under it. In other words, they would remain forever unattached, and I would have flushed $89.99 down the crapper.

The Big Guy has declared that evening's rant unfit for public consumption, so it will remain alive and smoking solely in my wife's memory.

I dare her to smile about it. You hear me, babe? Dare. You.

Three days before Christmas, we finally finished, hauled the empty boxes to the trash, and filed the instructions manual, just in case. We hadn't needed to make any calls to that 1-800 hotline—For amateurs. Told you so—but Denise, the cautious list-maker, wasn't taking any chances.

You'd be surprised how large 26" x 19" x 26" is when it's no longer numbers on a page. The Berry Happy House was so huge it had to be stashed under a sheet in our closet to keep it hidden from three-year-old prying eyes.

I admit, though, the end result was charming, even to me: a man who'd become jaded by endless nights of headache-inducing assembly time. The stucco exterior featured a trellis of strawberries, a functioning Dutch door, a white-railed porch with hanging swing, and an airing deck similar to our own.

Its five little rooms boasted clever details like a bay window, clawfoot bathtub, and mirrored medicine cabinet. There was a drop-down staircase to an attic of sweet "junk" that included a steamer trunk, cat bed, and telescope for spying through the pink skylight. In the bedroom, the bed glittered with faux brass and was dressed with plush strawberry-themed bedding. An ornate armoire held tiny hangers for Strawberry's duds. I could just imagine the clothing allowance I was going to have to set aside for berry-scented dresses and shoes.

The place came furnished with a grandfather clock, tulip-shade floor lamp, rocking chair, sofa with removable cushions, a china hutch with dinnerware, and a drop-leaf dining table with matching leafy side chairs. A lidded cookie jar would hold pride of place in the table's center.

There were plush rugs, striped towels, a red skillet on the old-fashioned kitchen stove, a green mixing bowl in the farmhouse sink, and a miniature butcher block table that mirrored the one Denise's parents had bought for us as a wedding gift. The place even had a mailbox that opened and closed —ready to accept teeny-tiny credit card statements.

I confess I lifted that sheet before going to bed, to peek one last time at our handiwork.

"Did some fine work here, James, my man. Rachel is going to freak."

I couldn't wait to see if she'd squeal in delight, or for once in her chattery life be without words.

I had only too happily—and maniacally—slashed this to-do off our refrigerator list before coming upstairs. Just two more items to go, I thought before nodding off, and we're ready for the holiday.

Chapter Void: Fighting Back

My world is narrowing. The pieces I can comprehend grow smaller and no longer fit together. Sound has become my sight. Words fill my mouth but lose their way when I try to speak. I feel little but pain: a relentless agony in my head that has grown so quickly it threatens to fill the space where once I embraced a wife, a daughter, a son. Parents. Sisters. Brothers. Nieces and nephews. Church. Work. Play.

Life.

Only one other sensation touches me.

Fear.

Fear that I will lose it all. Soon.

No damn way, man. No.

A voice sprinkled with static speaks near my shoulder. "He's combative?"

"Won't lie down. Fights us when we try to insert a line. Punching. Kicking."

"Not unusual for a closed-brain injury," says static man.

Not unusual for a guy with places to get back to. People to hold on to.

"Wife says to take him to Saint Vincent's."

"Riverside is closer."

"He's Doctor Meyer's son."

"Got it. Proceed to the center. We'll alert ER."

I am James P. Meyer… Senior. There's a Junior now. Get your freaking hands off. Going to see my kid. My kiddos. My wife.

"Transporting him now."

"Prone?"

"No. We've stopped fighting that. Got him in a neck brace. Strapped on the stretcher sitting up."

"Understood. ETA?"

"In ten."

"Hey! Hey! What's happening?"

Len? Is that you? Get these assholes off me, will you?

"Sorry, sir. Please step back. We need to close the doors."

"Thank God. Len! Can you take care of the kids? There's this guy. From the neighborhood, I guess. He's inside with Rachel and Jimmy. But they don't know him. Can you…?"

"Don't worry. Daria and Michael just pulled up. We've got this. Call…"

Wait! Don't turn those sirens on again, damn it. I can't hear. And hearing is all I have.

But the piercing wail ratchets up to smother everything. Its sobbing screech is all I will have for the next precious minutes. Minutes I could have used to tell everyone I loved them. Instead, it's nothing but crying and wailing and lost time.

Somehow, though, I hear her. Over the shrieking inside my head and out. "It's going to be okay, Jim. Hold on. I love you."

It's automatic by now. She says, "I love you." I answer, "I love you, too."

My mouth moves, but a gargle spills out. The right number of syllables. The right cadence. The wrong consonants.

She gasps.

"I know," she calls over the sirens, over the murmurs of the men holding me back from my life. "It's okay, honey. I heard you. I know you do."

Something cold presses against my wrist, moves slowly and rhythmically up my arm toward my elbow. A snip. Then another. And another.

No!

They are cutting off my new jacket.

Chapter Eight: All the King's Men

I want to tell you I fought hard and won. That guts and determination were enough to save the day.

I want to tell you my father stormed the fortress, gathered the medical experts and resources at his disposal, and made it all better.

I am desperate to tell you I was there when Rachel saw her dollhouse. When Jimmy laughed at his My Buddy doll. When Denise finally got a peek at the tiny opal and diamond ring I'd splurged on against her wishes.

Hell, I would be ecstatic to confess I go to work. Pay taxes. Mow the lawn. Wash the car. Bitch about politics.

Things like lighting skyrockets on the Fourth of July? Making love? Even arguing—then *making love again*? That would be beyond ecstatic, bordering on rapture.

Do you want to hear that I walked my daughter down the aisle to her soldier boy, Matt, and proudly shook his hand? That I danced a waltz with my son's beautiful Katie at their wedding... cuddled each of my grandchildren as they came into the world... still neck with my wife on the porch swing late at night... still tease my brothers and sisters... still eat Esther's Mac and Cheese as often as I can get it? Are you hoping I will pull a Stephen King and rewrite history so it ends happily ever after?

Oh, if only I could, even for one false but joyful chapter.

Because more than anything in the world I want to tell you that the first paragraph of this book is a bold-faced lie.

Okay, yes, some things are true: I did fight hard, and so did Dad. I *was* there to see those gifts delivered on Christmas day. And I was present for all those other precious moments in my family's lives.

But I could not walk or dance or hold.

Telling you I could? That would be the lie.

It's a miserable, cruel fact, but my Titanic did rake the iceberg, and all the king's horses and all the king's men couldn't put it back together again. Sorry for the mixed metaphor. But, frankly, Scarlett, I don't give a damn. I wasn't ready to die—and you won't be either, if you have time to see it coming.

So my advice? Do it all. Large acts of love, small acts of kindness. Every good thing you can think of. As often as you can—'cause, baby, we only get one shot.

Night was falling and dense snow with it by the time my father got to St. Vincent's. Denise was pacing in front of the Emergency Room doors watching for him. Her first words: "He's hurt. He's so hurt. And they won't let me be with him. Won't tell me what's going on."

Dad hugged her briefly, kept it nice and easy—the doctor with a capital D delivering comfort and confidence. Not a father with a capital F whose stomach was heaving with distress.

Parents are not supposed to outlive their children, and Bill Meyer was sure he would not. It was a pep talk he would give himself regularly over the hours ahead—one he would try to believe with all his heart. "They won't let you in because they're treating him right now. But I can find out what's going on. Sit, Denise. Try to relax. I'll be back as soon I can."

What he saw must have shaken his belief to its foundations. I don't know for sure, of course, because by then I'd dropped into a black hole of pain— was mixing up the past with the present. Was grasping at my happiest memories to hold the darkness at bay.

I am sure you'll understand, it is not a time I have ever wanted to revisit.

But anyone looking down from above would have seen nurses and doctors surrounding me, some trying to wrestle me down, others struggling to reattach IVs I'd yanked from my arm. I'm not a big man, but I was fighting for my life. Everywhere was organized chaos.

"Jim!"

My dad used his Father Voice. Stern and firm. A voice I'd respected and responded to since childhood.

"Stop that. Now."

And I did.

Just like that.

I settled, without another punch or kick, knowing I didn't have to fight alone anymore. Dad was here.

A harried ER doc shot my father a grateful glance. "Thanks. I didn't want to strap him down, but we need to get more X-rays. An EEG. He hasn't exactly been cooperating."

Dad stayed out of the way, but raised his voice. "He'll be fine for you now. Right, Jim? Let them take care of you, son."

He stuffed his hands into the pockets of the black topcoat he hadn't bothered to remove, snow melting on his shoulders and in his hair. "What's your prognosis? If you've got time to tell me?"

The doctor nodded, but kept moving, delivering commands to the rest of the staff. "Can't know for sure until we get more test results," he said between orders. "First x-ray was blurry, but I don't think it's a skull fracture. Can't feel a ridge."

Dad nodded. Kept the relief off his face.

"But it may be a closed-brain injury."

Relief fled.

"Hopefully, not brainstem."

Dr. William Meyer was still standing, but Jimmy's dad was collapsing to his knees. "Hopefully," he murmured.

He cast one more look around, reassured that the hospital he'd worked for his entire career would do everything it could to help his boy. Then he dared to step between a nurse and another doctor to grab my hand and squeeze. "Keep me posted, please," he asked the primary physician. "When you can, of course."

Three voices answered him from around the room. "Absolutely, Doctor Meyer." "Of course." "As soon as I can."

My dad turned away and let the chaos close back around me. I wanted to call to him. To tell him I'd be good. That I'd see him later. But the pain and the dark wouldn't let me.

My father shouldered open the swinging door and turned toward the ER waiting area. He got only four stumbling steps before he pivoted and took a different path, kept walking and turning corners until he found a quiet place with few comings and goings.

Only then did he slump against the wall and let his head drop.

This was bad, he knew. And it didn't matter how much training or experience or skill he had, whatever happened next was out of his hands. There was nothing he could do.

Nothing? He straightened. Lifted his head and inhaled. Nodded to himself.

Dad headed to his office several floors above, and made two phone calls. The first to Dr. Ned Lawrence, arguably the finest neurosurgeon in the region. The second to my mom.

"Pat," he said when he heard her anxious voice. "I think you should come."

She cried out—a short syllable of distress.

"Try not to worry. Drive carefully. The roads are bad. But come."

"Should I call Denise's mom?"

"She may have done that already, but let's be sure." He tried to infuse his words with confidence, but Patricia had been his wife for over thirty-one years. She could hear what he wasn't saying. Knew what he could not say. Not even to himself. Not yet.

"All right. I'm coming."

My dad hung up the phone, took off his coat, shook off his fear. Alone in the quiet, he folded his hands, bowed his head, and made one last call.

When his job was done, when he'd done the best he could, he painted a hopeful expression on his face, and went down to lie to my wife.

Chapter Nine: Mama

I am going to hit the rewind button again. No complaints
this time? I didn't think so. I'm in no hurry to see me die, either.

When our Rachel was born I called her my princess. I know a lot of guys hope their firstborn will be a boy, someone they can share their manly passions with one day: baseball, Budweiser, bad jokes. The usual. But a daughter is her own special joy. Maybe it's because men entertain the fiction that we still live in caves and our womenfolk require the protection of those who've been blessed with outdoor plumbing. Like it's some sort of club we can use to clobber predators that threaten the clan.

Or, heh, maybe that's just me.

Anyway, Rachel was my princess, a fragile damsel—or so I deluded myself —who brought out my inner knight.

Every day that first week, after we'd brought our noisy little beauty home from the hospital, I would run out the door after work, race at ticket-tempting speeds across town, slam on the brakes in my driveway, dash up the porch steps, throw open the door, and dance like a fool up the stairs to snatch my tiny piece of royalty from her crib and give her a smacking kiss.

Call me blind or stupid, but it took me about the same amount of time to discover I was leaving my wife standing in my wake, day after day, with her mouth hanging open.

See, it was Denise I used to maul first. With a tickle—which she hated.

With a kiss—which she did not. With an "I love you"—that she returned with equal ardor. Suddenly, my affections had transferred to another female. A female my wife could never hate, but for whom she could harbor the tiniest, meanest sliver of resentment.

Denny had not complained, but the hurt was there to see, if I hadn't been be-spelled by our darling little chatterbox. It slipped out from behind my wife's mask in week two.

I was just beginning my Fred Astaire routine up the stairs, front door swinging on its hinges behind me, when Denise halted me in mid shuffle-ball-change.

"Hey, ho, no, buster! Rachel didn't go down for her nap until late. Please, I'm begging you. Don't wake her."

My mouth twisted like I'd just sucked a lemon. Well, damn. Then one corner lifted in a wicked smile. "Hmmm. Okay then. There is more than one gorgeous female in this house, isn't there?"

Denise had turned away and was in the process of rewinding the sweeper cord when I slipped up behind her and placed my hands on her hips.

She wriggled out of my grasp. "You noticed, eh?"

Huh? (Have I mentioned having a male anatomy does nothing to improve our hearing—or our ability to reason?)

Denny straightened, sighed. And turned. She was smiling, but it was not as seductive as mine. In fact? My wife's smile was fricking fake.

Fake. Fake. Fake.

You'd have thought the woman had zero experience in front of the footlights. No Tony for this performance, no siree.

"What's up?" I asked, dunce cap perched atop my head.

"Nothing."

"Did I forget an anniversary or something?"

Denny scrunched up her eyebrows and pretended ignorance. Again, no applause from the critics. The Best Actress Award would be presented to some other fibbing wife.

"You just caught me trying to straighten this place up," she said.

Yeah. The place was a shambles, all right. Things probably got messy somewhere during that sneaky pause between Obsessive and Compulsive.

"Seriously?"

"Why? Can't I be busy? Can I not want to play sexy French maid just this once?" She jerked back around, returning her attention to the vacuum. "Your turn to be ignored, I guess," she muttered, slapping the last of the cord around the handle and knotting it in place.

I had a fleeting image of my neck there instead.

I ran through the checklist of possible offenses, real and imagined. It hadn't yet been a month since Denny's C-section, but I was already feeling the pressure of keeping my distance while her incision healed. Was it possible she was, too?

"Um. I haven't been ignoring you, hon. It's just—er—I thought we had to wait a while."

"Oh for heaven's sake, Meyer!" Denise yanked the sweeper off the floor and swung it toward the coat closet where it was stored. I resisted the urge to duck. "Did I not just say I wasn't in the mood? Forget it. Just forget it." She stalked across the floor—threw the door open, the sweeper in, and the door back shut. Yank. Bang. Slam.

New fleeting image. This time, my head.

Before I could think *postpartum*—or sign my own death warrant by speaking it out loud—my wife dropped to the floor, her butt on the bottom step of the staircase, her knees against her chest, her hands hiding her face. "Aw, Jim," she sobbed. "Oh, Jim."

Crying women don't bother me. Okay, that's a lie. They do, but they do not scare me away. I crossed the room and settled beside her, risking amputation to circle my arm around her waist. "What, babe? Tell me. Whatever it is, I'm sorry. Okay? All my fault. Completely. Guilty on all charges. Just…" I rested my cheek on the top of her bowed head. "Cry it out. Then tell me, so I can fix it."

It took a couple of minutes and an equal number of shudders, but finally she managed to choke out an explanation.

"I'm ugly."

Huh?

"Are you kidding? You're beautiful, honey." Okay, maybe the denim was unraveling in a ragged hem on her shorts; maybe the *Dark Shadows* T-shirt had faded to *Faint Shadows*. She still looked great to me.

"I'm fat."

"You are not. You just had a baby." I would have confessed I loved the added lushness to her curves, but women just don't seem to like hearing stuff like that. Cuddle all you want, men, but always say the pants make them look skinny.

Denny's next sentence barely made it past her vocal chords, it was so soft, so filled with fear.

"I'm not the same woman you married."

"Agreed." I lifted my hand to her chin, tilted her face up so she'd meet my eyes. "You're better. Seriously better. Every day. In every way."

She studied my face. Like she was looking for something she'd lost. I couldn't imagine what—then, finally, she sold me a vowel.

"You love her more than me now."

I think I've said it before, but I always considered Denise to have the brains in our partnership. That afternoon, I realized I had more than my share. I could have laughed. Could have joked off her concern. I mean, how ludicrous could she be? Love Rachel more? Love Denise less? If that wasn't laughable, nothing was.

But I didn't make light—though it went against my nature to clamp down on the comedy. Instead I kissed her on the nose. "Wrong, woman. First, middle and last. So damn wrong."

"No?" she whispered.

"I love our daughter. Of course I do. How could I not? I mean, come on. We made her, you and I. Together." I pressed my forehead to hers. "I couldn't have done it without you—wouldn't have wanted to with anyone else. Okay? But that together thing? That makes you number one. For freaking ever. Maybe longer."

I leaned back, grasped her shoulders, and gave her a shake. "If you ever forget it again? I'm going to…" I had to dig to come up with something harsh enough to use as a threat. In the end, wiseassery prevailed. "I'll mess up your sock drawer every day for the rest of your life."

She gave me a watery smile that turned into a laugh, then transformed into a wiggle of eyebrows and a pouty lower lip. "*Oui oui, monsieur,*" she said in a disgraceful French accent. (Yeah, no Supporting Actress Award either.) "I vill not forget, *mon ami.*"

You know what? Turns out there are lots of ways to make up—even with stitches in your belly. But you're going to have to take my word for it.

After that I made a point of greeting Denise first as soon as I got home from work. A hug, a kiss, an annoying poke in the ribs. An "I love you— what's for dinner?" It wasn't always major or mushy. Just something that would prove, by its constancy, exactly where she stood in the hierarchy of my heart.

Even later when she was buried in grief, my Denny Lou would remember that. It would remain for her the one eternal truth of our life together—a final message from me that she was first. She was last. She was always.

Now, as for my second sweetheart? Some of the gilt wore off Princess Rachel about the same time she began to speak in words as opposed to coos and screeches. (Always one or the other. And I do mean always. Did the kid ever sleep?)

My daughter's first royal decree at age three months was "pretty." No kidding. I'm told that an adjective is rare, but Rachel was ever a groundbreaker. She made sure we knew it wasn't a fluke by saying it nonstop for a month, signifying anything that caught her attention. Eventually, however, she began to use it solely when we were in the car at night passing a McDonald's. Not sure why, but those glowing arches made such a big impression on our poet laureate she'd decided they warranted their own designated name. McPretty's.

Rachel's second word was "mama." I naturally was disappointed, but not surprised. The girl knew who was responsible for supplying breakfast, lunch, dinner and the occasional late night snack. I couldn't blame her for wanting an ironclad way to summon her next meal.

But Rachel's third word?

Nope. Not dada. Or dahdeeeee. Or even a half-hearted da.

Plug.

Meaning pacifier. A freaking pseudo-mama, for God's sake.

In time, my daughter would acknowledge my parentage by uttering the sound "dada"—but it would be a distant fourth in her lexicon.

Denise tried to console me with logic. "We didn't use the word often enough around her, honey. I mean, I don't call you daddy or dada, do I? I say Jim. She can't manage the *jay* sound yet or you would have been first."

Nice try, Denny Lou.

No. Not a nice try. Blatant bullshit.

Okay, okay... loving blatant bullshit.

Bottom line: I never stopped adoring my daughter but I never fully forgave her. Especially since she was an otherwise precocious wordsmith. For example, it didn't matter that we told her over and over that those fuzzy brown rodents in the yard were squirrels, she would demure. "Tails," she would correct us. Firmly. "They are Tails." And olives? Nuh-uh. Those were "Red Noses." Tasty little red noses she would pop in her mouth all day if you let her. And honestly? How can anyone with eyes and a brain deny it? They *are* tails. They most definitely *are* red noses.

But dada? Maybe I didn't look like one. Or maybe she was having trouble saying "Furry Faced Other Parent Who Honks Like a Goose." In any case, I had to accept I'd finished out of the money.

Ah, but Jimmy! I was determined our second child would be my salvation. After all, he was the offspring who'd inherited my eyes, my face, my barking laugh. He was the seed of my loins. The chip off my block. Junior to my Senior. Certainly James Patrick Meyer, Jr. would recognize the special bond we shared. Would absolutely not let his old man down.

Not if the old man had anything to say about it.

I started whispering dada in his ear in the delivery room. It was the first thing I said to him every morning, and the last thing I murmured to him every night. I made it an addendum to his bedtime prayers: "Now I lay me —and dada—down to sleep." The poor kid heard a string of endless dadadadadadadadas with every diaper change. Hell, I would have called each bite of food that passed his lips dada if I hadn't been afraid he would try to chew off my finger when I passed him the salt one day.

"Dada, Jimmy," I crooned to him one morning as I hoisted him out of his crib and over my head. He greeted me with a gale of baby giggles. "Say dada."

He smiled down at me, deposited a string of drool in my open mouth, and waved his pudgy hands.

Then I swear to you I saw a lightbulb form above his dark curly head.

"Dada?" I prompted. "Can you say dada, kiddo?"

His brown eyes glowed. He curled his bow-shaped lips into a teddy bear grin. And as angels sang *alleluia*, he spoke his first word.

"Mama!"

Denise heard my agonized cry all the way down in the basement where she was slogging her way through another load of dirty diapers.

"Jim!" she screamed. "What's wrong? What's happened?"

"Damn," I muttered under my breath. "Nothing," I hollered back while my son pounded my cheeks with tiny clenched fists. "Stubbed my toe," I called out.

I tucked Jimmy against my hip and glared down at his grinning face. "We are going to pretend you didn't say that," I ordered him. "Dada."

"Mama!" he answered gleefully.

"Do you want to drive a car one day?"

"Mama?"

"Don't count on it, kid. When it comes to car keys, it's a man's world. Dada rules. Get it?" We locked eyes, a classic stare-down between dueling generations. "Curfew? My domain, too. Dada."

"Mama!"

I pressed my nose to his. "You're pushing it, buster. Allowance? Gone. Your first beer? Not until you're twenty-five."

"Mama, mama, mama."

"Aw, Jimmy. I was counting on you, buddy." I tried to pout… and the little turd laughed. Laughed!

"Dada?" I coaxed as all hope faded.

He giggled. Snorted. Rocked his head back in a passable imitation of my father's uninhibited guffaw. Then punched me in the jaw—with a pretty good left hook, too.

"Mama!"

"Dada," I insisted.

He chortled. He cackled. I'm telling you, he even threw in a honk and a titter for good measure. And between each snigger he repeated like a chant: "Mama! Mama! Mama!"

Then I got it.

"Dada! Dada! Dada!"

He bounced in my arms. Lifted his hands like tiny starbursts over his head. Slapped them down on my nose.

"Mama! Mama!"

He was making a joke. My kid. My genius son. He knew exactly who I was and what I wanted him to say—and was poking fun at me.

I couldn't stop the tears from filling my eyes as I hugged him tight. Stupid eyes.

Truth? That shared joke? Beat the hell out of dada any day.

I knew I could count on him.

Chapter Void: The D Word

Time is a river. That's the best way I know how to explain it. For the living it appears to have a beginning and an end: we are born and we die. Each day finds us in the middle, moving from one point to the next. What's that thing people say? Stop and smell the roses, because what you see at this moment? It's already disappearing around the bend behind you.

I was in a coma that was growing deeper with each struggling inhale. For me, time was still a river but I was no longer floating on top of it. I was part of it. And when you *are* the water, you experience it in its entirety. Beginning, middle, and the fact that it doesn't end at all.

I was becoming one with time. Still a single molecule, but being absorbed into a vast sea of eternity. I could see myself learning my first word. Taking my first steps. Starting my first job. Making love for the first time. And the one hundredth.

Was that my son going off to college? Hey, Rachel! Is that my first grandson... my first granddaughter... and my second? New houses. New spouses. New holidays piling up one on top of another. Events weren't so much *gathering* around me as they *were* me.

I wasn't the dearly departed yet, so a lot of what I felt and saw was still changeable—but I could also see God was not going to intervene.

It's called free will.

The Big Guy gave it to us as our most precious gift. He allowed us the right to choose, and that's why he declines to meddle in our affairs—even when he might wish to with all his infinite heart. From the silent womb of my coma I could see the prayer circle springing up in St. Louis; could hear my brothers and sisters bartering with the Savior to do a little more saving; could feel rosary beads sliding between anxious fingers. I could see Daria, a Rubenesque madonna, crying and begging as she rocked my babies in her lap; could see my father-in-law Len with sad Danny Kaye eyes staring into the dead fire of his wood stove, refusing to believe his God would deny him the pleasure of my company on Christmas Eve.

The Big Guy saw and heard and felt it all. And he cried, too.

But he would not make a miracle. The fact is, he seldom does. Miracles are dangerous things. All of the choices made freely by all the people of all the world had led to this moment. Big and little. Good and bad. All the paths that had been taken, right down to which sperm met which egg at which time. All of it made up the water in the river. Altering one outcome would alter them all.

So God cries, just as we do. But he will not take away that most precious of his gifts to us.

On this occasion, however, the Big Guy would give a single molecule of water named Jim the opportunity to make a final choice of his own.

Dr. Lawrence is the first person to say the D word out loud.

My dad and mom, Denise and her mother are sitting side-by-side on a long couch inside a private room off the ER. A plastic bag emblazoned with the St. Vincent Medical Center logo sits upright between Denise's feet. Her hand is tight around the handles. Periodically she releases them. Then grabs hold again. Inside are the things they'd removed from my body: my belt, splattered with white paint from our renovated bathroom; my wallet with its treasure-trove of photos taken moments after our children's births; my boots, the laces slashed; a single fur-lined leather glove; my jeans and shirt and new grey jacket a piecemeal of ragged ribbons. Every now and then, Denny slips a hand inside the bag and fondles the raw edges of that jacket, like a security blanket.

I'll buy him a new one, she is thinking. *As soon as he's better, I'll rush out and get another one just like it.* Before Christmas, she is sure. I'd be better before Christmas. Anything less is unimaginable.

"Jim's brain is bruised," Dr. Lawrence explains from his perch on the coffee table in front of them. Even seated, he is an imposing man: thick sandy hair beginning to silver, and intense eyes; a serious face suited to his calling; central casting's top candidate to play the role of neurosurgeon and champion. "It's swelling," he says. "But his skull is not damaged—which is a good thing and a bad thing."

My father cuts his eyes to the side to where my mother sits silently, nodding. The warning is ignored—or else Dr. Lawrence isn't one to sugar-coat the truth. "It is going to continue to swell over the next three days," he continues, "and it's not going to have anywhere to go."

Denny's fingers stray again to the torn jacket. "What will you do about that?" she asks him, her tone halfway between a plea and an order.

He looks her straight in the eye. "Nothing," he admits. "There is nothing I *can* do. It's up to Jim now."

Everyone turns to her, as though they are waiting for her to demand another answer. Like maybe she, as my wife, has the authority to demand more.

"Okay then," she says. "What does *Jim* have to do?"

Lawrence leans forward, his gaze fierce. "One of three things is going to happen, Denise. Some people with a closed-brain injury wake up perfectly fine—a little memory loss, perhaps; don't remember the hours leading up to their accident—but otherwise, right as rain." He places a hand on her knee, but when she pulls away, he nods and straightens. Gives it to her the way they both prefer: undiluted. "Others wake up after three days with serious handicaps, depending on what portion of their brain has suffered the most damage. They might not be able to speak, to walk, to feed themselves. There could be a year or more of intensive therapy ahead—which could make Jim *almost* right as rain. Or," he adds after a pause. "leave him with permanent disabilities."

Denise's head is working out the problem. I can see it in the way her brows pull together, her pupils dwindle to tight pinpoints. *I'll go back to work,* she is thinking. She'd retired from teaching when Rachel was born. *My certification is still good. Maybe do some subbing.* She is making a list, her chin dipping with each new item: set up a schedule to get Jim to therapy; find daycare for the kids; contact Whitmer to see if there are any openings; find out what equipment Jim might need—a hospital bed? A wheelchair?

She shudders, but draws a cleansing breath. She can do this. Will do anything.

"Or," Lawrence is saying again. He shifts his eyes to my father, then to my mother, and to my mother-in-law in turn. In the end he settles solely on Denise. "Or," he repeats, "the swelling will be too much. It will crush Jim's brainstem…"

Denise squeezes her eyes shut.

"And he will die."

My mom gasps. It is the only sound in the room. Even the river of which I am a part seems to stop moving for a heartbeat.

Denise opens her eyes. Sees the future and chooses the direction she will take. *Let him live,* she prays. *I'll take care of the rest. Let. Him. Live.* "Can I see him?"

Lawrence nods. "In a little while. He's being moved to Intensive Care."

"Will he know we're there?"

Of course I will, sweetheart.

"He's unconscious, " Lawrence explains. "We're keeping him that way until the swelling peaks, so he's more comfortable. But even people in a coma tell us afterwards they could hear their families speaking to them."

Denny inclines her head in acknowledgement. So calm. So calm. So freaking terrified, but hiding it under a mask.

Oh, Daria is going to hate that, I know. Will want to shake her sister until she wails and cries. But that will never happen, because this is so my Denny Lou.

"That's good, " she says. "I want to talk to him." *Tell him I love him and I've got this covered. Tell him to focus on only one thing. Coming home.*

"Soonest," Lawrence promises. Then he stands. "He's got a lot going for him. He's young. Strong."

Denise cuts him off. "And he has every reason to live."

Unfortunately, I also had one very good reason not to.

The dream came flooding back to her the moment Denise entered the ICU. The room they had put me in was sectioned in two by a hospital curtain. To her right through a crack in the drape, she can see a frail old man, propped up in his bed, eyes open, staring as she passes. She starts to smile a quick greeting before she realizes it will be wasted.

He's dead, she thinks. She doesn't know how she knows, but she does.

To her left, I mirror the old man's posture. I, too, am in a hospital bed: Sitting up. Legs extended. Arms at my side. Eyes slitted.

Naked.

My family had been expecting one of those snazzy open-backed hospital gowns, but I am not wearing one. Not even a blanket. From the hips down, I am attired in a pair of black rubber inflatable pants. Nothing else.

"His temperature rose too high," a nurse explains without being asked. "We removed everything we could to help keep him cool." She adjusts the drip on a nearby IV, one of many in a forest of IVs. She glances toward my legs. "His blood pressure is dropping a bit, as well. So." She nods at the hissing pants, returns to her duties and her charts. "The air inside is cool and the pressure forces the blood up and into the body's core." She catches herself and softens her recitation. "Into Jim's body."

Even my father seems confused. This isn't a tool he's ever needed in the environment of a delivery room.

The nurse knows who he is. Probably is telling my family more than required because of it. "It's more important to keep the circulation moving around the vital organs than the legs. Jim's heart? His lungs? This will help protect them from damage."

"Why is he sitting up like that?" Denny's voice doesn't break, but I know her too well. Her distress hits me harder than the fall ever did.

"We're trying to minimize the swelling in his brain by keeping his head elevated." The nurse turns to the bank of monitors piled at my side. Scribbles numbers. Taps a dial. Returns to her scribbling. My heart rate is a bit erratic. They can see that. But my father will reassure them it is not unusually weak or crazy wild. My breathing is ragged, but that is to be expected, considering my trauma. I have not yet been intubated. That indignity will come later. Soon. But later. My temperature hovers at one hundred and two degrees Fahrenheit. High, but manageable. Just. For a time anyway.

"But why does he…?"

My wife stops herself. She was about to add "…look like he did in my nightmare?" The nightmare where one glance had told her the man she loved was dead.

I wasn't. Not yet. And maybe not at all.

So she leaves the sentence unfinished and focuses on the other: on "maybe not at all."

I am doing the same. Am thinking long and hard about it from the depths of time's river.

The nurse finishes her paperwork and says what they always say to the families who gather here in the world of Maybe He Will or Maybe He Won't. "You should go home now. It's late. Get some sleep. We'll take good care of him." She is speaking to my father when she says the rest: "Jim is receiving the best care we can provide. He has the best experts and the finest neurosurgeon watching over our shoulders, to make sure we do." She smiles, a small tentative twitch of lips. "You can go home knowing he's in great hands."

Everyone exchanges cautious glances. Each of them comes to me to kiss my cheek, squeeze my hand. To tell me they'll be back in the morning. To sleep well. That all will be better soon.

Denise makes sure she is last. I feel her cool lips on my feverish cheek. She wants to kiss me on the mouth. I know it, even try to turn my head to return the kiss. She does not and I cannot. She's afraid of hurting me more. Doesn't realize nothing ever can again. "I'm staying," she tells me. "I'll be right outside. Don't worry about a thing, Jim. Just sleep and get better. That's your only job." She straightens. "I love you, you know. I've got your back. I'll take care of everything."

The nurse ushers them out. Denise gives me a last look through the open door.

"I'll take care of everything."

She sure will. We are a team. Have been from the first, when we were just partners putting together a show. Have remained so as we put together a love, a life, a family.

I would do the same for her, if our situations were reversed. I'd find a way to pay for the extra care she would require. Would work two jobs if I had to. Would bring her home where she belonged, no matter how desperate her condition, how heavy her needs. (We'd promised each other that, back when we were sure we would live forever.) I would feed her. Make special meals—puree them if that's what she could swallow. I would listen patiently to her words when they are not words at all. Only grunts or vacant stares. Would try to understand and respond. I would bathe her. Dress her. Change her diapers. Rearrange the house to accommodate the mounds of equipment she might need to just open her eyes and breathe each day. Would hold our kiddos on her lap as she lay in a hospital bed instead of our marriage bed, reading to them—to her—from storybooks that would age with their development, but would remain a confusing blur to her scrambled mind. And I would do it until the day I died.

Denise is only thirty-three. That could be a very long time.

I am seven years younger.

Since arriving at the hospital and settling into this muddled sleep I've had little to do but listen. I am Wild Bill's son, a medical celebrity of sorts. Outside my father's hearing, staff members have been talking. Gossip and opinions are bartered like currency around my bed.

"I heard he fell off a roof. Landed on his back."

"What the hell was he doing on a roof with all this snow?"

"Putting up Christmas decorations."

"What? Was he nuts?"

"Stop it. This is Doc Meyer's kid."

"Yeah. Horrible thing."

"What are his chances?"

"Not good. If he landed on his back…"

"Probably bounced the back of his skull."

"Brainstem injury."

"If it were me? I wouldn't want to come back from that."

"Not everyone ends up in a vegetative state."

"Not sure that wouldn't be a blessing."

"How do you figure?"

"Memory loss? Not able to reason? Loss of speech? Inability to read? To plan? To complete a task?"

"Had a patient a couple years ago? Came partway back but couldn't control her temper. Shouted obscenities at her baby. Stole the family car, drove to Indiana, rammed a light pole."

"Round-the-clock supervision. Rehab costs a mint, I hear."

"Poor bastard."

"Poor family. He has kids."

"Doc Meyer's son."

"Shit."

I second that.

I might not have been able to see or speak anymore, but I sure as hell could hear. Didn't like it much, but I heard every bitter word. The Big Guy didn't have to say to me, "Here's your choice, kid." I was of the river now, and could see all the possible outcomes stretching out around me.

I did not want to die. But I did not want to become one of Denny's lists either. I wanted to come back whole. There just didn't seem to be a lot of whole floating around.

Oh, honey, you're going to hate me for even thinking this. I'm hating myself for twisting and turning it in my head, examining it to see how it might fit. But we have insurance. You won't lose the house. The kids will remember me the way I want them to. You'll hurt, but as the years pass, you'll heal. You won't grow to detest our life. A life you never bargained for. Or be driven into the ground by guilt for not being selfless enough to shoulder the burden. Day after day. Month after month. Year after grinding year.

God forbid—and I mean that, Fella—you might even find someone new to love one day.

Shit indeed.

If I decide to stop taking backstrokes toward the surface, to let the hereafter pull me under for good… you'll be mad at me. Furious. But only for a time, right? You will forgive me. Eventually. You'll have to. It's how you roll, as the kids will one day say. You can't stay angry forever. Can you?

You love me.

I love you.

I would give you all the best things life has to offer, if I could. But if I can't? If my body will be too damaged to give you even some of the best?

Well. I do have an escape clause.

In sickness and in health. The vow I forgot. The loophole in our contract.

Come tell me goodnight, my darling. And begin to forgive me. Please.

If it's the last thing I do, I'm going to give you the world.

I just won't be in it.

Come, babe. Please come.

Chapter Ten: Hear After

First words.

They take time for a newborn to grasp. To mimic. To learn. And finally to speak in a way that is understood. Pretty. Mama. Dada. Tail.

Denny. Come. Sorry.

Love.

It's possible, I imagine, for some of us who die to never learn the new language. After all, we've become a different kind of energy. Our "life" is no longer physical. (Yeah, yeah, we're ghosts—if that's the only way you can wrap your head around it.) We don't go around shouting *Boo!* because we don't have lips to form a proper B. Besides, it's tacky, okay? In poor taste.

I suspect, as well, that not everyone who dies has the same motivation to speak that I did. The people they leave behind may not be open to listening —or cannot bear to.

I coded three times before Denise finally heard me calling.

Dad had convinced her to try and get some sleep—to get away from the ICU for at least a while. He'd given her the key to his office and explicit instructions to the Intensive Care staff to call there if anything happened. Reassured she would be notified in case of an emergency, Denny and her mom had bedded down on cots in one of his examining rooms.

The first time my blood pressure bottomed out, the staff were too busy handling the crash to call her.

The second time, they were still working to save me—but they also were pretending to forget. Calling the wife of the soon-to-be deceased to break the horrible news? That could be put off a little longer yet.

At some point, as I continued to make the alarms scream and quiet and scream again, someone's finger hesitated before tripping the switch that might have silenced the machines for good. A second someone had reminded them all who I was.

Suddenly, restarting the heart of Dr. William J. Meyer's son... intubating the lungs of Dr. William J. Meyer's son... plugging the body of Dr. William J. Meyer's son into every life-supporting device known to man? That was paramount.

A phone call to the guy's wife? Not so much.

I wasn't going to make it. I was dying. Again and again. But no one wanted to be the one to say it. Let alone allow me to go peacefully. Does this sound bitter? I don't mean it to. I understand what those doctors and nurses were up against. As Dr. Lawrence would tell my wife later that morning, "I recommend leaving Jim on life-support one more day. We have to give him time to come back. If he can."

But they had instructions, damn it. I wanted my wife to be with me one last time, and they weren't reaching for the freaking phone! A nurse dared to mention it but was silenced by a lot of Are You Kidding Me? looks.

They thought they were being kind, letting Denise keep her hope alive one night longer. I get that. But I knew my wife better than they did. Not being here by my side when she felt I needed her most would tear her apart. It wasn't going to do what was left of me any good either.

Motivation. It's a powerful teacher.

I started calling for Denise after the second code. She was my other half—and she was only two floors above. Surely that wasn't too far for my love to reach. Certainly I could make her hear me when she was that close.

Denise.

Nothing.

She couldn't possibly be sleeping. How could she be? But it had been a traumatic day. Maybe…

Denny Lou? Denny!

Still no answer.

This psychic crap was just that. How could I make her hear me? Make her know how important this was?

At that moment? When for once I would have welcomed an instructions sheet? Nada. So I guess it's true: you really do reap what you sow, because *Ghostly Communication for Dummies* did not manifest.

Then it hit me. I'd said it already, hadn't I? I knew my wife better than anyone. And what I knew was my woman was a list maker. A careful plotter. The spouse who left no task undone. *That* was my Denny. So, what would get her here the fastest?

Sweetheart? Honey? Wake up, babe. There's something you forgot to do.

"What's wrong?" Esther asked.

Denise was sitting up, swinging her feet off the cot and onto the floor, fishing around with her toes for the shoes she'd shucked an hour before. "Um."

"Can't sleep?"

"Uh. No." Not finding them, she slid off the side of the bed to her knees, began to grope underneath in the dark. "That's not it. I have to."

Her voice didn't trail off like you might expect it would. She simply stopped.

"Have to what, honey?"

Denise didn't answer. Only huffed in satisfaction as she dragged the missing shoes out and into her lap. "I have to."

She extended one leg, stuffed a sneaker onto her foot. "Have to go down for a minute."

"Down? To ICU?"

"Yeah."

"They said they'd call," her mom reminded her.

"They might forget." Both shoes on, she pulled herself to her feet, started toward the door. "Besides."

Esther rose as well, letting her blanket slip unheeded to the floor. "I'll come with you."

"It's okay, Mom. You don't have to. I just."

This time, Denise seemed to realize she hadn't completed the thought.

I gave her a nudge.

She turned to her mother and stared, her eyes the only things glimmering in the dark. "I just."

"What?"

Her mom moved to join her, slid an arm around her waist. "What, Denise? What is it?"

Denny tilted her head to the side, listened intently for a moment. "I forgot to tell him goodnight."

"No, dear. You're wrong. You did. I heard you. Besides. It's after three. He's asleep."

"Doesn't matter," my wife insisted, and pulled away, turning to the door. "I told him I love him, but I didn't say goodnight. He would expect that. He *won't* sleep until I do. Besides…" She listened intently again.

I was getting through!

"I told him I'd be nearby." Her eyes widened as she stared back at her mother over her shoulder. "I'm not. Nearby. And I need to be. I have to tell him goodnight. Now."

She yanked open the door, headed for the exit of my father's office. "Take the key, Denise!" her mom called after her. "Wait. Let me get it. I'm coming."

I'd done it. She'd heard me. She was on her way. I could hold on that long, at least.

The door was closed when my wife got to my room. It had not been when she'd left me—they seldom are in Intensive Care. Denise hesitated. She wasn't sure she could just walk right in, so she knocked.

A man opened it a crack. I do not know if it was a doctor or a nurse—don't care much either way. I am only grateful my wife didn't have to encounter him again after that night.

He slapped a hand against the jamb: entry denied. "What?"

"Um. My husband is in..."

He cut her off. "We don't have time for you right now."

She stumbled back, her face collapsing in fear. "Has something happened?"

"Would the door be closed if it hadn't?"

I swear, if the Big Guy had allowed me just five minutes inside my old functioning body, that jackass would have been flat on his face on the floor, a stethoscope tied around this neck, and a probe up an uncomfortable orifice.

"Now, just a minute," Esther interrupted, Mama Bear to the rescue. (Thank you, mother-in-law dearest.) "That is uncalled for. You are making a difficult situation worse." She paused, considered where she was, and was perhaps deciding to edit herself. Then again, maybe she was soaking up spill-over from my thoughts. "You are an ass," she continued, more strongly. "This woman has every right to expect decency, no matter what has happened. But maybe Doctor Meyer will find your behavior excusable. What do you think?"

It was Mister Rude and Thoughtless's turn to hesitate. Additional time for cognitive thinking didn't help him much, though. Or maybe he didn't have the extra cylinders needed for courtesy.

"We are busy."

A monitor began to wail behind him. "Hear that? It means his blood pressure has zeroed out. Again. We'll come get you when we can. Now go." He began to close the door in their faces, but paused. "Please."

Then he shut them out—away from me and the alarm that continued to bawl in protest.

My wife's eyes, flickering with terror, tried to burn holes through the wood to reach me. When they couldn't, she lifted her hand, let her fingertips graze the surface.

Let them fall away.

"Oh," she whispered. "Oh."

She turned—her movements jerky and uncertain—to search the hall behind her, the large waiting area at its end, the darkened far-off corners of a hospital all but asleep. Not finding what she was looking for, she began to whimper. "No," she cried, softly at first but growing. "No."

Esther took Denny's elbow, began to steer her toward the empty waiting room.

"Noooooo. Noooooo. Noooooo."

Oh, my darling. I am so sorry. Please. Please. Please. Don't. I won't go yet. Not until you can see me one more time breathing. I'll wait until later, okay? Just please. Don't.

Denise's cries would ring out through those empty halls the rest of the night, over and over—long unbroken no's that cut off only when she ran out of breath. Then would start again every time a new alarm shrilled from behind my closed door.

Oh, baby. I'm so sorry. My first words from the other side... and I couldn't have bungled them more.

The sun rose on my last day. I didn't see it, but I felt it. There is something mystical about that yellow star making another appearance after the endless hours of darkness. It's like you can feel its warmth in the marrow of your bones even before the first rays crest the horizon. Our early ancestors welcomed sunrise as a daily salvation. The stalkers that haunted the night couldn't hide in the shadows anymore. With the sun in the sky above, homo sapiens had a fighting chance against the predators that would feed on them.

The sun brings light. Warmth. Renewal. It banishes fear for a time. It ignites hope. It's always darkest before the dawn, they say. But after the dawn... anything is possible. You just have to make it through the night. We brought those cliches with us out of the caves, and have never lost them.

The grey dawn of December twenty-second filtered through the windows of the ICU waiting room, and Denise stopped crying. She shoved back all thought of death, insisted to her mother she wasn't hungry—to go grab breakfast without her—and began to haunt the closed door of my room. As soon as the day shift allowed it, she rushed in.

Machines buzzed and bleeped and hummed around me. I shuddered that Denny should have to see me like this. Needles pricked my arms, slithering fluids into my veins. My lungs inflated and fell—but I had little to do with it. A thick tube had been snaked down my throat. I couldn't have spoken to her if I'd wanted to. Grunted maybe.

Wouldn't that have been a special greeting?

They'd lowered the head of my bed at some point during the night. Probably easier to perform all the life-saving crap they'd used to keep me on this earth a little longer. Okay, okay. No more bitching about it. They thought they were doing what I would want—or at least what my father the important doctor would want. And now that I realized how not-strong my wife was going to be on the inside, I was happy to have a few more hours to help shore her up on the outside.

So I was breathing. Blood was pumping through my heart. My skin was warm, no longer feverish, but a comfortable and steady 98.6. I wasn't staring dazedly through half-slitted lids. They'd managed to close my eyes to approximate the look of sleep. (They wouldn't be able to keep them shut, though. A small desperate part of my brain would pop them open now and then. Seeking one last look.) A glance at the monitors would have shown Denise my respirations were steady and regular. No hint of variation. That my BP was likewise locked in its proper place. If any green line spiked at will on any screen, it was my heart rate—which was still managing to travel to the beat of its own drummer. For now, at least. But the rest? As regular and textbook as General Electric could make me.

Last night, I'd promised my wife I would hang in there, would keep breathing, so she could see me that way one last time. And I'd kept that promise.

Be careful what you wish for.

Denise did not touch me during that first brief visit. It really wasn't me stretched out before her. It was a puppet attached to a lot of lines and tubes and strings, a marionette forced to keep dancing at the whim of medical science.

I heard her swallow. "Why is he doing that?" The question was directed to one of the nurses.

"His hands?"

"Yes. Why is he clenching them? Over and over like that? Is he in pain? Why is he in pain? Why haven't you done something to…" My wife's warrior was emerging, prepared to do battle to protect me.

"He is not in pain," a woman interrupted gently. "It's a kind of rhythmic seizure. His brain is reacting to stimuli of some sort. It's not unusual among people who've experienced this kind of trauma."

I felt Denise shudder, a soft rustle of clothing against the sheet that covered me. They'd ditched the rubber pants, thank God. Had made me appear comfortable. I couldn't feel comfort or any other damn thing, but for Denny's sake I was pleased that they'd made me look more like a normal patient and less like a desperate experiment.

"It's sometimes a good sign," the nurse continued. "It can mean a portion of his brain is beginning to respond because it's trying to come all the way back."

Aw, geez, first last night's Mr. Gloom and Doom. Now this morning's Pollyanna. Bad timing all the way around.

Denise said nothing.

She moved closer. I could smell her perfume, mixed with pungent sweat from an anxious night spent in the same clothes. I welcomed it.

"He can hear you, you know."

After a moment Denise cleared her throat, and spoke in a whisper too faint for any ears but mine. "I don't think so," she murmured. "But just in case... I love you, babe."

It didn't matter that I had no control over my body anymore. I knew my cue, and muscle memory kicked in. *"I love you, too."*

Shit and double shit. A four-syllable grunt, just as I'd feared.

"Okay," she stammered softly. "Okay."

Then she left me.

I didn't know if I'd made things better, or worse.

She never spoke to me alone again in that life. Family and a scatter of friends began arriving over the course of the morning, everyone wanting to see me for themselves.

Denise would escort them, entering my room on a wave of optimistic support: "He's going to make it... Prayers have been flying all night... God would never let this happen to your kids... Jim's too good... Too strong... Too young..." But inevitably she would be pulled away from me again on an outgoing tide of silence and tears.

Hope's a slippery thing. Difficult to hold onto when the truth keeps punching you in the face.

Only my children did not visit. I was grateful for that—really did not want them to see me like this—but I couldn't help wishing with all my heart that I could see *them*.

Apparently it wouldn't disrupt the river of time to grant me a parting request, because the Big Guy delivered. Between one ragged heartbeat and the next, my kids called to me and I ran to join them.

Rachel and Jimmy were not at home, and it took me a few blinks to clear the haze before I figured out where they were. With Denise's Uncle Don and Aunt Carol.

Of course. That made sense. The family lived just a mile or two from our house on Elm Street. Daria must have enlisted their help. I'd never been there, but I recognized the faces, cued in to Donald's hearty laugh. The man was bold and boisterous; his wife soft-spoken and somber—the kind of person the Bible said would inherit the earth.

Was Don singing? Yes. And Rachel was joining him. *You are my sunshine… my only sunshine…*

Small correction. My daughter was doing more giggling than singing. I drank in every detail as I watched her dance around their living room, blonde hair swinging out in a short fan, a whirling dervish of glee.

On her great-uncle's shoulder a white cockatoo was doing its own dance, sidling back and forth as it added its piping voice to the song. *Sunshine… My only sunshine…*

Oh, what a good image to treasure into eternity: Rachel, happy and joyful. Laughing and twirling and sharing a duet with a bird she would probably say was no bird at all. A creature that finally, to her clever mind, had been named exactly right: Sunshine. Bright and merry Sunshine.

But where was Jimmy?

Oh, on Aunt Carol's lap. With a baby bottle.

What the?

He was turning it in his pudgy hands, as if he were thinking the same thing; examining it like it was a prehistoric artifact. Which, to him, it was.

Jimmy had been breastfed, and then weened directly to a cup over a month ago. His face clearly said, What is this chewy nipple thing? Then he shrugged. Seriously. He *shrugged*. A gesture so like my own, I had to grin. Then my little bottomless pit did what he always did best. He stuffed something he assumed was edible into his mouth and made the most of it.

Oh, wow. Another blessed image.

What the hell was I giving up here? Why wasn't I trying harder to pull the pieces together? To stay with my family, damn the consequences?

Then Rachel left off singing and wandered to her brother's side. "Dada's at the hospital," she told her great-aunt. "He went in a big light-up truck. He's hurt, but doctor's gonna fix him. Mama said."

She smiled. So innocent. So sure. "We'll go get him. In the Mazda. He'll come home all better and play with us."

Yeah. That was why not. Because the pieces were never going to go back together the way they'd been. Dada was never going to be "all better."

Rachel and Jimmy and their mama deserved a whole dad.

I sent them a silent kiss, and closed my eyes. *Sorry, babies. Your mom will build you a good strong memory of me. Much better than a broken thing. Trust me on this. I know all about broken things that can't be fixed.*

I love you—be good. I'll be watching. Promise.

By afternoon, Denise was locked into the role of Dark Hostess, ushering people to and from my bedside, saying all the correct things at all the correct times. Not arguing with anyone who insisted I could still come back to her. Not agreeing with them either, I noted.

Very carefully, very deliberately, not crying.

My wife—soon to be my widow—was a consummate actress following a script written by etiquette and delivered by a zombie.

A few people exchanged glances behind her back. *Doesn't she feel anything?*

Of course she did. If I could tell, why couldn't they? Yes, my Denny appeared calm, but her expressions were carved in wax. True, her eyes seemed alert and dry, but they didn't look directly into yours. They were fixed on some flickering dial just over your shoulder. And maybe she wasn't trembling the way you wanted, but just watch her fingers twitch anytime a line on a monitor zigged instead of zagged, or a gauge began to hum in a different key. Denise's focus wasn't on you—or even on me anymore. It was devoted to the machines. She was watching, watching, watching; all the while talking, talking, talking.

So much easier than thinking.

For one brief moment, she broke character, daring to slip her hand inside mine. My muscles contracted, and my fist clenched.

"Look!" someone cried. "He knows you're here!"

Denny jerked away, wrenching my arm over the side of the bed to dangle amidst the tangle of lines and tubes. My touch was false—and she knew it. With indecent haste, she blundered past my guests and into the hall.

Why couldn't I get this dying thing right? I was killing the woman I loved as surely as the pressure on my brain was killing me.

"Doctor? Doctor Lawrence?"

I could hear her out there, cornering the one man she hoped could give her answers. *Someone should be with her,* I thought. *Some things are not meant to be heard alone.*

The tethers on my body were slipping, so I could step away if I wanted. I'd done it more than once already. But what was it doing to that lump of clay every time I broke the connection?

Hell, did it really matter anymore?

I sat up, the motion lifting me out of the bed and toward the ceiling—floating just like they say we do in those stories about near-death experiences. My place was at my wife's side, damn it, not hovering overhead like the Goodyear blimp. I thought myself down to the floor faster than you can say, "Sir Isaac Newton," then slipped through a wall and into the hall.

My wife and my neurosurgeon stood facing each other across from my room.

"Doctor," Denise said for the third time—like a talisman, a magic chant—her hands clasped together at her waist.

I wondered if she realized she was praying.

"I look at Ji…"

She halted, my name catching in her throat. Then tried again: "I look at my Jim. But. I don't *see* him. It's like… the man I knew—the man I *know*? He's not there. Am I wrong? Tell me I'm wrong."

The *please* cried silently at the end of the sentence.

The neurosurgeon heard it. How could he not? But he was too good a man to lie. Lawrence gave it to her straight like a shot of bourbon.

"Denise? I think you see what I see."

The wax splintered. The clear eyes dimmed. But Denise stiffened her spine and refused to tremble.

When she said nothing, Lawrence nodded and turned away.

Denny tried to move, too, but stumbled. Then steadied. Took a step. Then another. Knees locked, but carrying her forward.

I wanted to tell her it was all right to let me go. That it was all right for *her* to let go. To cry. To scream. To hurt. How the hell was I going to do that with the switch between my head and tongue offline?

The answer slipped out of a door into my wife's path.

Patricia Meyer, a woman who'd always had eyes in the back of her head, had a sharper pair in her heart. She took one look at my wife, and laid a hand on her arm.

The touch started a process Denny had been holding in check. She exhaled —a long windy sigh. Had she been holding her breath so very long? She leaned forward, teetering on the edge—still fighting to keep the pain padlocked inside a lead box, inside an oak chest, inside a granite tomb, inside a broken heart.

She gasped: "Mom. What should I do? The highs… the lows… It's so damn… *hard*." Climbing a mountain of hope one moment. Plummeting into a pit of despair the next. A soul could get whiplash. Even my strong, stubborn wife had limits.

Everything began to come undone: the carelessly glued edges ripping apart seam by seam. "How, how, how," she wailed. "How do I keep riding the ups and downs. Mom. How can anyone be expected to stay on this…this… *rollercoaster* forever!"

My mother was hurting, too. Even a dead man could see it. But that woman? What a saint. What a miracle. What a lucky man I'd been to have grown up under her care and love.

"Denise," she said, "don't ride it any more. Get off. Now." She lifted a palm to my Denny's cheek and let it rest there to catch the tears that I could not. "Give yourself some peace. Your babies are going to need you."

God but I love you, Mom. Thank you.

She'd given Denny permission to let go.

And me, too.

I wrapped myself around them, tried to gather them up—though it was as useless as trying to gather their cries.

Down the hall, in a room buzzing and humming with everything but life, a green line on a heart monitor flattened for a handful of beats. Then resumed. This time steady. Each peak the exact same height. Each interval in between the exact same length. Inhumanly perfect. Like all the other lines on all the other monitors.

The hardest recovery was about to begin.

Chapter Eleven: Do Not Disturb

Back in 1979 when Denise Meyer was still Denise Tomanski, coming out that she was dating me was like jumping into a pool of piranhas. Friends, family, people she'd gone to school with, the cheerleading squad, a guy panhandling on the corner, maybe the Channel 13 weatherman: everyfreakingbody had an opinion.

Most people speculated that Denise had been chasing me since my high school years, and was one of those teachers who would end up featured on *A Current Affair*. A handful said they accepted our relationship—but were already squinting, prepared to give my Denny Lou the stink eye when she turned out to be a tramp of the highest order. We would not have been surprised to see a billboard outside her apartment reading: Shame on you, Hester Prynne. Shame.

Good grief, folks, I wanted to shout. *Get a life and a scandal of your own, please.* I was having enough trouble keeping the woman in my corner as it was.

One guy expressed his "support" to Denny face to face: "Meyer? Good for you! If that's what you want, go for it. But, baby… he's so *small.*"

I was just shy of five-ten, one-fifty soaking wet—but only if I were holding a five-pound weight. Mr. Snide was six-two, two-fifty plus change. Every man alive of Denise's acquaintance was *small* in comparison. Not to mention—but I *will* (Hey, insulted manhood here.)—the Incredible Hulk had been chasing my woman since she was in high school, to no avail. So, fella, swallow those sour grapes and go home to your wife. I'm the guy Denise loved, and that is no *small* thing in anyone's book.

Do I sound a smidgen bitter? Not my usual cheery self? Sue me. I may be dead, but I'm still a guy—species *Maximus Territorialus.*

In the end, only our parents fell solidly on our side.

I'd thought I was keeping things discreet, not flaunting our relationship while I waited to see if Denise would succumb to guilt and kick me to the curb. Discreet, my butt, I guess. About a month after our first "date"—a movie we attended with a group of unsuspecting friends (cagey cover, eh?) —the phone rang at Denise's apartment.

I remained sprawled on my stomach on the floor, watching the tube, while Denny rose from the sofa to answer it. I didn't pay much attention.

Until she kicked my foot. Hard.

I rolled over with a silent *ow*—just in time to see her eyes widen. Denise had the phone tucked to her ear, and was stammering something I couldn't quite catch. She wiggled her fingers at me in a come-hither gesture—obviously wanting me to get up. Get over there. Now. Maybe faster than now.

As I was climbing to my feet she bounced her chin a handful of times like a bobble-headed doll, and mumbled, "Of course, I'd love to. Sure." Then she met me halfway, and thrust the receiver into my chest.

"It's your mother."

I tried not to fall back to the floor while performing a two-handed juggling act with the handset. *How did Mom get this number?* More importantly, how had she known I would be on the other end of it?

I put the phone to my ear, and waited to hear what would come out of my mouth.

"Uh, yeah?"

Master of oratory, that's me.

"Hi, Jim. I just invited your girlfriend to Easter Sunday dinner. We'll be eating around two, after church. Will you guys be there?"

My brain still wasn't connecting the dots. "At church?" I asked.

"Well, of course, church. But I meant dinner. With your family. Your brothers and sisters will be here. Good chance for Denise to get to know everybody better." She didn't give me time to make up an excuse. "See you at two."

I don't know for sure, but I think I heard the corners of Mom's mouth turn up. "Or at Mass."

"Right," I agreed. "Mass. Dinner. Family. Got it."

"Bye, Jim."

"Uh, bye, Mom."

And that was that. Lack of matrimony notwithstanding, Denise had been invited into the Meyer tribe. Have I mentioned how neat my parents were? Can't say it enough.

Now, Leonard Tomanski? He scared the bejesus out of me. As Denise's father, he had every right to want to throttle the young upstart who had dared mess with his little girl. I mean, if some guy began spending serious time with my Rachel, and brought a load of rumor and scorn down around her head? The punk would be mulch.

Don't. Hurt. Our. Kids.

I think there's a T-shirt.

Safe to say, Mr. T was a man I did not wish to cross.

To make things worse—was that possible?—I liked the guy. He and Esther had been assisting with Denise's shows for several years: constructing sets, hanging wallpaper, crafting props—the usual bits and pieces that make up the backstage world of theater. At various times, I'd even raided their house for tables and chairs to furnish a set, and on one back-spraining occasion a refrigerator.

Len and Esther loved helping out as much as I did, so it was inescapable we would bond—her father and I especially. Take a big scoop of Danny Kaye, toss in a pinch of Ronald Reagan and a dash of Henry Winkler. Stir briskly then stretch the dough until it's long and lanky. You have Lenny Tomanski. Add to that the fact that the man was an electrician, a maintenance technician for General Mills? The guy who could keep the Cheerios guns firing? How could I *not* think he was cool?

Stop. Don't bother to Google it. Some brands of cereal really are shot from guns. How do you think those little Os get so puffy and crisp? Or, wait. Maybe that's how they get the tiny bullet holes. In any case, I was a squealing fanboy.

Mostly, though, because Leonard Tomanski invented the switchblade gun.

Right this way, down memory lane, if you please, back to the show that started it all, *Wait Until Dark*. To your right, you will see the script, and in fine print, a notation for a tricky illusion. To your left, is the director, one Denise Tomanski. Watch closely now as she dumps said illusion into our young hero's lap.

The special effect the script called for was supposed to allow the villain to hurl a knife at the show's heroine, and miss, just as she cuts the lights plunging them into darkness. Normally at this portion of the tour, the clever Stage Manager delivers the goods, and takes his bows. But you can hold the standing ovation, because this one had me stumped. Yeah, me. The original Inspector Gadget. Hard to fathom, but true.

For a week, I'd mulled and imagined and conjured up one gizmo after another, then crumpled each sketch into a tight little wad of frustration. Seven days of intensive imagineering? Zero options for throwing a sharp implement across the stage without turning the leading lady into shish kabob.

Enter, my genius father-in-law-to-be. On day eight of How the Hell Do We Do This Thing, Mr. T showed up with a spring-activated pistol contraption he'd built himself. Talk about assembly skills. That baby impressed the boxers right off my butt.

Imagine, if you will (said in my best Rod Serling impersonation): a metal tube and trigger mechanism. (Add patented Serling pause here.) A mysterious device that can be attached to the back of a stud supporting one wall of the set. Inside the barrel? A thin spear of metal resembling (cue theme music)... a switchblade. A device that would only work with a keen eye, precision timing, and a little help from… The Twilight Zone.

Okay, I'm done fooling around. Thank you for your patience.

Lucky for Denny, she had James Patrick Meyer behind the scenes. It would be my job to stand out of sight backstage, eyes on the action, finger on the trigger. When the evil Harry Roat, Jr. pretended to hurl a prop knife, the actor would palm it, and I would open fire.

The fake blade would pop through a hole in the wall, becoming visible to the audience so quickly it looked for all the world as though the "thrown" knife had struck there. Damn thing even quivered as though it had impaled itself in the door jamb. The thunk of it hitting the stop-plate inside Leonard's "knife gun" added an extra layer of scary to the FX.

Brilliance par excellence, Mr. T. I bow to your expertise even now.

Every night during curtain calls, Len Tomanski and I would grin at each other across the footlights: me through a crack in the side curtain, him from the second row where he would be applauding madly. As I said, I liked the guy, and he me. We had a lot in common. Like two fuses in the same electrical box.

Of course, that was before I began dating his daughter…. before I was spending an occasional night at her apartment, or her at mine. Okay, more than occasional.

Once he found *that* out?

Well, maybe Denise and I were still new at being a "we", but I did know this: if her father objected, that would be that. His opinion mattered more to her than anyone's. James Meyer would have ended up with a metaphorical switchblade vibrating in his broken heart.

Minutes after my mom ordered—er—extended an invitation to Easter dinner, Denise decided it was time to tell her parents about us, as well.

Gulp.

I told her I'd be happy to come along.

Denny only smiled. "You are such a bad liar, Meyer."

She exaggerated. I might have been lying, but not badly.

I insisted I should come. She insisted I should not. I persisted. She countered. Lather. Rinse. Repeat.

Which would have gone on indefinitely if she hadn't pointed out that my being there might make things more difficult.

Denny and her folks played on a bowling league once a week, and always met for burgers beforehand. If she broached the subject then—sort of dropped a word or two about our relationship into the conversation—well, they would be on neutral ground, in a public place. With food as a buffer, she figured the risk of yelling or thrown cutlery would be minimal.

"But if you show up," she argued, "Mom will sense something." Sort of like a Great White does when chum meets water.

Put that way, I had to concur. Jim Meyer should stay home. Or on a deserted island, whichever was farthest out.

On the designated evening, between a sip of Coke and a nibble of French fry, Denise screwed up her courage and said—super casual, like she was asking for the salt or something—"These fries are flat."

Her father nodded agreement without looking up from his plate. He passed her the shaker.

"Oh. And I'm dating someone new."

Her dad lifted his burger, took a bite, chewed and swallowed. Esther, in contrast, lowered her sandwich. Peered through slitted eyes. "Oh?"

If you knew my mother-in-law you know exactly how much meaning could be stuffed inside that single expletive.

Denise nodded, swirled a second fry through a mound of ketchup, put it in her mouth. "Uh-huh."

Esther thought that over for a moment as though it were the Dead Sea Scrolls, lifted a spoon to pretend she was going to eat, and elbowed Leonard in the arm. He missed his mouth with his second bite of hamburger. "Hey! Wha...?"

"Denise is dating someone."

He shrugged, gave his daughter a fond smile. "So what else is new?"

Esther was undeterred, her ESP in overdrive. "Someone we know," she decided, based on nothing.

"Yes," Denise confirmed. She gave them each a moment's consideration. "Someone you know quite well."

Leonard returned to his supper; again, less than riveted. His daughter was about to reveal her choice of bachelor in the Dating Game of life, and he was busy contemplating the benefits of yellow mustard over Grey Poupon. If I'd been there instead of hearing about it after the fact, I might have wondered just how many old boyfriends littered Denny's romantic landscape that her father was totally unconcerned about the prospect of yet another one.

"Dad?"

He raised his head. "I'm listening." (He was never any better at lying than I was.)

Denise drew a deep breath, held it, then dove into the deep end. "It's Jim Meyer."

Her mother dropped the spoon she'd been holding suspended ever since her daughter had uttered the words "dating" and "new" in the same sentence. Len didn't hear it fall. He stared at Denise for so long, she told me later she wondered if he'd had a stroke.

"*Jim?*"

"Yes."

"Jim from the Whitmer shows. *That* Jim?"

"The same."

"Really?"

"Really."

He turned to his wife. "You okay with this?"

"I'm very okay." Esther leaned in as though preparing to do battle. "Isn't it about time?"

Denny squeaked. "About *time*?"

"We saw it coming ages ago," Esther confirmed. "Didn't we, Len?"

"Dad? Do you hear what she's saying?"

Her father laughed. "It's Esther. Of course I hear her."

"And you're fine with this?"

"Fine?" He picked up his drink, took a sip, then lowered the glass.

Now, I should point out, Leonard Tomanski was as addicted to jokes as my father. When Daria's husband-to-be Michael asked if he could have her hand in marriage, Len had responded, "Sure. But what am I supposed to do with the rest of her?" So when his oldest daughter lobbed a straight line that night, the man couldn't resist flexing his funny bone so he could spike it back.

"Not exactly *fine*," he said. "More like…" He picked up his fork to return to his dinner. Stabbed an adjective. "Relieved."

Then he stabbed a fry. Chewed. Swallowed. Considered. "Yep. Relieved." Swapping the fork for his burger, he wound up, aimed, and scored. "What's hard to believe is you're *finally* bringing home a guy I like."

Was that the sound of Mr. T giving me his blessing? The way Denny had described the conversation to me later, it seemed to be. Still, I figured I should refrain from saying thanks right away. Wait a year. Or two. Just to be sure. In case he changed his mind.

After all, this was the man who figured out how to fire a switchblade through a wall.

You are no doubt wondering why I'm telling you this after it can no longer matter to the story. Am I avoiding talking about the obvious? That those days are gone… and me with them?

No. Because those memories were precisely *why* I could leave the woman I loved.

Ask any doctor or nurse who has dealt with patients caught in the grip of a coma. Some of us hang on long after we should because we feel we have unfinished business. Those same doctors and nurses will tell you that all it sometimes takes for us to die is a sincere promise by our survivors that they're going to be all right. That it's okay for us to leave.

My mom's assurance to Denise that she could get off the rollercoaster was one of those messages. The other was my knowledge that the four people who'd supported us in the beginning were there to do it again: Bill, Pat, Len and Esther—along with a waiting room filled with brothers, sisters, their spouses, and friends. Even more were on their way from near and far. Dozens of caring souls. My family. Her family. Our family.

I could go without fear, because my Denny would not be alone.

I had never been more wrong.

There wasn't anything I could do about it, and in my defense I had never died before so how could I have known?

See, grief isn't only about tears. It's about shock and denial, anger and guilt. Those are not emotions that make you want to throw your arms around someone. Throw a punch, maybe. An ashtray, sure. Give the widow a comforting hug? Not so much. Not early on. She's not the one you're crying over right that second, now is she?

It was no one's fault, but my darling was about to take her first steps down a long bitter road, and she was going to discover it was not only dark. It was empty.

Dr. Lawrence met with Denise and my parents to discuss the series of EEGs he'd ordered to determine if anything was still sparking in my head. There would be two scans taken hours apart, the first to register brain function, the second to make sure the results from the first were reliable. When he finished going over the procedure, my parents left the conference room, fingers linked.

Denise lingered a step behind, her gaze falling on their clasped hands.

Lawrence touched her shoulder. "A moment, please, Denise."

He gestured her back to the chair she'd vacated.

Face filled with questions, Denny returned to her seat, knotted her fingers in her lap. I tried to twine mine between hers.

Lawrence pulled up a chair at her side, scooted it to face her. "I wanted to go over a couple of things with you. Alone."

Denny dipped her head, not quite *yes*, but *go on*.

"I wish I had a more optimistic prognosis," he began, "but I believe Jim's EEG is going to show you one of two things: that he has no brain function, or not enough to sustain a normal life. I expect he will never be able to breathe on his own again."

Denise's face drained of expression.

"It will be up to you to decide what happens next."

More blank acceptance, less understanding.

"Denise," he repeated. "You."

She pressed her lips together, a thin slash of confusion.

"Not Jim's father. Or his mother. Not his doctor. You. All of us may have an opinion, but legally we have no say in Jim's future."

She blinked, the pieces falling into place. "I'm the one who has to decide whether or not to turn off his life support. Is that what you're telling me?"

"Exactly. It may not be easy. Your father-in-law is a doctor. Your family is Catholic. He and others around you may have a very different opinion from yours. I just wanted you to know that. Before the EEGs. Before I have to ask you that question."

Denise pushed up from the table, palms flattened there for a moment as she steadied herself. Then she straightened, and shook the doctor's hand, like he'd handed her a stock tip or a free pass for the parking garage—not the responsibility of making a decision that would turn a whole lot of worlds upside down.

I stepped to her side, wishing I could put my arm around her shoulders, but the best I could do was shadow her as she left the room and wandered away.

I had seen my wife do a lot of wandering over the last twenty-four hours, and it didn't surprise me. It was part of her nature to walk when she was troubled. Any time we'd had an argument...

What? You didn't think we argued? Yelled? Threw the car keys down the stairs (me) or threatened to get a divorce (her)? Hell, people, we were *married*. Real life married, not sitcom married. Yes, we fought, maybe less than some couples, and we always made up—but not until after Denny Lou had gone storming out to walk around the block and cool off. I'd learned to be patient.

Denise didn't know that my father had slipped away for a private moment of his own. Couldn't see him, standing around the corner in a hushed hallway, only a few footfalls away.

But I did.

This was not the confident doctor who'd strode into the Emergency Room two days before. With no more medical miracles in his bag, William Meyer had been reduced to a father about to lose a son, a man unable to conjure up even one small bit of magic to stop it.

My dad's back was turned. He didn't see my wife step around the corner, didn't hear her falter, then move closer.

"Dad?"

He jumped, pivoting to face her.

Denny was biting her lip.

My father was way too still.

So alike in their pain, I thought. So similar in their need to hide it.

Each of them pulled it together: she with an inhale, he with an upward shift of his shoulders. Neither realized how identical their postures, how interchangeable the fear in their eyes.

"Do you have time to talk?" she asked. "About the EEG?"

Dad grumbled something that sounded like *sure*.

"If it comes back flat—"

Denise fumbled, swallowed a knot of air that stuck painfully in her throat. "If it shows there's no function? What... ? What would that mean? To you?"

His answer was abrupt—brushed with anger. "It will mean he's brain dead."

My father's tone must have startled him as much as it did me. He paused. Grimaced. Then forced himself to say the rest, perhaps before he was prepared to. "It will mean he's gone."

This brittle intensity was not my dad's way. But Denny had stumbled into a whirlpool of helplessness that Bill Meyer the father had not intended anyone to see. She swayed from the sucking force of his pain. "I know, I know," she hastened to correct. "I didn't mean..."

I told her to take a breath, but she'd beaten me to it. This time, her words dared not tremble. "You know about medical things. I don't. I want to know if you think he would have any chance coming back from that. Because Jim and I talked about this. If he can't? I want to let him go."

It would mean breaking a promise to me, "but I won't take him off the vent, if you or Mom say otherwise."

My father slumped, his anger falling away, his shoulders dropping with it. It was the lowest I had ever seen him before, or ever would again except at my mother's funeral. He wasn't upset with my wife for asking the question. He was angry that *anyone* was being forced to ask it at all.

"No," he murmured. "We wouldn't disagree with that. Is that what you need?"

Denny nodded. There was a moment when I thought my wife might reach out to my father. That my father might reach for her. But it passed like smoke from a guttered candle. Denise took a step back. Nodded again. Said: "Thank you."

Then she turned and walked away, pretending not to notice that my dad had already done the same.

I stood caught between them, one hand lifted toward my father, the other straining to reach my wife.

It was my first glimmer of what lay ahead.

The people I loved who Denny would need to cling to in these first horrible days? They were going to be filled with their own despair. They would not be ready for her. Not yet.

I couldn't help Denny. I couldn't help Dad.

I was Dead Me now. And that guy couldn't help anybody.

When the results came back from my EEGs—both scans as flat as Lawrence had predicted—Denise gave permission to shut off life support.

It put her in the crosshairs of a lot of grieving people.

Some shots were aimed as sly asides, others were in-your-face accusations. *They don't mean this, honey,* she told me, hanging on to the ragged belief I could still hear her. *They just need to slap at someone.*

Why my Denny had to be that someone was beyond me. I would have been slapping back, but my wife addressed every comment with an evenness that, from where I stood, looked like she'd been given a full-body injection of Novocain.

"No, of course I will never keep the kids away from the family. Why would I? They are Meyers."

"Of course I knew what Jim was doing."

"It wasn't snowing yet. He didn't *know* it was slippery. I didn't know."

"I'm sorry you feel that way. I hope you'll change your mind."

"I'm sorry if I was too harsh. I can't seem to find a softer way to say, 'He's gone.' I hope you'll forgive me."

"You're right. I should have stopped him."

"You're right. I should have paid closer attention."

"You're right. He shouldn't be the one who died."

"No, I'd never let them shut off the machines before his brother gets here."

"No, I don't *want* to."

"Yes, I'm *sure*."

"I would never do that."

"I don't mean to."

"I'm sorry."

"I'm sorry."

"I'm sorry."

That was a lot of apologizing. And for what? I wondered. Did my wife fear her accusers were right? That it was her fault for not preventing my accident? Her fault for surviving instead of me? What bullshit.

My mother found us in the farthest corner of the waiting room, Denise turned away from the rest of the family, seated on one of those rigid wood-and-vinyl sofas the Spanish Inquisition must have invented. I hovered behind her, trying to shelter her as she hunched over her knees, shoulders winged forward, hands balled in a knot between her thighs.

Mom sat down beside her.

"I don't expect you to understand this right now," my mother said. "Or for it to be any comfort yet." She ducked her head, looked up through her lashes at Denny's blank gaze, forcing my wife to meet her eyes. "But your father and I cried and talked a lot last night. About you. About the kids. Do you know what we decided?"

Denise blinked. Shook her head, bracing for whatever new pain might be coming.

"That if this horrible thing *had* to happen to someone in our family, if it couldn't be avoided? Then we were grateful it was you."

Mom cupped her hands over Denise's, squeezed lightly. "Because *you* were the one we knew would be strong enough to deal with it."

Say something, I urged. But Denny remained mute. My mother nodded, as though she'd heard volumes. With a final squeeze, she stood, and walked away.

Denise watched her go. Tipped her head as my parents came together. Studied them as they wrapped their arms around each other, leaning in to share the burden of my death.

With a wince, she rubbed a fist against her chest, then shifted sideways to distance herself from the image. It didn't matter. She couldn't help but see what I saw.

All around us other family members were finding each other. Heads were bowing, foreheads touching. Arms were opening to comfort. Shoulders were being offered to accept tears. Every person in the room had sought and found someone to help hold them up.

Denise sat alone in a room full of couples.

"Face the truth," she muttered to herself—no longer to me, I noted. "This is how it's going to be from now on." Anytime her heart might threaten to explode from the horror trapped inside, she would have to be the one to tamp it down. When her body squirmed with a need to run and hide, she would be the one to tell it, Breathe deep. Endure.

"You can do this," she said aloud to that scared woman. "But…"

It would be so much easier if, like all these other couples, *her* other half were there to share the weight. If I could come sit beside her.

But this was her life now. Separate from the world of couples. "He's never going to be there again."

She tested the word: "Widow." Didn't like it. But that was what she was. A widow.

With two small children.

When Denise finally acknowledged me again, it was to swear at me. *Damn you, Jim. I don't want to be strong. I don't want to be the person they think I am. I don't want you to be gone. Come back, damn it. Now. Right now.*

A television played high up in a corner, the sound turned low and ignored by the people huddle together in twos and threes around it. No one was paying attention to the vocalist on the screen lifting his voice in *Oh, Holy Night.* Or to my woman sitting alone nearby.

The song was reaching its crescendo, was about to drift down like snow to a gentle end. When you're part of the river, not floating on top of it, you are aware of *everything* the water touches: past, present, and future. So I knew what the singer was going to say when his performance ended: a special message to his own wife seated in the audience.

I'd reached Denny before, hadn't I, when I'd called for her to come to the ICU? Maybe I could again, to let her know I was still with her, if she'd only listen.

I hovered at my darling's shoulder, leaned in, prepared to whisper. As the last chord faded, the singer spoke, and I joined him in soft harmony.

"Merry Christmas, sweetheart."

Denny jerked—spun around on the cushion.

Excitement burned in her eyes for a moment, her gaze darting left, then right. But she peered through me, not even a wink of hesitation.

I wasn't there. Only the bare wall of a hospital waiting room.

Denise squeezed her lids shut—twin slits of denial—wrenching her head back and forth, as she tried to shake me loose.

Look at me, babe. Listen. Please.

It seemed she heard me, but when she opened her eyes, they were empty of hope.

Denny squared her shoulders, thrust out her chin, and twisted forward to face the room. Oh, man, did I know that look. My woman was mad. Spitting mad. Mad as a hornet, mad as a wet hen, mad at *me*.

I should have been cringing, but I wasn't. You can't be angry at someone you don't believe in, now can you?

"Oh no you don't," she snarled under her breath. "That's not going to be enough. Come back, damn you. All of you. Not just some spooky assed voice. Come back. Right now. All the way back. Or… or… damnit… *stuff a sock in it.*"

I had to stifle a laugh. She'd used one of my favorite wisecracks. Had dared to hurl it at me, even through a haze of grief. Okay. I was on familiar ground now. Denise was stomping away from me, as she had during other disagreements. Yes, this time it was going to take a long while for her to cool off. Would require a lot of coaxing to get her back.

But, no problem. I'd been patient before. I could be again. *Take all the time you need, babe. I love you, you stubborn woman, and I will never give up.*

Besides. Now? I had forever.

Chapter Twelve: Aftershocks

I was taken off the respirator on December twenty-third.
Neither Denise nor my parents were allowed in. Dr. Lawrence assured
them it was not a memory they would want haunting them. That they
should hold on to the good stuff. My life. Not my death.

Denise didn't fight his decision. She had known for over twenty-four hours
that I wasn't in that room anymore. Her biggest fear? That she was wrong.
That they would turn off the switches and I would struggle. Would feel
pain or panic. That I was still hiding somewhere inside that empty shell.

Her biggest hope? That she was wrong. That I'd take a great big greedy
gulp of air… smile, and live. That God would straighten all this out if she
just kept believing life could be normal again: *I'm being strong. I've done
everything right. Can we have him back now, please?*

She stood in the hallway, clutching my mom's hand, clinging to that secret
prayer. Lawrence returned in a surprisingly short time, moving directly to
them. "He didn't stir. No heartbeat. No respirations." My father nodded.
My mother sighed. Lawrence turned to Denise. "You did the right thing."

She sagged, thanked him for everything he'd done (and all he had wished he
could do), then left with her parents to go collect our kids.

That night she broke the news to Rachel that her father wasn't coming
home.

Cuddled on her mother's lap under the soft green shade of her canopy bed,

Rachel listened to the explanation, lips pursed in thought, pupils too dark in her pale round face.

"The doctors tried, Rach. They tried hard, but your dad was so hurt they couldn't make him better. He died and he can't come home anymore—though he wanted to more than anything."

My daughter looked up with those sharp knowing eyes, and patted Denny's hand. "We can go get him," she said. "We can drive the Mazda to the hospital and grab him back."

"Oh, honey. We can't." Denny pulled our daughter tight, kissed her head. "They tried everything. They couldn't fix him. But I'm still here. And Daddy will be watching us from heaven. We just won't be able to see him or hear him."

Rachel considered this. "Forever, Mama? You gonna be here forever?"

Denny didn't hesitate. "Yes, baby. Forever."

My princess thought about this some more. "They musta used the wrong destructions," she said. "Get the Mazda."

I never understood Rachel's belief in my boxy blue car as a superior beast to her mother's racer-red Sebring. It was smaller, less classy, and laid up for repairs more often than not. Maybe it was because whenever we needed to fetch something important, we relied on its hatchback to do the job. I'd brought Rachel's swimming pool and her sandbox home in the Mazda. We'd used it to gather up groceries, pegboard for her playroom, and Christmas trees. In her young eyes, it was a Tail versus her mom's squirrel—the right vehicle for serious work.

Whatever her reasons, Rachel held onto the belief that Mama could make everything right if she'd just get in the right car and bring me back in it. Would persist in her belief for fourteen days, eight hours, and eleven minutes, to be exact.

Side story. (You didn't think that would change just because I died, did you?) When Jimmy was about four and old enough to understand what had happened to his father, he wanted to go to the cemetery and bring me home to bury in the backyard. But not alone. He wanted to inter a big ol'

Harley-Davidson beside me—figured I might like to be a Midnight Rider or something. A ghost with cool. Me and James Dean.

If you have no children yet, be warned: they will break your heart in ways you can never expect. But that bittersweet moment was still years away. Denise had to deal with Rachel's loss first.

During the day, Rachel never frowned or shed a tear over my death (sound familiar?), spent her waking hours stealing her brother's toys, and renaming all of God's creatures to her exacting standards. Business as usual. But at night? She stopped waking up to play.

The wail would erupt around two in the morning: a high-pitched siren of pain that would have Denny rushing to our daughter's room. There, she would find Rachel sobbing, tears streaming from beneath closed lids, her little body writhing, fluttering fingers picking at her blanket. Bawling. Thrashing. Calling out for me.

In her sleep.

To quiet our daughter's grief, Denny would snatch her up and swaddle her in Grandma Meyer's quilt. Then rock her for hours on end or, exhausted, tuck her next to her on the empty side of our bed.

Desperate, she bought Rachel a storybook titled *The Fall of Freddy the Leaf*. It had received glowing reviews about how it helped small children understand and deal with death.

Rachel threw it in the toilet.

She didn't need a book to tell her what death was like to a three-year-old. It was loss. It was unwanted change. It was a hole in a place that had once been filled. She also didn't need advice about how to express her feelings over this unacceptable development.

Two weeks after Christmas—fourteen days, eight hours, and eleven minutes, to be exact—my little girl plunked herself down in front of her new dollhouse. She searched the interior until she found its resident, slipped a pudgy hand around Strawberry Shortcake, bent the doll's legs into a sitting position, and set it down beside her.

"Watch," she said.

Rachel plucked a ruffled pillow off of Strawberry's brass bed, squeezed it between her thumb and finger a couple of times, as though she were plumping it up. Then leaned to her left and shoved it between the slats of the heat register.

Our Elm Street house was old, the metal registers darkened with age, their grillwork wide and ornate. Rachel waited a moment, then lifted Strawberry to the wrought-iron grid, pressed the dolly's face against it. Waited some more. With a nod, she put the doll back down, and reached for the little red skillet. It scritched and scratched as she shoved it through the grate and watched it disappear. "See," she said. "See."

Some pieces took more work than others. The berry-scented towels and rugs and blanket slipped away like silk. The little red hangers that she plucked from the wardrobe fit through the space with ease. The pretty green bowl, however, had to be turned on its side, and forced through the narrow gap. Rachel got on her knees and flattened her palm against it, leaned forward, putting every ounce of her thirty-two pounds to the task. She pumped her little muscles, grunted, and was rewarded when the bowl popped through and fell. The brass bed had to be yanked apart: headboard, footboard, frame. Insert, drop, goodbye.

I hunkered down beside my little girl, wondering if I could stop her. Or if I should. Her movements became more secure, her face more serene, the longer she worked. And it was work, make no mistake. The twisty tulip floor lamp had to be shifted from side to side and corkscrewed through the vent using fine motor skills that did not come naturally to a three-year-old.

Do you have to do this, kiddo?

"Gotta," she said.

Then she unhooked the swing from the front porch, growled softly as she bent it into a manageable shape. Then wiggled it back and forth against the wall vent until it, too, met its fate. She even tried to peel off a decal with her stubby nails, but that bit of destruction defeated her. Everything else? Anything that could be twisted, shoved, squished or crammed into a small enough wad? Rachel dropped it out of her life.

Lost it forever to the flames of the furnace in the basement below.

I could almost hear her thoughts as she dusted her hands of the whole affair. "There. Make *that* better, you stupid adults."

When Denise found what she'd done, she crumpled to the floor next to the remnants of my last gift to our daughter. Rachel crawled into her lap. Patted her cheek. "Don't cry, Mama. It was no good now. I didn't want it. Don't cry."

Denny didn't scold her. How could she? Mama was just as angry. There was no room for Berry Happy in their home. Not anymore.

There wouldn't be for a long time.

I left the hospital along with everyone else on December twenty-third. Christmas was looming and I had a project to complete. What? You were thinking being deceased exempted me from our to-do list? You thought wrong. I wasn't about to let a little thing like being dead stop me from sinking that two-pointer.

I owed my wife a present. If Denny had ever needed something pretty and sentimental and impractical—a clear message that I loved her?—it was now. But, despite my daughter's faith in it, I didn't think there was enough magic in the little blue Mazda to get Dead Me to Bailey Banks & Biddle before closing.

I needed an assist.

A dozen family members had gathered in our house on Elm Street—a kind of pre-funeral wake. I wandered among them, brushing against people as I passed. Some rubbed down goosebumps. But that was it. No one looked up and said, "Hey, Jim, how's it going?"

Pay no attention to the little man behind the curtain, I muttered in frustration.

One important person was not present.

I found Denny outside, standing ankle-deep in white stuff: no coat, arms crossed against her chest, staring up at the roof. The snow was thick on our walk and driveway. Without me to do it, no one had thought to shovel. If I couldn't even delegate a job like *that*, how the hell was I going to persuade someone to head over to the mall?

The one person who ought to be able to hear me—*had* heard me a few tantalizing times at the hospital—was shutting me out. She couldn't do that forever, could she?

Stop this, babe, I tried. *It isn't helping.*

Denny shivered. Was it from the cold, or was she shaking me off?

Jimmy's hungry, I lied. *Come inside.* It wasn't quite a lie. Jimmy was always hungry.

My wife lowered her head, shuffled her feet. "I hope there's something to feed the kids," she murmured to no one in particular.

That was encouraging. Maybe she could hear me, in her way. I gave it another shot: *Come on. I'll help you.*

With a last glance at the roof, Denise moved toward the house, and I followed.

Inside, the kitchen counters strained under a mountain of casseroles and cakes that had found their way to our door. *Good,* I thought. *Plenty to choose from.* The kids might be ready for a snack, but my wife hadn't eaten since lunchtime on December twentieth. Seventy-two hours without food... and no one had noticed but me. I reached for a plate, thinking I'd load up a few of her favorites. My fingers passed through it.

Right. Have to rethink that.

Denny stared at the space where my hand had been, then jerked her eyes away, switching her focus to the refrigerator. As was her habit when it came to food, she hesitated. As was mine, I gave her a tickle. *Go on,* I teased. *Calories are not Satan.* I added a gentle push.

Denny didn't feel it. *Shit.* Neither did I.

But, again, she stood a moment, biting her lip, staring at the refrigerator door.

She reached for the handle. Then spun away. "Any pasta salad?" she asked.

"Jimmy loves pasta." Someone answered they thought there was, and Denise began to forage through the Saran Wrapped buffet on the counter.

My sophomore English teacher, Mr. Lattimore would have been proud. I could finally relate to that short story I'd read in his Science Fiction class: I had no mouth and I really freaking had to scream.

I was about to turn away from the refrigerator myself, when something made me pull up.

Well, son of a gun.

Despite all the comings and goings, it was still there.

Did I mention two people knew about the opal and diamond ring? Correction. Make that one-point-five people. Denise had only been guessing, so that made her the point-five. Rachel had ridden on my shoulders through the mall the day I picked it out, making her the full one. As a teenager, she would say that the feel of my frizzy hair in her hands was her last clear memory of me. Unfortunately, still ten years shy of that teenage mark, toddler Rachel wasn't going to be much help.

Ah, but *this*.

I stared at my handwriting on the long strip of paper. Legible, for a change, and unmarked. How could I point it out to Denny? Make her understand? I stared some more. Kept on staring, my brain drafting idea after idea. Did more staring than achieving, though. I had no mouth, and no hands either, so options were a teensy bit limited. Zero, in fact.

Wait! If not the mother… maybe my pint-size personal shopper could be useful after all.

I wiggled my jaw back and forth, priming the pump. Cleared my spectral throat, and gave it a go. *Rachel!* I imagined calling. *Can you come give daddy a hand?* Two of them, if you're not using them at the moment.

My three-year-old wandered in from the dining room, clutching a sticky green-and-red reindeer. Hmm. Someone wasn't guarding the cookie stash. Had my daughter heard me, or had she come in search of milk to wash down Rudolph?

Rachel licked at the colored sprinkles. Then peeked over the top of half-eaten antlers… eyes flitting around the room. I leaned low to reach her ear.

Hey, kiddo. See that? Up there. On the frigerator. (It's always best to speak to children in their native tongue.) *Wouldn't that be fun to draw on? Go ahead. It's all yours, sweetie.*

Rachel blinked. And lifted her blonde head to study the slip of paper.

Good. This was good.

Rachel's Mama opened the *frigerator* to place a pan inside. The long narrow sheet fluttered: *"Come and get me."*

Gramma *Manski* pulled out a platter of cold cuts, and it fluttered again. *"Whatcha waitin' for?"*

Aunt *Day-uh* kept it dancing, too, swinging the door wide time after time to stow tins of cookies, fudge and brownies.

Rachel waved back, and licked another layer of frosting off the cookie.

Go on, kiddo. It's not too high. No one will care. See how busy they are?

With a tiny hop, Rachel snagged the prize and tugged it free. The magnet of the letter C (for Christmas) went flying.

"Oh, honey," Denise scolded. "Leave that alone, please." She reached for the paper, but my daughter shoved it behind her back.

"No! Wanna draw a pitcher." (In case you think she meant picture, you forget who you are dealing with.)

Uncle Len passed by, carrying the still-life Rachel really had in mind. "Let her be," he advised. "This has to be boring for the kids." He switched the pitcher to his other hand and reached for my daughter. "Here, Rach. Let's throw that out and go play a game."

Not exactly what I'd had in mind. *Won't you be happier at the kitchen table, kiddo?*

Rachel ducked away and scuttled into the breakfast nook, where her mother was setting out paper plates and napkins.

"Mama? Where's my purple crayon? I wanna draw a pitcher and see if it pours." Like *Harold and the Purple Crayon,* one of Rachel's favorite bedtime stories. Mine, too.

Mama wasn't paying attention.

Give her a hug, Rachel. Mommy needs a hug. One way or another I had to get that paper into Denise's hands. *Tempus* was *fugiting.*

Rachel threw her arms around her mother's legs and Denny staggered, trying not to trip over our baby fullback. "Oh, sweetie. Not now, please."

"But mommeeeeeee. I want to draw."

I held my breath. Well, no, I didn't, but old habits don't die just because we do. Exasperated, Denise reached down and lifted Rachel onto her hip. "You *have* to draw? Right now?"

"Yes, yes, yes!"

"Okay." But before letting our Picasso have her way, she cupped Rachel's hand and tipped it to see if there was anything important on the scrap she was holding.

Denny paused. Then read the words aloud.

" 'Pick up Denise's gift.' "

It was the only item on our Christmas 1983 to-do list that didn't have a slash mark or a squiggle through it.

Rachel tried to tug free. "Can I make a pitcher, Mama? Can I?"

Denise's eyes never left the list. She answered without thinking. "Sure, sweetie. Of course. Whatever."

Then she disengaged our daughter's tiny fingers from the paper and moved it out of reach—eyes still tracking the single item left undone. "But this paper is too small. What do you say we find another one? A bigger one."

"And all my colors?"

"Right. Absolutely. All your colors."

"Yay!" our daughter cheered. Denise didn't seem to hear, was still studying the list, chewing on her lower lip.

"Len?" she called. "Can you check on something for me, please? I'm not sure, but Jim may have…"

The time, babe. Hurry. Notice the time.

She glanced at the clock on the stove as she passed. "Oh, geez. You may have to hurry… They could be closing soon…"

As Denny Lou vanished around the corner into the dining room, I leaned against the kitchen wall, crossed my ankles, folded my arms, and grinned.

Slash. Crumple. Two points.

My father drove Denise to the mortuary to pick out my casket. Her brother told her how I really fell. Jimmy kept banging on the airing deck door, calling, "Dada, dada, dada." Rachel wouldn't say her bedtime prayers. My mother-in-law asked what kind of dish Denny was going to bring to share on Christmas Eve. A relative dropped the *Why didn't you stop him* question on her—for a second time. And that was all after Denise had spent hours phoning close friends to tell them I'd died and asking several to be pallbearers. Oh, yeah, she also filled out the form for my obituary—which she was told would run on Christmas Eve.

December twenty-third might not have been the shittiest day my wife had endured that week, but it was a photo finish.

Outwardly, none of it seemed to affect her. She kept her chin up (way too), answered everyone calmly (through grinding teeth), and was heroically patient with the kids (who would have tested Job). She resisted the sales pitch to purchase an expensive bronze casket in favor of a cheaper model in polished wood—even after the guy explained that bronze would be superior at protecting my earthly remains from the elements. With a murmur to my father to make sure he felt the same, she pointed out I wasn't using them anymore, so there was no reason to spend thousands of dollars to keep them springtime fresh. (That last part is me talking. Denny was more diplomatic.)

Through it all, Denise wore the gift I'd given her, twisting it around her finger anytime she feared she would start to cry or yell or do something too human. Time and again I watched her stroke the small opal with her thumb, or glance down to catch the glint of tiny diamonds. Both actions were designed to rein in her emotions.

I wanted to snatch it off her hand and do a little yelling of my own. But this was my Denny; she was going to deal the way she always did. Behind a mask.

After the house had emptied and the kids had been coaxed to sleep, my wife walked down the hall to our bedroom, pulled off her clothes and let them fall where they would. She made no move to pick them up, or to kick them aside as I'd been prone to do. She did not turn on the lights. By touch alone, she groped for the hook on the inside of the closet door.

And found my robe.

She'd bought it for me the Christmas after we were married. Black velour, trimmed in deep burgundy bands around the cuffs and lapel. Somewhere, there's a photo of me wearing that first-Christmas gift. Beaming a first-Christmas smile. Arm gesturing to our first-Christmas tree.

Pressing the robe to her face, she inhaled deeply, then rubbed the nap across her cheek.

I wanted it to be me.

Moving as though her bones were made of crystal, she slipped her arms inside the sleeves and wrapped the warmth around her.

Why couldn't it be me? Why wasn't it me? Why, Man, why?

Moving through the debris of her castoff clothing, Denny stepped away from the closet and toward the three windows that looked out over our porch roof. Holding my robe tight to her waist with one hand, she reached for the latch on the middle window. The window I had often used as an exit when I didn't want to haul out the ladder to perform some simple task— like string Christmas lights around the sills, or return Santa to his hook. I'd used it, too, when I and our brothers replaced the porch shingles.

Denny flipped the latch to the left, fingered it lightly, flipped it back to reset the lock. A sob got away from her, but she swallowed the next one through sheer grit. "Oh, Jim," she whispered, "why didn't I know?"

Because I never said. Because you never saw. Because why would you question it, really?

"I would never have let you do it."

Len, Len, Len… you should have kept your damn mouth shut. Knowing would do her no good, would only pour gasoline on her smoldering guilt.

Until I'd heard her ask the question a handful of times, I hadn't realized that she'd gotten it wrong. Denise had believed I hung *all* the second-story Christmas decorations from right out there—from the porch roof.

"Who closed the bedroom window?" she asked the first time to a handful of blank stares. "Did Jim close it behind him when he went out?" Her sister only shrugged. Denny tried a third time: "Whoever did close the window, thanks. The snow would have blown straight onto our bed."

Her brother Len tossed down his napkin, then stood to stalk into the kitchen, unfinished food still on his plate. He'd gotten as far as the door, when he spun back. "Denise, he did *not* go out the bedroom window."

Her brow furrowed. "I don't understand. I mean, our ladder wasn't in the driveway. He wouldn't have needed it. He always climbed out the window for the small stuff."

Len tipped his head back, stared hard at the ceiling. His throat worked. His father reached out to stop him, but too late.

"He did not go out the window, because Jim did not fall from the *porch* roof." He lowered his gaze. "He did what he *always* did. *You* needed the lights changed on the *top* string, so he had to get on *top* of the house, Denise. The top."

"But how…?"

I saw when understanding dropped into place. "He went out on the airing deck?"

"Yes."

"Through the door in Jimmy's room?" The door our son had been banging on all afternoon.

Let it go, Len. Please. Stop now. It's enough.

The bastard wouldn't listen. "Yes. Onto the airing deck above the breakfast nook and up the antenna tower."

Denny's face began to crumple, but she ironed it stiff. "Jim. He… walked… across the peak. To the front of the house. He didn't fall from…"

"No." Len turned away and disappeared into the kitchen. His voice floated back, "So please stop asking about the goddamn window."

Now, in the dark of our bedroom, she gazed out at snow that glittered with false cheer. "So you couldn't have grabbed the eavestrough with your hands," she said to me.

She'd noticed that, huh?—the two shallow indents in the aluminum. Probably spotted them while standing in the driveway studying the roofline.

Not the way you're thinking. Like her brother, I wished she would drop the subject.

"Did you dig in with your heels?" She nodded as if answering her own question. "I'll bet that's just what you did."

She tugged at my robe until the lapels overlapped near the base of her throat, cinched the belt, flipped up the collar so it would hug her neck. I wished it were my arms.

Finally, she turned away, shuffled back through her discarded clothing to a plastic bag propped next to the heat register—where I usually dumped my stuff at the end of every day.

She hefted it into her arms and moved to the bed. Sat cradling it. The blue St. Vincent Medical Center logo stood out against the bag's white surface.

She sat unmoving for so long I wondered if she had nodded off sitting up. She'd gone without sleep for as long as she'd gone without food. But she was all too awake. Groaning, as if in pain, she grappled with the handles to pull the bag open. Yanked at them, fought with them. Then twisting sideways on the bed, upended the contents next to her.

My boots and paint-splattered belt slapped together—a sharp snap in the silence. One black leather fur-lined glove tumbled free. My wallet and socks thumped down beside it. She shook the bag. My jeans, T-shirt, jacket and underwear fell with a muffled whomp; all had been cut to make them easier to drag off an unconscious man. Denise touched nothing, only sat staring down at the pieces and parts of the last moments of my life.

"They didn't have to cut the jacket," she said. "The arms would have zipped right off." It was one of the reasons she'd bought it; I liked to wear a down vest when the weather warmed. "I suppose you would have bitched about that." With a sigh, she tugged the largest half of the jacket into her lap, stroked it gently. "If you had lived."

Her fingers caught on a bulge inside a zippered pocket.

More clues. More reasons I wished she'd just let it go. Knowing what happened wasn't going to bring me back. The truth would ease her mind one day—but it would only add to her distress tonight.

She plucked at the zipper to free what was inside. Reached in, then snatched her hand away as though she'd touched an open flame. On her second attempt, she slipped two fingers into the gap like tweezers… and pulled out a green Christmas bulb.

"Take them out of the box," she recited, like some sort of weird catechism. "Put the loose bulbs in your pockets. Make sure you can't drop them." She fumbled a blue bulb out next. Then found the other half of the jacket, repeated the search in a second pocket. One yellow. One red. "Be prepared. Don't fumble around once you're up there."

She lowered her face into the remnants of my coat. Mumbled into it, her voice annoyed. "Being careful, weren't you, Jim? About everything except what counted."

I'm sorry.

She jerked as though I'd struck her.

Lurching to her feet, she snatched up the plastic hospital bag and began to jam everything back inside. Boots, glove, mangled clothing. She punched each item one at a time, so hard, so furious, a corner of the bag ripped open, revealing the taunting gleam of a silver zipper.

With a growl that rumbled up from deep in her throat, she staggered into the hall, tripping and righting herself as she moved down the three steps to the stairway landing. Like a basketball player at the foul line, she lifted the bag over her head and, strangling a scream, prepared to hurl it into the black below.

Baby.

Tears welled in her eyes, but she forced them down, rubbed out any that dared escape with her shoulder.

I reached for her face, cradling her cheek, a thumb ready to stroke away her pain if she would only let it fall.

I felt skin. Her skin. Soft. Smooth. The smallest bit damp. Real.

It moved beneath my fingers.

Before she could think, *This cannot be*, she turned her face into my palm, lowered the bag to her chest, and hugged it tight.

It was almost good enough. The best we could manage. Maybe it had something to do with need, or desperation, or how recently I'd died, but I would never be able to touch her this way again.

Denny slumped to her knees at the top of the stairs. "Oh, Jim," she sobbed. "Oh, Jim."

In the morning, Denise thought better about throwing everything out, and salvaged my belt and wallet to store for safe keeping.

She has them still.

The rest she tossed in the trash out back. Did it quick, like yanking off a bandage, racing inside so she couldn't change her mind. A garbage truck would haul it all away before she had time to notice that there were now only two blown lights at the peak of our house where once there'd been three. By then it was too late to check if any of the bulbs in my pockets had been duds. "It doesn't matter," she would murmur. And I would agree.

On the night of December twenty-third as the clock ticked over to the twenty-fourth, Denny awoke from a dream that I was standing outside our house at the curb. That if she would let herself fall back to sleep, she would see me turn around, smile, and wave.

She pulled the covers over her head. "Don't come to me in dreams," she ordered. "Please." She twisted and thrashed, corkscrewing her body, until she could no longer see the empty side of our bed. "I can't bear it."

All right, I promised.

In the river of time, a part of me still stands on Elm Street, my back to our house.

Chapter Thirteen: Love Letters

There are things you come to expect at Christmas Eve Mass: incense, carols, mounds of poinsettia, satin vestments trimmed in gold. What you don't expect is to have your widow tag the Big Guy with a few four-letter words, along with a couple in the six- and seven-letter range.

I had never died before or I might have seen it coming. I'm not sure I could have kept it from happening. Like Rachel and her dollhouse, some things stop being good for a while. Even God.

Before you get all holier than, you should know this isn't a rare occurrence —especially among people who've had someone ripped out of their life without warning. The Supreme Being they thought loved and protected them didn't step in to save the day. He ignored all those prayers begging for help. In the face of such betrayal, even the most devout can start thinking of God as god. It's kinda hard to remember that capital letter when you're crying yourself to sleep every night.

A shame, really, since those are the times when we could use him most.

Denise had bundled the kids up and driven to an early Christmas Eve service at Holy Rosary Cathedral. Figured it would be easier than dragging them away from Santa's presents in the morning. That's what she said, anyway. It was a bit of a copout. The actual Holy Day of Obligation in the Catholic faith is the twenty-fifth, or midnight Mass on the twenty-fourth. I wasn't going to argue about it—even if I could; I was just happy to see *Church* on her to-do list.

I watched from one of the bell towers as my wife climbed out of the Sebring, hooked Jimmy's legs around her waist, and took Rachel by the hand: three tiny figures bundled in coats and hats and boots shadowed by the majestic Notre Dame-style architecture soaring overhead. Snow had been shoveled to the sides of the stone steps, creating buffers of white glowing in the night. My family trudged up between them, candlelight flickering down through the Gothic rose window, painting them with diamonds of ruby and gold and sapphire. I met them out front, my hand melting into Denny's as she pulled open the high carved doors.

The deep voice of a pipe organ pulsed out, a sleepy soothing moan. The voices of a choir joined it, raised in harmony. *This is what she needs,* I thought. *What they all need.* The familiar hymns. The triumphant gospel. The joy and ceremony and peace.

But when Denise stepped over the threshold into the church proper, and began to touch her fingers to the holy water… she stopped in mid-dip. Rachel tugged at the hem of her mother's coat. Jimmy squirmed in her arms, trying to eat the mittens off his fingers. And Denny frowned.

She stepped away from the fount.

So, okay, I thought. She's got two good excuses not to make the sign of the cross, and they're named Rugrat and Rugrat Junior. *No biggie.*

The three of them moved into the aisle, Rachel skipping ahead toward the front of the church where we'd always sat as a family. But Denny pulled up short. "How about here, Rach?" she said. "Someplace different."

Rachel skipped back, not questioning the choice of pew. But I did. My family was as far from the altar as they could get without ending up back in the vestibule.

Kids get fussy, I reasoned. She doesn't want to disrupt the other parishioners. Sure. Makes sense.

But my wife did not genuflect. Didn't remind Rachel to drop a knee, either.

Denny plunked down in the pew with a solid thump. Yanked the top button of her coat open. Blew hair out of her eyes. Bounced Jimmy on her knee in a horsey ride that was entirely too bronco for his taste. I wanted to apologize to someone, but couldn't figure out who. To Denise for leaving her to handle this alone? To God for treating his service like it was a tetanus shot?

I was waiting for the kids to pick up on Mom's vibe and start climbing on the seats or slamming the kneelers against the marble floor. But Jimmy didn't fuss. His sister sat quietly gazing around at the colored lights. *Thanks, guys,* I told them. That should help.

But Denny's frown deepened, her lips disappearing in a slash that clearly said pissed-off-mama. On any other Holy Day we would have been grateful to have the kids so quiet and content. Denise was irritated.

Babe? What is it?

It didn't take long for the buzzer to go off. *You* want *them to make a scene, don't you? You* want *a reason to take them home.*

"Don't see why I have to drag little kids through this whole Silent Night Holy Night rigamarole," she muttered under her breath. "They don't get it, anyhow. Too much for them to handle."

You mean too much for you to handle.

She tried to calm herself—I could see that—took a handful of slow breaths, and shifted Jimmy to her other knee. But when he didn't complain about it, snuggled in like a teddy bear, my wife huffed and puffed.

Try an "Our Father," I suggested.

She lifted her eyes to the altar and the crucifix suspended above it, opened her mouth to murmur the opening words.

But something entirely different hissed out: "You don't deserve the name, you bastard."

All the air left the building at once. I could almost hear the sucking sound as it vanished into the bowels of hell.

Denny's mouth hung open, like it had a mind of its own and she was helpless to shut it.

Stunned, she glanced around to see if anyone had heard. When no one waved a hex sign in her face, and the ceiling didn't fall on her head, she turned her gaze back toward the front of the church.

Me? I was still ducking.

This time, Denise singled out the plaster baby Jesus swaddled in a manger at the side altar.

"I'm supposed to celebrate?" she spat. "Seriously? After what you let happen to us? That's not fair. Not right. It's... it's..."

The choir above us lifted its voice in *Oh Come All Ye Faithful* and Denny stopped her rant.

Not to sing.

To cry.

Not in sorrow.

In hell-hot fury.

"Joyful and triumphant my ass," she seethed, tears flowing down her cheeks and off her chin. "You let us down. You let Jim down—a man who deserved your help more than anyone alive. You... you... you..."

I'd wanted my widow to finally let go, to stop carrying her pain locked up behind closed doors. This? It broke my heart. The lock had shattered and though I could see her spine stiffen and her shoulders knife back, there would be no fixing it tonight. A kind of madness had seized my Denny, and her mutters became audible.

First a four-letter word. Then another. A thesaurus of profanity flung at the heavens.

A woman in the pew ahead turned.

Denise scowled her back to her rosary.

Then Denise stood, hoisted Jimmy to her hip, and took Rachel by the hand.

"Is it over already, Mama?" our daughter asked.

"Yeah, honey," she answered as she steered them toward the exit. "It is so over."

Denise would not enter a church voluntarily for the next three years. And when forced to for a wedding or funeral, she stayed as far away from the action as propriety allowed. Every time, she cried anew, her anger and tears unquenchable.

Here's the thing about the Big Guy. What she said did not piss Him off. It's not His first rodeo, not the first time a grieving soul has taken a shot at Him. He's used to it. He *gets* it. And He's patient. You can try to shut Him out, but He's not shut-out-able. It hurts Him, not because we're lashing out unfairly, but because He feels our loss as keenly as we do.

I'm not going to batter you over the head with more capital letters. Just wanted to make a point that's personal to me. No lecture intended. In fact, the Big Guy doesn't care if you're atheist, agnostic, dedicated Baptist, Catholic, Lutheran, Buddhist, Jew, Hindu, Muslim or NAME YOUR RELIGION HERE. Life's a journey, it's a much nicer trip when you have a moral compass of your choosing.

I did tell you about free will, right? God lets us live our lives without pulling our strings. Even if it means not saving a much-loved child from death or pain. It isn't a matter of who deserves his love and attention more. He adores us equally. It is not his job to smooth out the road. Only to be there to catch us and hold us up when it gets rough.

Denny needed him, but she was damned if she was going to admit it. If he wasn't going to be the kind of God who would save a good man from dying, then he wasn't the god she needed to help grapple with the wrecked life he'd dumped on her. She would continue as she'd begun: raging and crying in private.

Truth? She was upsetting me more than the Big Guy. I mean, if she didn't believe in him anymore, that sort of meant she didn't believe in me either. Right?

Well, hell. That ain't gonna happen, babe. Not if I have anything to do about it.

Ah. But what to do? I'd already tried speaking to her and she'd told me to shut up. I tried touching her and it made her collapse in tears. I tried to smile encouragement to her in her dreams. Got the door slammed in my face.

This was turning out to be a two-man job—but the Big Guy had been put on Denny's Do Not Call list.

I needed a creative partner with mad problem-solving skills.

Are you thinking who I'm thinking?

Christmas Eve at my in-laws' house went better than anyone expected. Kids have a knack for seizing happiness with both sticky hands and dragging the rest of us laughing along with them.

There were seven crazy kiddos in the basement rec room that year, playing tag around the tree, warming their bums at grandpa's wood stove, and cadging snacks while parents pretended not to notice.

Have you seen the snapshot? The whole tiny posse, dressed in their holiday finery, row upon row of them sitting on Gramma *Manski's* basement steps: Jenny fashionably clad in velvet and tulle... Danny in a corduroy sport coat (Hah! That wouldn't happen again.)... his sister Kristy prim and proper in dainty blue... brother Lenny in a snazzy bowtie (ditto that "Hah!")... my Jimmy with his tongue sticking out—hoping someone will drop a crab puff on it... and "Little Chris" who would remain Little Chris long after he topped six feet. Did I forget my daughter? Oh, she was there, at the top of the heap, giggling with contagious joy.

It's a wonderful photo—a precious memory. So wonderful, time has wiped away the fact that I am nowhere to be seen.

For once though, in that long week, it didn't seem to matter. Gifts were exchanged, opened, and admired. Food was savored. Beverages downed. I was pleased to see my wife enjoying both, though in tiny bites and stingy sips.

Grandpa Tomanski had the fire burning fiercely in the Ben Franklin, and as usual people had congregated around it, some on the sofa, others on overstuffed chairs. The furniture had been recycled from the upstairs living room during a recent redecorating effort: green-plaid New England styling that was past its freshness date, but had been broken in to fit a variety of butts and slouches.

Dad T returned to his fire frequently throughout the night, poking the flames higher, churning up the bed of ashes, as I'd hoped he would. The heat grew, the smell of scorched iron with it. Logs disintegrated into cinders.

Dad stoked. I dabbled. The ideal team for my first FX project from beyond.

Denny had chosen to curl up on the rug nearby; had joined in as carols were sung, jokes were told, and laughter rang out without strain. She'd added her voice to those that tumbled exuberantly over the top of others, and for a precious few hours, no one, including her, thought about the funeral that lurked three days away.

I figured my timing was just about perfect. She couldn't deny me when she was feeling so good, especially not with a roomful of witnesses to convince her what she saw was real.

As the sugar level in their bloodstreams peaked, the grandkids did what grandkids do everywhere when they're wired on cookies and cola. They screamed and ran and fought and played. All of it at decibels that threatened eardrums. No one hushed them, everyone seeming to relish the racket. And why not? Sorrow didn't stand a chance against it.

At one point when the mayhem had reached Olympian levels, Rachel darted around the coffee table at Denny's elbow, kicking discarded wrapping paper and empty boxes out of her way. She was going to break her cute little neck if she didn't slow down. Denise leaned out to grab her, and missed. "Jim," she called out. "Could you…"

It wasn't like anyone stopped and stared. Not exactly. But something left the room. My wife snapped her mouth shut, shifted to her knees, and caught our daughter on her next pass, as if nothing had been said. Around her, conversations stuttered back into gear. Laughter rekindled. Kids shrieked again with unbridled joy.

But not long after, Denise packed up our children and went home. Gave the excuse she'd asked some of my brothers and sisters to come over to help put out the gifts from Santa. She had over an hour before they were due to arrive, but for her the party was over.

Wait!

She escaped despite her family's protests and hugs.

Damn it.

I considered following her. Then figured, *What the hell, the show must go on.*

She was leaving before the finale, but maybe my go-to guy could get her back for an encore.

When I caught up with Denny again, the Meyer side of our family had come and gone. Our house was dark, illuminated solely by tree lights. The children were nestled, their sugar plums dancing, the gifts my wife and I had accumulated for them a giant sunburst extending out from the Christmas tree.

The wife herself? Bent over the side of the bathtub heaving up what little she had eaten. I rubbed her back until the purge spent itself. Couldn't feel her muscles as they spasmed, but I could see when they eased. She settled back on her heels with a small hiccup of air. Maybe I was getting the hang of this no-touching thing.

Denise wiped at her mouth with the inside of her wrist, cranked on the tap to let the mess wash away.

Can we say Neat Freak? I teased. My heart wasn't in it, though.

She stood, swaying and shivering. *You're cold, babe. Get my robe.*

I don't know if it was my coaxing, or common sense, but she did as I asked. Then moved quietly through the dark and down the stairs. In the living room, she lowered herself to the sofa, choosing to sit in the middle—as if too much empty space on one side or another was an invitation for someone to join her.

Don't worry, babe. I'll keep my distance until you're ready. Which I hoped wouldn't be too much longer.

I settled at her feet, legs crossed yoga fashion, and watched over her. Waiting for the call.

What is taking so long? I know you guys saw it. I hadn't left until I was sure someone had.

Still the phone remained silent.

I have a distinctive signature. If you've seen it, you know. It's halfway between a scrawl and a contrail in a windstorm; the *M* in Meyer the part people can actually read. The rest is guesswork.

It had taken me an hour to whip the ash and cinders in my father-in-law's wood stove into the proper formation: two enthusiastic humps etched in black on the inside back wall, followed by a tail that curled up, then faded off in a scatter of glowing embers.

I was pretty proud of it. It was unmistakably my M, about one-foot square and more than legible in the glow of the dying fire. So why wasn't someone calling Denny to tell her about it?

Minutes continued to tick away, and my wife's eyelids fluttered. Wrapping herself more firmly in my robe, she leaned forward—almost kissing distance—and began to rise.

Come on, Dad. Call. Her. Now.

She was crouching at the foot of the tree to pull the plug when the phone finally rang.

Thank God.

Denny hesitated. Calls that come late at night seldom bear good news. But this was 1983, and we didn't have an answering machine. Curiosity made her shake her head, stand, and turn toward the kitchen.

Her voice was hesitant. "Hello?"

"Denise? It's Dad."

Her tone sharpened. "What's happened? Who's hurt?"

"Nothing like that," he assured her. "Listen, everyone thinks I shouldn't tell you this. That it might upset you."

Ah, so that's what happened.

"But I believe you'd want to know."

"What, Dad? Know what?" One hand was gripping the receiver so tightly the plastic crackled in her grip. The other hand was twining the phone cord round and round her fist.

"That your husband isn't gone."

Denise sucked air between her teeth, a hiss of shock, then tipped her face to the ceiling, eyes slitted in pain. Her lips moved and I read them easily. "Oh no. Oh no. Please, no."

Her worst fears had come true. I hadn't died peacefully when they turned off the vent. I was vegetating somewhere—and they hadn't wanted her to know.

Oh damn.

Leonard continued on, unknowing. "He left us a message," he blurted, his pitch high and excited. "In the stove. In the ashes. His name."

Denny stopped praying to the ceiling and lowered her head, features creased in confusion. "A message?"

"Yes! A huge M, honey. Clear as hell. Everyone can see it. No question at all. Jim may have died, but he hasn't gone."

Whatever Dad had expected, it had not been silence.

"Did you hear me? Jim wrote his initial in ashes on the back wall of the wood stove. He wants you to know he's still with you—with us." He gave her a few more moments to take it in. "Do you want to see it? Your mom could come stay with the…"

"No."

The word was spoken softly. Didn't snap out, like a whip. It stung nonetheless.

She tried to gentle her rejection: "Sorry, Dad. I believe you. I'm just…" She fumbled around for an excuse. "In bed."

"Denise? We're not making this up. If you'd only see it…"

She swallowed, closed her eyes. "I can't. I'm sorry."

"Well, okay…"

Her father's sorrow and disappointment were apparent—to say nothing of mine.

Denny leaned against the wall, cradling the phone against her ear with two hands. "All right, Dad. What if you *tell* me about it?"

I waited next to my wife, fingers crossed, the murmuring of her family audible in the silence of our kitchen: voices were speaking in hushed whispers; glasses and plates were clattering as someone cleaned up; music played softly from a radio tuned to an all-holiday station.

At last my father-in-law came back on. "Well, your sister says to tell you it's most definitely Jim's handwriting." *Well, of course it is.* "Says she'd know it anywhere."

Denny curled into herself, put her back to the glowing tree in the room beyond. "His name."

"No. Just the M. You know. The big loopy initial—like in his signature."

"Could you be seeing it because you *want* to see it?" she offered gently. "I mean. It would be understandable."

Leonard's exhale was uneven, frustrated. "I suppose. But if you came back over…" His voice trailed off.

When the answer he hoped for didn't come, he spoke again. "Okay, then. I'm sorry I woke you, honey. Just… Well… It's so damn clear."

"His M."

"Yeah."

"Not *Jim*. Or his whole name."

I was pacing now, back and forth, carving a half circle around my wife. *My last chance, Dad. Come on. Please. Just… just… describe it better.*

"A great big loopy M," Denny's father said.

I stopped my jitterbugging. Had he heard me?

"With a tail that sort of tips up at the end," he added.

Yeah, that's more like it.

"Then vanishes in a trail of glowing cinders."

I pumped the air. *Go, Mr. T, go!* That was it. Exactly it.

Denise frowned. "Like a squiggle."

"Exactly," he replied, his enthusiasm peaking, along with mine. "A glowing squiggle. Like he meant to maybe write the rest. You know. But maybe one letter was all he could manage. Are you sure you don't want me to come get you?"

My wife's frown had twisted into something more considering. I waited. Hopeful.

"No, Dad," she said.

No? Really?

"But thanks. I do appreciate you telling me. I believe you." She paused, about to move the receiver away from her ear. "A capital M with a squiggle?"

"Absolutely."

"Thanks, Dad. That's good. Uh, tell everybody I was glad you called. Okay? It doesn't upset me."

So why is there a tear sliding down your cheek, woman? Call me *a bad liar?*

It should have made me sad to see it, but it didn't.

"Merry Christmas, honey."

"You, too, Dad. Merry Christmas."

The line clicked over to a dial tone, but Denny continued to stand with the phone in her hand—chewing her lower lip, shoving the errant teardrop aside with an impatient swipe of her wrist. "Jim?"

Yeah?

"Is it really you?"

You know it is. It's in your scarf drawer. With all the others. Go look.

The dial tone dissolved into that annoying wah-wah wail that practically yells at you to hang the damn phone up already.

Denise placed it back in its cradle on the wall and walked through the dining room to the living room archway where the Christmas tree stood, pulled the plug on the lights.

She was still chewing her lip as she mounted the stairs—had it nearly chewed off by the time she'd finished checking on the kids, picking up a dropped unicorn, a discarded dinosaur, then snugging blankets back into place.

You're stalling, woman.

"I'm stalling," she muttered to herself. She entered our bedroom, pulled back the comforter on the bed, began to slip out of my robe to hang on its proper hook.

Instead, with a huff of surrender, she shrugged it higher on her shoulders and drew the belt more tightly around her waist. "Okay, okay, okay. What can it hurt?"

She spun on her heel and stepped to the dresser, drew open the top righthand drawer.

On one side: a neatly folded stack of scarves; purples, greens, golds and rubies, all collected in separate matching bands like a rainbow of silk.

Opposite, almost as neatly gathered: a pile of greeting cards; some store-bought, some crafted in crayon, a bunch for Mother's Days, three for anniversaries—one for Halloween. The most recent card was on top.

Denny lifted it from the drawer, let her eyes wander over the illustration of red roses touched with glitter. *Happy Birthday to My Darling Wife.*

She opened it, turned toward the window where light from the snowy landscape would illuminate the message. It was the same handwritten note she would find on all the cards in the drawer:

All my love... M

A loopy M with a tail that rose and twisted away like a contrail in a windstorm. The *e* that was intended, no more than a squiggle. Recognizable as an entire word only to her. "Me," she whispered. "All my love... Me."

She argued with herself repeatedly that it just could not be.

But she slept with the card on my pillow beside her that night.

Chapter Fourteen: Sticking

If you're a guy with brothers, you've got scars. What? You say you're wound-free? Then your male sibs live out of state. Or your pants are on fire. Brothers don't discuss or bicker. We fight. It's part of the code, dude.

I was seven, I think, during the Battle of the Bloody Nose. (Bill? Tom? Correct me if I'm wrong.) I do know one or both of my brothers had to have been old enough for Mom to trust babysitting.

Why do kids think they can get away with stuff when their parents are away? The mice may play, but Sylvester will always spot the clues. A broken lawn chair stuffed in a garbage can. Bird seed in the cracks of the coffee table. A single brown beer cap nestled in the brown carpet beneath the brown shadow of the brown dining room table. Yeah, Junior, I'm looking at you.

On the occasion of the beer cap, Denise and Rachel had just returned home from a tour of a New York art college. It took Denny less than two steps inside the door before she said, "Your brother had a party." Jim's goose was cooked before he felt it hit the frying pan.

Wow, my sidetrack just had a sidetrack. I refuse to apologize. After fourteen chapters, I assume you've learned to keep up.

Anyway, back to the Battle of the Bloody Nose.

Bill is my oldest brother, a year behind my sister Jan. Medium build, glasses, dark hair like me, smart—brain developed by IBM. About five-ten. Tom is next in the hierarchy. Medium build, glasses, dark hair like me, smart—brain grown in a beaker at the Mayo Clinic. Taller than Bill by a hand span. All things considered, they should have been best buds, right?

"I'm older."

"I'm bigger."

"I've got you by twelve months."

"I've got you by twelve inches."

"You gotta do what I say."

"Make me."

Forget everything Bill and Tom had in common, one was born first and the other was born taller. For *brothers,* that's all that's needed for a fist to fly.

Man, it was great!

There were punches and jabs. Grapples and headlocks. A karate chop here, a kung fu kick there.

I was the littler, skinnier brother, stuck between my sister Kay and my younger nemesis Mike in the pecking order. While Bill and Tom spent their waking hours battling for position as top dog, I'd spent mine buffing up my skills as an irritant. "He's a weeny, Tom. You can take him." "The bigger they are the dumber they are, Bill. Whoops, look out for the coffee table. He's gonna blame you, for sure!"

As nicknacks tumbled and furniture toppled, I waded in close to the action, slinging taunts designed to keep the warring parties punching. Nothing better than watching two siblings duke it out. I was having the time of my life.

Until one punch missed its target and found my nose instead.

Yow, man. There's a reason self-defense classes teach women to go for the schnoz. It freaking hurts.

And it bleeds. Copiously. On shirts. Pants. Shoes. Carpets. Walls. Anyplace a little kid can whirl as he tries to get out of the fray. Look up "mess" in a thesaurus and pick the worst option. Then double it.

A truce was called by the two oldest brothers so they could clean up the evidence.

The middle brother, however? Not cooperating. No way, buddy. While Bill and Tom scrambled to wipe up the DNA, I fled to Mom and Dad's bedroom and plunked myself down on their bed.

"I'm gonna sit here and bleed until they get home," I hollered. "Then you'll be sorry."

Bill looked at Tom. Tom looked at Bill. Both came down the hall, their two sets of eyeglasses peering around the doorjamb to get a good look at bloody, dripping me—and the as-yet pristine bedspread.

The truce became an alliance.

I fought like a terrier, but was out-sized and out-numbered. My brothers wrestled me into the bathroom and onto the floor, me swinging and kicking the whole way. One of them sat on me. The other grabbed a washcloth and scrubbed at my face. I didn't make it easy for him, though, dodging his hand and whipping my head from side to side. I'm pretty sure they had to do some scrubbing of the floor and tile in there, too.

Eventually they won the war, but I do believe they eyed me with more caution in the future. I was smaller, but was champion in my weight class for stubbornness. With the proper motivation, I would stick like a burr and fight with a will.

Denise was about to discover the same.

Our local newspaper ran the article about my death on Christmas Eve. Might seem harsh, but it's just the way things timed out. I won't argue I wasn't newsworthy: a guy who had fallen while decorating his home for the holidays, in the middle of a recent snowstorm, leaving a wife and two children to open their gifts without him. Who could blame those editors, really?

The story ran six-column inches on page twelve, beneath the fold—which, all in all, showed considerable restraint. Also to the paper's credit, it was factual—not lurid as it might have been. Nonetheless, details were missing or incorrect. Our decorations had been hung with care over a month before; I wasn't "putting a light on the roof" when I fell. The article also failed to mention that temps had reached the mid seventies less than twenty-four hours prior to my accident, so there was no snow on the ground at the time. But for readers who were perusing the story while sipping their eggnog, and casting a glance at the drifts outside their windows? All they could think was, "What the hell was wrong with that man?" The story also said I fell thirty feet. It was more like twenty, though I wasn't counting at the time.

Denny began receiving phone calls shortly after rising with the kids on Christmas morning. Most were from second-tier friends who had not made it onto our families' call lists. "I must say, Denise, I was hurt not to have learned of Jim's death from you personally. I mean, really? Do you have any idea what it was like to read about it in the *paper*?" Never mind that some of these folks hadn't spoken to me or my wife in years. "But it's okay, dear. I'm so sorry to hear of your loss. So. What happened? Exactly?"

Jostling for position among the lookie-loos was one call from a monument company. The perky telemarketer wished my widow a "Happy holiday! May we send you some information about our services?" True story, except for the name of the company: **VERY MERRY GRAVESTONES** may have been the speediest competitor out of the gate, but they wouldn't be the last.

By the time our kids had been fed and dressed and carted out the door to visit Grandma and Grandpa Meyer, Denny was at low ebb. She'd tossed my birthday card back into her scarf drawer, scolding herself for her foolishness. In the rational light of day, a message from her late husband in a wood stove? Wishful thinking. Or so thought my wife. Belief was going to require more than a wisp of ash.

I settled on a sister for my next effort.

When Dr. Lawrence banned Denny and my parents from ICU the day they unplugged my life-support, my oldest sister Jan defied him.

Can you see her there? She's the one in hospital scrubs, just outside the door to my room: Jan Humble nee Meyer, a nurse at St. V's, dressed precisely as you'd expect for an employee who belonged there. Maybe she's about to check a patient's vital signs, or deliver meds.

She isn't, of course. She's there to tell me good-bye.

You wouldn't know by looking that Jan is part of the Meyer clan. Line up all of my brothers and sisters and you'll see variations on the same cookie-cutter theme: six out of eight of us sport dark wavy hair, and have faces that will age into versions of Mom or Dad. Only Mike and Jan found a blond chromosome in the family gene pool, and only Jan could pass for someone else's kid if she tried.

That's why I know my sister could have slipped into my room without notice, if she'd wanted. But Jan is bolder than that. Determined not to let me die alone, she shoved the door open, and walked in without comment, challenging the staff to order her out.

No one did.

I stepped aside and let her pass as she approached the bed. I cocked my head, trying to see what she saw. But there was just this empty shell, some other guy's body, heart and lungs doing their thing to a mechanical beat. I'd stopped thinking of it as me the day before.

For Jan? This was still her little brother. Not yet gone.

It's okay, I tried to say. *That's not me, but I'm close.* So close, if she shrugged, our shoulders would melt into each other.

"Jim?"

She reached for the hand lying inert on the bed. "I love you, you know?"

Well, sure, I know. Sibling rivalry aside, all brothers and sisters know that. A word to the living: if you don't get there in time to say the words before we die, it's okay. We remember more than the pinches and punches and orneriness.

Jan rubbed at her eyes with her free hand.

Aw, geez. She was crying.

I shuffled my feet. A sister crying? Over her annoying baby brother? That wasn't something I was prepared for.

Jan wiped at her eyes a second time, waiting as the medical staff disconnected the wires and lines, shut down the machines. The room hissed into silence, and she gave the limp fingers on the bed one last squeeze.

Damn, she was still batting away tears—now with both hands. It made me itchy to do something, anything, to make her feel better.

"Ow," she said. "Let's not lose the other one, shall we."

Other one? Oh, right. I'd almost forgotten. Jan had misplaced one of her contact lenses two days before. Hadn't she tracked it down yet?

Well, hell. I was my oldest sister's Mr. Fix It, the brother she called when something broke down. She and her husband had split, so she often needed a hand changing a light fixture, repairing a railing—or, on one scary-funny afternoon, extracting her daughter Brooke from inside their bathroom. My niece had accidentally locked the door and couldn't get it open again. Uncle Jim to the rescue!

Was there time to fix one last thing?

Jan turned away from the body on the bed, ready to let me go.

I gave her a shove.

My hands—what still felt like my hands—passed right through her.

But Jan did stop. She crossed her arms over her chest, and rubbed briskly, like she was scrubbing away a chill.

Turn around, Jan. Look.

She did. Seemed confused, but did it anyway. Excellent!

But she didn't spot what I'd done.

No worries. That happens sometimes when you're trying to be theatrical; you just need to pump up the lighting.

I tipped my eyes toward the ceiling and the overhead fluorescents. Gave them a gentle zap.

The light fixture pulsed.

And Jan gasped.

Christmas Day, my sister made a point of cornering my wife before the party could get into full swing. Denny had settled into a chair in the corner of the den. Jan grabbed one catty-corner to it, and leaned in close. "Mom didn't want me to tell you this…"

Sheesh, there's a lot of that going around.

"…but I decided you should know anyway."

Not exactly, Jan. I decided she should know. But potato patahto.

"I didn't want Jim to die alone—and I knew you didn't want that either—so I ignored Lawrence and was in the ICU when they took Jim off life-support."

Denise blinked. *Steady, honey.*

"He died peacefully," my sister assured her. "He would want you to know that." Then she paused, her lips thinning as she tried to decide if she should tell the rest.

Yes, you should. You really should. Because this is the important part.

Finally, she nodded, brow set in determined lines. "Something weird happened. Before I left. After they had… Well. Anyway. I… found something. Just lying there as if it had been there the whole time."

Denny knuckled away a crease between her brows. "Jan…"

"Hear me out." My sister scooted closer, practically out of her chair. "Remember how much they moved Jim around? While he was in ICU?"

"Of course I do." Denny's confusion was inching into the red zone. "They had him sitting up for a while, then on his back."

"Right, right. And they changed his bedding."

"They took off the blood pressure pants…"

"They bathed him, put him in a hospital gown."

"Yes, but what does that…"

Hang in there, hon. This is good.

Denise blew out a breath. "Okay, yes. They told me they were going to do all that. So he would look… presentable, I guess. For anyone who wanted to…"

Jan was nodding, the intensity in her eyes cutting off the rest. "I found my missing contact lens."

"Wha…?" Denny squinted at the change in topic, shook her head. "Wait? What?"

Jan grabbed my wife's knee and squeezed. "It was gone for two days. I'd looked everywhere."

"That's great, Jan. In ICU? It probably fell out during one of your visits. Lucky thing…"

Jan squeezed harder. "Not just in ICU."

Denny stopped squirming. Narrowed her eyes at my sister. "But." She shook off the idea that had popped into her head.

Jan was bobbing with excitement. "Uh-huh."

"Jan," Denny said. "That's not possible."

My wife and sister locked eyes. Jan lifted her brows in a facial shrug. "Yeah. I know."

See, my sister's missing contact hadn't been found *just* in ICU. It hadn't been located on the floor. It hadn't been on a tray or table. Not on a chair or a window sill.

Jan's missing lens—a circlet of nearly invisible glass the size of a pinky fingernail? Had been found winking under the pulsing fluorescents of ICU... on the arm of James Patrick Meyer, Sr.

Mother Nature wasn't happy about my death—or so my Denny said on the day of my funeral. Temperatures had plummeted to minus-frigid, and had stayed there the full week, transforming the snow and slush in the streets into ankle-high granite mountain ranges. Fortunately, my wife didn't have to worry about navigating the gullies, because the mortuary had provided a limousine. It was her first time riding in one, but she would have gladly given it a pass. You can't appreciate the comfort of plush Corinthian leather when you are struggling not to think about who is riding in the hearse up front.

Denny didn't own a lot of black clothing—which is kind of funny since her closet today has a definite dark side. She borrowed a black velvet jumper from her mom and added a white silk blouse with puffy sleeves and a bow at the neck. I loved that blouse on her. Is it weird to say your wife looked lovely at your funeral? Her parents were riding with her, decked out in their own solemn colors. Me? Denise was burying me in my one good suit: a slick grey tweedy thing that made me look like JR Ewing.

If that was what I was going to be stuck in for eternity, I would have preferred my usual, please.

Recycled energy doesn't require a fig leaf, of course. But for you guys out there reading, lets put together an ensemble to remember me by. Not the suit. And, while I got a kick out of it, not the "Get a Charge Out of Life, Kiss an Electrician" shirt Denny tried to hide from me all the time. Let's make it my favorite navy tee, the one that's faded to grey-blue and matches the jeans that have been washed so often they feel like suede. Add the thick brown belt with the Star Trek buckle and my tennis shoes, and I'm good to go. Think I'll keep my beard, too. Had it when I died and I will no longer have to shave it off when the weather heats up.

That feels better, thanks. More like me. If I ever get a chance to show myself to my wife again, this is how I want her to see me—not the cold, stiff, suited-up corpse we buried.

It was just the four of us in the back of the fancy limo that morning: me,

Denny, Len and Esther. Denise had offered to include my parents, but Dad wanted to drive the two of them himself. Denny didn't bring the kids, knowing it was one memory of their father they should not have tucked away in a dark corner. She hadn't brought them to the viewing the night before for the same reason.

Nearly everyone else I'd ever loved or known had come for the funeral. A caravan of cars bearing purple flags that snapped in the cold clogged the street alongside the mortuary. Many more were illegally parked on side streets, the parking lots having been jammed hours before the service. When Denise and I arrived at Holy Rosary Cathedral, we found more vehicles packing that lot as well: mourners who had chosen to bypass the closing of my casket and head straight for the Catholic Mass for the Dead.

Yeah, I know. A church service. It was going to be one of those times my wife was forced to enter the house of her newly discarded god. Only one thing kept her from howling her anger and defiance: the knowledge that I *was* a believer. With no faith of her own left—for now—it was mine that got Denny through the service intact.

Right up until our friend Tina stood to sing the recessional hymn.

As my pallbearers accompanied my casket down the aisle toward the icy light outside the open doors, *Ave Maria* soared around us. It was a touching reminder of our wedding—and one arrow too many. My wife and mother broke into pieces, clutching each other, as they followed behind.

This isn't a memory Denny dusts off on a regular basis. Hardly ever, in fact. She's telling it now because... Well, closure, I guess. Or... what, honey?

Oh. She'd like people to know I was loved.

That's nice. But, truly? The people who mattered had shown me how they felt while I was alive. Their actions and words during my life said love each and every day. A tribute from them after my death wasn't necessary.

Something to remember about living and dying, I guess.

Eventually my processional made its way from the church to the cemetery. No one counted the number of cars, but someone said later the Toledo Police sent out a couple of cruisers to help keep the traffic moving and to clear the jams caused by our passing.

I was buried at Calvary Cemetery—or I would be, in a couple of days. The ground was so solidly frozen, workers had been unable to break through the ice to dig my grave. Heavier equipment was being brought in to handle the job, but it hadn't been available in time for my interment. As my wife stepped out of the limousine, she was informed I would be taken into the cemetery chapel for a short prayer instead.

Denny scowled. Were they thinking I could be left there? Alone? Over several nights?

The man from the mortuary gave her a there-there pat—the demeanor of a male who'd dealt with anxious widows too many times to count. Denise narrowed her eyes—the look of a warrior goddess who would skin him alive if he didn't take her seriously.

In tones crisp enough to cut glass, she informed him I was *not* going to be dumped like a box of castoff clothing to sit alone and cold for the next few days. I think he caught a sunburn from standing too close to her righteous flame, because his pat turned into a quick squeeze, followed by a professional handshake. "I promise, Missus Meyer. The body—er—James will be transported back to the funeral home today." He waited for her reaction. Got none. "I'll see to it personally. And... I will call you as soon as the cemetery contacts us, so we can return to finish his burial." Another pause. Another silent frown. "Properly. With all due respect." He faltered one last time. "Will that be acceptable, ma'am?"

Denny nodded, sheathed her sword, and walked up the steps to the chapel.

See why I married her?

The building was small, capable of holding only a fraction of the people who were trying to come inside. It was all over in minutes. A prayer, an explanation about the weather, an announcement that anyone wishing to return on a future day could contact the mortuary for details. Denise, our parents, brothers, sisters and their spouses filed back out, the echoes of their entering not yet faded, squeezing past mourners who were still standing on the steps.

My family climbed into their various vehicles and began to move slowly away… passing a double line of cars jockeying along the cemetery's narrow road… rolling past mourners who'd found parking spaces but had not yet reached the chapel on foot. As they drove under the arch at the cemetery's entrance and out onto the main road, their mouths dropped open—no one able to speak. A seemingly endless line of vehicles, purple flags snapping, stretched along the byway, exhausts puffing white clouds of condensation into the cold air.

My family was leaving, and the end of the procession had yet to reach its destination.

Grief is a seesaw. People riding it can teeter on the edge of normal one day, then drop into despair the next. There's no telling what will tip the balance.

Denise had held it together at my funeral. Had brought our kids to the luncheon afterwards—held in the same hall where her mother had hosted Denny's baby shower—and had shared reminiscences with guests. She'd even smiled now and then. (Though the truly observant could tell the expression was painted on.)

When she returned home that night, she whipped up a real dinner that wasn't microwaved or donated by church ladies, bathed the kiddos, tickled them into their PJs, and read a bedtime story. I noted she didn't pressure them to say their prayers. But, all things considered, she'd weathered the worst.

The next day she found dozens of sympathy cards in our mailbox—and opened them without flinching. Some contained gifts of money. She settled the munchkins down in front of Mister Rogers, and pulled out her stash of thank-you cards. Filled them out without a single tear dotting the envelopes.

"I can do this," she said to herself. "It's bad, but I'll manage."

Day Two Post Funeral passed without a breakdown.

Day Three did the same. Grief was losing, she thought. She could beat it.

On Day Four, Rachel followed her mother around the downstairs as Denise vacuumed the carpets and dusted the furniture. When her mom finally dropped down onto the sofa with a sigh of accomplishment, Rachel climbed onto her knee.

"*Mom*," she said, in a tone that implied it wasn't the first time she'd said the word. "*Look.*" She stuck out her hand, two fingers pinching a tiny ring of plastic. She poked it into her mom's tummy. "It fell off."

"What fell off, sweetie?"

"The pull thingie." She lifted it into the air and waggled it back and forth in her mother's face. "From my Speak and Say. It *broke!*"

Denny took it from her fingers with one hand, stroked Rachel's bangs out of her eyes with the other, and thought, *Need to book a haircut soon.* Then she shifted her gaze to the circle of plastic, nodded absently. "Aww, that's okay, baby," she soothed. "Daddy will fix it when he gets home from work."

And just like that, the seesaw slammed my wife to the ground.

Rachel gazed up at her with a sneaky dash of hope in her eyes.

"No. Wait. What's Mama saying. *We* can fix it. *We* can. All by ourselves. Okay, sweetie? We've got this. We do."

It broke my heart to see her swallow her tears, knew she was doing it to protect the kids. When I put my hand on her wrist and tried to tug, she didn't feel it. But she didn't shrug me off either. *The needle-nose pliers,* I coached, as she climbed to her feet. Rachel landed on the floor with a one-two dance, anticipating a new adventure. *Phillips screwdriver. They're in the junk drawer,* I instructed.

Denny went to the kitchen, and pulled open the drawer on the butcher block table.

Ah, progress. She was hearing me, even if she wasn't truly listening. But after shoving items back and forth and not grabbing the tools I'd suggested, she slammed it closed again. "The tool bench," she muttered. "Mama's going down in the basement. Wait for me, okay?"

I knew they weren't in my tool bench, but I'd find something that would work. *Don't sweat the small stuff, babe,* I tried to tell her. *Don't let it rattle you. I can help you fix it…*

If she'd let me. If she'd ask.

Denny stomped down the steps—not a good sign—and plodded heavily toward my bench. Instead of opening drawers to begin sorting through options, however, she halted, squeezed her eyes shut, clamped her hands across her mouth like the monkey that speaks no evil.

And screamed.

It was a deep strangled cry that tore my heart out, a cry she was smothering so our babies wouldn't hear.

Aw, geez. Don't bottle that up, babe. Let it out.

But Denny was already choking it down. Gagging and swiping at any tears that dared to leak down her face.

"Mama?"

I tried to put my arms around her, but she spun through them and away. "Yeah, Rachel. I'm still looking. Okay? Stay up there. I'll be back in a few."

Oh, how cool and collected my wife could sound when she was hiding behind a mask. Well, that wasn't going to cut it. Not anymore. She was going to listen to reason—or her gut was going to explode. If not to me, then to someone who carried weight.

"Mama."

"I said I'd be…"

"The phone, Mama. I can't reach it."

Wrapped in her grief, Denny had missed the jangle of the phone on our kitchen wall. She lifted the hem of her shirt and swabbed at her face, then turned and dashed back upstairs.

"Mama…"

"I hear it, Rach. Thanks."

The woman on the other end of the line spoke without waiting for a hello. "Denise?"

"Uh, yeah," my wife stammered. "Mom? What's up?"

"I was going to ask you the same. Is everything all right? The kids?"

I swear my mother could taste trouble in the air, with or without a nudge from me.

"They're fine. Good as gold."

Mom chuckled. "That can't possibly last." She paused, lost the laughter. "And you? How are you?"

"Okay. Not bad, really. You know."

Mom sighed. "Yes. I do know." She waited, the better to make her point. "You wouldn't hesitate to call me, would you? If things weren't, you know… 'Okay'."

Denise didn't answer right away, but Mom and I were patient.

"Mom…"

"It's horrible, isn't it?"

Denise shifted her weight until her body was turned into the corner that divided the kitchen from the breakfast nook: hiding her face from Rachel who watched with bird-sharp eyes, muffling her words from Jimmy who'd crawled out to join them. "It sneaks up on me," she whispered.

"The tears?"

"I'm afraid to let it out. I think I'd just start wailing and never stop. Scare the kids. I mean, *Mom,* they can't see me like this. Not like this. All falling apart. A weeping mess. What a thing for them to remember: their mom— the whiny sniveling useless hopeless screaming wreck?"

The rant had gushed out of her mouth, climbing the register to near hysteria.

"God," she finished, blowing out air in a gusty sigh. "I'm sorry."

My mom sighed, too. "What for? Being human?"

Denny hiccuped.

"Denise, would you have expected Jim to hold it inside? Would you have forced him *not* to grieve?"

"Well, no. But…"

"Hmm? But what?"

"But maybe not in front of the kids."

There was silence on the line long enough for Denise to ask: "Mom? You still there."

"Oh, yes. I'm here. I'm just waiting for you to hear yourself."

Denise turned back to face the room, our children sitting on the floor, still watching, curiosity etched on their faces. "What? What do you mean?"

"Honey," my mother said, "do you really want your children to grow up thinking their mother *never* cried for their father?"

Denise dropped into a crouch, two-handed the phone to her ear. "But."

"No but. You loved him. I loved him. They loved him. Crying for him is good for all of us."

Denise reached out to brush at Rachel's over-long bangs. "And if I…"

"…crack open and become a—what was it?—whiny… squalling, sniffling whatever?"

Denny laughed a bit. "Well, yeah."

"If you let some of it out now and then, I imagine that won't happen. But if you feel it coming on, put the kids in a room with their toys or down for a nap. Close the door and call me. We'll scream together."

Denise plunked down on her butt, twined her legs, and waved the kids into her lap. "I was being stupid, wasn't I?"

"No, you were being a woman who's lost her husband. Feel better now?"

"Much."

"Good. Come for dinner Sunday."

"Mom?"

"Yes?"

"Why did you call?"

"Hmmm. I think Jim told me to."

Denise's hand slipped on the receiver. She caught the phone before it fell, and pressed it more firmly to her cheek. "You think so?"

"You don't? Goodbye, Denise. Kiss the kids for me."

Denny cradled the phone against her breastbone and looked down at the treasures clambering over her legs.

"Your grandma is amazing," she told them.

Yeah. That.

Chapter Fifteen: The Calling Plan

If cellphones had been introduced by the time of my death, Denny would have been forced to add Dead Me to her family plan. Dropping a coin into a metaphysical payphone was turning out to be a great way to drag my wife away from her depressing thoughts, or to throw a body block at any problems that cropped up—you know, the day-to-day crap I would have taken care of if I'd still been around.

Like, for instance… the time she couldn't locate the insurance policy she needed to collect on my death benefit. As she was sitting hunched over the file, pulling out folders and growling in frustration, I had our insurance guy ring her up. Say: "Hey, Denise, I was wondering if you'd like someone to go with you to Social Security to fill out the forms for your government benefits. I'd be happy to drive you. Oh, and I could bring copies of your insurance policies, while I'm at it. If you could use them?"

It took my surprised wife five minutes to collect the contents of the folder that tumbled from her numb fingers, scattering papers everywhichplace.

By the way, how long has it been since we took a side trip? That long, eh? What do you say we hitch a ride with Denny Lou down to Social Security. It'll be worth it. Promise.

Quick scene change: overworked, bored, government employee sits at a typewriter, hands poised above the keys. "Social Security number of deceased?" she asks, her tone indicating she's said this three hundreds times this week alone.

Denny reads it off the notecard in her hand.

A spate of mad typing follows, nine digits long. "Social Security number of surviving spouse?" employee asks before the last key falls.

Denise rattles hers off from memory.

Bap bap bap bappity bap bap bappity.

"Any offspring?"

"Two," my wife replies.

Keys hammer.

"Gender? That means what sex are they." Employee does not look up. Hands are paused again to await the answer.

"One girl. One boy."

More keys hammer.

"Ages?"

"My daughter Rachel is three. My son Jim is eleven months."

Hammer, hammer. Hammer some more.

"Are either employed?"

It is now Denny's turn to pause.

"That means do either of them have a job."

"I know what it means," my wife says.

"Answer?"

"Rachel is *three years old*," Denise repeats. "My son Jim is *eleven months*."

Employee spares applicant a glance, eyes narrowed. "Do they have jobs or not?"

Mother of my children stares back, eyes so narrowed they are about to cross. "Jimmy has a paper route, and Rachel is starting at McDonald's next week. Drive-thru. We're so proud."

I'm betting you're not one bit surprised that Denise had to stop said government employee from typing up the answer. They must not teach sarcasm at Social Security Clerk School. Or hand out a sense of humor.

See. Told you it would be worth it. Now, where were we? Oh yeah. My calling circle.

Flash forward to the time my wife got all weepy watching Jimmy sleep— twisted up about how we were never going to have that third kid we'd talked about. For that one, I had to hunt up a good friend to come to the rescue. Laura put in a call on the spot to tell Denny she and Marty were pregnant *again*. "A third!" she lamented to my wife, with a laugh. "What the hell were we thinking? Or drinking! We should never let them outnumber us, you know." It made my Denny grin, which was my goal. But it also helped her reconsider the what-ifs of our life with a practical eye.

Then there was the scary moment.

I still get chills thinking about it.

In the words of Alexander—one of Jimmy's favorite storybook characters —it had been a terrible, horrible, no good, very bad day. No less than four monument companies had telemarketed Denise, one of them reciting from a prepared script: "If you ever loved FULL NAME OF DECEASED HERE, Missus FULL NAME OF SPOUSE HERE, you won't put this important decision off another day. FULL NAME OF DECEASED HERE deserves the best... and that's a marble testament to your love from MONUMENTS R US.

Mind numbing is a polite term. Emotional bludgeoning is more accurate.

So it should have been no surprise to find the love of my life standing at the airing deck door that evening, staring out blindly through the foggy panes. What *was* a surprise? She wasn't moving. Not a muscle. Not an eyelash. Just looking. Not hearing the kids behind her as they tore through the upstairs tossing toys at each other and the walls. Not thinking. Or for the first time, not letting me *know* what she was thinking.

That damn antenna tower was only steps away to her left. What was she doing? What was she mulling over that was so secret she had to build a Great Wall of China around it?

I got my calling circle together and started demanding someone pick up the phone and dial. But when the telephone in our bedroom shrilled, Denise ignored it.

Come on, come on. Answer it, woman. Get away from the door. Close it. Lock it.

Did I mention Rachel was on my speed dial? My darling daughter dropped a truck on her brother's foot—purely by accident, I'm sure—and trotted into our bedroom.

" 'lo?"

"Rachel? Is that you? Hi, kiddo. Is your mom there?"

I had never noticed before how similar my voice was to my friend Jeff's— you remember Jeff? Of The Con? Chapter Five, if you need a refresher.

Anyway, it must have been similar. Or maybe it was because the caller knew Rachel's name and called her kiddo. I don't know. But the result was electric. My daughter tossed the phone on the floor and pounded down the hall toward her mother, who was continuing to hold vigil with her black thoughts. "Mama! Mama! It's Daddy! Daddy's calling. Hurry!" She clutched at Denny's shirttail and pulled with all her might, little heels digging into the carpet as she leaned back tugging and yanking. "Mommeee!"

Hope flickered across my wife's face. Then died into darkness. "Oh, Rachel. Honey, it can't be."

You *get* Rachel by now, right? You know my kid isn't going to give up. "You find out," she ordered her mother. "*Could* be. Daddy would call. If he could." She switched her grip to her mother's hand and began to lead her down the hall. "Long dish-ants," she added. "Find out, Mama. Talk."

Denise was no match against our daughter's pint-sized determination. She let herself be bullied into our room.

Before she could get the phone all the way to her ear, she heard a man's sobs. "Oh, Denise. I'm so sorry. I don't know why she thought that. God, I never... I wouldn't... Christ, I'm sorry, I'm sorry."

Denise sat down on the edge of our bed, switched the phone to her other ear as she looked down at Rachel. Our daughter was jiggling from foot to foot, eyes eager. "Jeff?" Denise said into the receiver. Then added for those tiny ears: "It's Jeff, honey. Daddy's *friend*."

Rachel's smile didn't falter. She nodded so hard her hair danced. "Yes! Jeff calling. 'Cause Daddy *said*."

Denny gave her a halfhearted nod. "Okay," she agreed, not wanting to dim that optimism. "Sorry, Jeff. It's all right. Rachel is fine. Uh. Why did you call?"

Rachel clambered up on the bed to follow the conversation, plunking her butt down hip-to-hip against her mother.

"I... I guess... I'm not sure," he said. "It just popped into my head that I hadn't seen you since the... in a while now." She could hear Jeff breathing, the ragged inhales of a man struggling to explain something that doesn't make sense. "Here's the thing," he conceded. "I just wanted you to know if you ever need to talk, or want to go out for a beer, maybe grab a pizza, and —you know—catch up. Or cry. Or... whatever. Well, I want you to call me. Doesn't matter what time of the day or night. Call. Okay? Just. Well, do it."

"Jeff."

Rachel had popped to her feet, was standing on the bed now, arms circling her mother's neck. She leaned close to catch the words spoken at the other end of the line.

"Jim would want you to, Denise. And I want you to. Okay? That's it. That's all I called about."

Rachel bounced once, released her mom, and jumped to the floor—headed out to do battle with her brother once again.

"Are we cool, Denny Lou?" Jeff asked.

"Yeah," Denny sighed. "We're cool. And thank you. More than you can know."

"I guess I do. So, then, okay. Later?"

"Later."

As Denise hung up the receiver, Rachel called out from her brother's bedroom. "Door was open, Mama. I closed it."

You sure did, baby. Thanks.

Every future Christmas my family would ever have was saved by my sister-in-law Daria.

I'd known my wife was still reeling from the previous horrible very bad day. I could see it in her eyes, had no doubt she was running out of duct tape to hold her emotions together. When she opened the day's mail, I had to add my own "oh shit" to hers.

Visa was canceling her credit line.

The form letter was short on details, stating only that if she wished to receive an application to have the account reviewed, she could contact Mister Rulebook before Arbitrary Date, 1984, at 1-800-FATCHANCE.

I'd died without a Will, so my estate—What a glamorous word for pittance, eh?—was tied up in probate. Our bank accounts had been frozen upon my death, and weren't to be released for weeks yet. The benefits from Social Security and my life insurance were still a month out. Denise was relying on credit to keep the household afloat until all the hoops had been jumped through. She was on the phone before the Visa envelope fluttered to the floor.

Give 'em hell, babe.

Turned out, what she had to give them was proof she could afford their terms—and maybe a notarized letter stating our children were marketable commodities.

"But," she reasoned to the chunk of ice on the other end of the line, "this was *my* account to begin with. I opened it at least *six years* ago. My husband was added after we were married. We have insurance, we have money in the bank; it's only tied up temporarily while my husband's estate is put through probate. I don't understand how you can shut me off, just like that."

"It's quite simple," he replied. (Was that a calculator I heard tap tap tapping in the background?) "When the man of the household dies, we assume his surviving spouse no longer has the resources to maintain the credit we've extended."

"Are you saying that if it were *me* who'd died, Jim would not be receiving this letter?"

"Statistics show that it is the male who is the primary breadwinner."

Denny was livid. "But. It. Was. *My* account. Not Jim's. I made more money than he did. This is unfair. Perhaps," she seethed, with fire in her eyes, "even illegal."

"Not at all," Mister Rulebook answered in even tones. "As long as we allow you to reapply for credit, we are perfectly within our rights."

The form letter was now a ball in Denny's hand. I would not have been surprised to see it condense into its chemical components, maybe even solidify into a hunk of carbon. Then into a diamond.

"I see. Well, that changes things." Was the warrior goddess getting her mad on? Oh, I dearly hoped so.

"I'm glad to hear that. Would you like me to send you an application?"

"I don't think that will be necessary," she returned. "I'm sure there are other credit card companies that would be more than happy to have me. With or without a big strong man to prop up helpless little ol' me. Good day."

Denise hung up with more control than I would have expected. If it had been me? Phone, say hello to wall. And maybe shake hands with the house next door.

Over the next hour, a self-christened Miz Meyer worked her way through a list of recommendations from our local bank manager, finally settling on a card with better interest rates than her old one—and more respect.

With the problem put to bed, she rose from the kitchen table where she'd launched her battle plans, and took in the state of the house.

Right, hon. Like it's total chaos. I mean, whoa, is that throw pillow a millimeter off center? Disgraceful.

My humor fell on deaf ears. And would have even if I'd been capable of speaking out loud. Denise was boiling with outrage that had been seasoned with a shot of humiliation.

The phone rang—and not of my doing.

"Hello," a chirpy female sang out. "Who am I speaking to, please?"

"Denise Meyer," my wife said, stubbornly leaving off the Missus part.

"Hmmm. Would you be the wife of James Meyer… James Patrick Meyer?"

"I would," she sighed, slumping back into the chair she'd just vacated.

"Excellent! I'm calling from the billing department at St. Vincent Medical Center. Can I assume you received our statement itemizing the services your husband received from our facility?"

This made Denny sit up straighter. "Actually, I did, and intended to call. There's a charge on the bill that is in error. I'd like it removed before you send it on to our insurance company."

The deviation from the woman's prepared remarks seemed to throw her. "Oh? And what is that?"

"You charged us a television fee."

There was a shuffle of paper, a relieved exhale. "Yes. I see it here. Three days television usage. It's quite correct."

"It is *not* correct. Are you aware my husband was in Intensive Care? In a coma? *Trust me,*" Denny enunciated. "A television was not high on his list of needs."

"But you, perhaps? His guests?"

Uh-oh. Countdown to blastoff was in my Denny's eyes.

"I repeat. Intensive Care. Coma. No. Damn. TV."

"Hmm. Well, I will pass your concerns on to my supervisor. Is that acceptable?"

"Sure. Your name please? I want to pass *it* on to my insurance carrier with my complaint about over-billing. I promise not to drop the word 'fraud' into my conversation with them. I assume *that* would be acceptable?"

Silence. And a bit more silence.

"I think I can expedite this, Missus Meyer. Let's just remove the TV charge, shall we?"

"Let's."

"Now, where were we? Oh, yes. The real reason I am calling is that I note the holder of your medical insurance policy was not the person who signed the forms upon release from our facility."

"That's right," Denny said. "I signed them, before the body was released to…"

"But, see, that is the problem. We need the primary holder of the policy to sign off. And that would be your husband… James Patrick Meyer… correct?"

"Yes, but…"

"Only the primary policy holder is authorized to sign. We cannot bill your husband's medical insurance company without his signature."

"Well, I wish he could do that…"

"I can send you a new form and a return envelope, but that will hold up payment. Could your husband stop into our office…"

"He cannot, though I wish he could. You're not listening. My husband is…"

"I don't wish to be rude, but I'm afraid *you're* not listening. I really need your husband's signature. The sooner the better."

I swear I could hear the pop of a small aneurism inside Denny's head. "Sure, sweetie. I'll just go dig him up, strap him in the car, and drive on down. Is it okay if I hold the pen in his cold dead hand for him? I'm pretty sure I can forge his signature well enough that he won't complain."

The woman's previous silence had been a trailer for coming attractions.

Denise waited her out.

When the clerk found her voice again, the chirpiness was as dead as I was.

"Oh."

"Yeah, oh."

"I'm so sorry Missus Meyer. I believe your signature as his next of kin is sufficient. Thank you for your... Um. Thank you."

"Right."

I gotta give my woman credit. She hung up the phone for the second time that day without ripping it off the wall.

So, you're thinking: this sucks and all, but where do Christmas and Daria fit into the mix? Has our intrepid explorer wandered into uncharted territory again?

Just setting the stage, my friends. Context is everything.

Denny sat longer this time, staring at the wall without seeing it. You know how bad news always comes in threes? I think she was waiting for another call. Jimmy sent her back into action by demanding a midday snack to stave off starvation. Lunch was a good half hour away; a boy could collapse from malnutrition.

Denise rose, made her way to the kitchen and dug up a banana. One rage-fueled dice and slice later, the kids were settled in front of Big Bird with their snack bowls, and my wife could begin her housekeeping.

I watched her move from chair to sofa to table to lamp, and for the first time in for-never found nothing to dust or straighten.

"Right," she said to no one.

Then she stalked up the stairs. I beat her to the top and was waiting in our bedroom, thinking maybe she was going to change the sheets. She turned away from me, moving with relentless calm into Jimmy's room. I jumped ahead to wait for her by his crib, but again she surprised me, hanging a right to the storage closet in the far corner.

Where we stored our Christmas decorations.

Oh, man, nothing good can come from this.

She didn't rip the door open, but the set of her shoulders told me she could have had it off its hinges without much effort. She bent, grabbed the handle of a jumbo plastic storage box, backpedalled it into the bedroom, then swung it up into her arms.

Don't do it that way, honey. Drag it.

Too late, I realized she was *trying* to make this difficult. She wanted to fight with something, and had decided, Why not with the holiday that had started it all?

She got to the stairway just as Jimmy crawled up the last step and into her path. She didn't trip over him, but it was a near miss. She canted her head to the side, peered at him around the lip of the box. "Whoops," she said. "Sorry. Mama's taking down the decorations."

She slipped past our son and maneuvered the box sideways down to the first landing. I couldn't tell if that was where she lost her grip or if she just decided to let it all go, but the box sailed out of her arms and through the air. A big blue bomb's away. It landed halfway down the staircase, corkscrewed, then skidded the rest of the way to the bottom. The container detonated with an atomic thud against the coat closet door, the plastic lid popping up and spiraling back down, ending up cockeyed across the top.

Honey?

She was shutting me out, but I didn't have to read her thoughts to know what she intended. Without a word, she turned back toward the upstairs hall, and set off on her mission to wipe one horrendous holiday out of their lives.

She started in our bedroom, gathering up the Christmas Cat pillow her grandmother had made, the muslin wreath Denny herself had embroidered, and the ceramic dove she'd won at Daria's baby shower. Then she cut a line to Rachel's room where she added the tiny tree we'd decorated with the kids, tucking it under her arm. Tinsel trailed behind her as she entered the bathroom and snatched the holiday towels off the linen dresser, scooped up the red Santa-shaped guest soaps with the fingertips of an already over-filled hand.

For the time being, Denny skipped Jimmy's room and descended to the landing. There, she thrust her arms forward, sending the lot of it clattering out and down. One of the items made it inside the storage box. "Three pointer," she muttered. Jimmy leaned out, chipmunk cheeks bulging with banana, to get a better look at Mama's new game. She toed him back. "Careful, kiddo. Mommy's cleaning house."

Leaving him to munch and watch, Denise focused on his room next, plucking up the miniature nativity scene, and the electric candle in the window—which reminded her of the other two that graced the upstairs. Return trips to the bathroom and Rachel's room finished the job.

This time my wife got creative, pitching each item one at a time. Clack. Snap. Rumble thump. Bam. She missed the storage box, but nailed the strike zone on the coat closet door three out of four fastballs.

The pile at the bottom of the stairs was hip deep. "Okay," she told our son. "That's done. Let's take care of the tree."

Denny lifted Jimmy to her shoulders, and carried him down through the debris, stomping on anything that dared come underfoot. She settled him next to his sister and added an extra helping of fruit to their bowls before zeroing in on her next target.

The Douglas fir we'd chosen that year was lit in all its holiday glory. The kids loved to watch it twinkle, liked to laugh at the clown tree-topper their Aunt Daria had made. I'd spent a week of lunch hours finagling a way to add a light inside each of three plastic balloons that could be clutched in his hand. They, too, blinked in merry sequence—red, green and yellow, unaware their minutes were numbered.

Denise didn't bother bending over to remove the plug from the socket. She snaked her arms between the branches of the tree, wrapped her hands around the trunk, crouched, and with a sharp inhale, hoisted the thing fully decorated into the air.

As she lugged it toward the front door, the plug snapped free of the wall and water splashed out of the base in a sloppy trail across the carpet. The kids were agog. I never knew what that expression meant until that day. I gotta say, gog is pretty damn accurate.

If Denny hadn't had to set the tree down to open the front door, the phone call might have come too late. But she did, and it did not.

She glanced over at the kids. Rachel's face was twisted in thought—probably trying to come up with a name for a mother gone mad; Jimmy's hand was in his sister's snack bowl, taking advantage of the distraction.

Denny smiled serenely. "A day for chitchat," she said to them, her voice measured and calm. She left O Tannenbaum stranded where she'd dropped it—thankfully, upright—and moved to answer the ring.

"Denise?"

"Yes."

"It's me."

"Of course it's you." Denny chuckled. "I recognize your voice." The snicker was off, though, and her sister caught it.

I think I mentioned before, my sister-in-law is a madonna-like woman: warm and mothering. She may not have had a supermodel figure, but she was super in every way that counted. A full-sized angel of love, intuition, and common sense. I could see her shaking her brown gypsy hair before she spoke, already anticipating trouble. "What are you doing?"

"Right now?"

"No, next summer. Of course, right now."

Denny blew her bangs out of her eyes, leaned a shoulder against the wall, crossed her ankles. "I'm taking down the Christmas decorations."

"No. You are not."

"Of course I am."

"No. Stop whatever you are doing. I'm coming."

"Why?"

"To help."

"Don't need any."

"Too bad. Go sit down and don't touch another thing. I'll be there in ten."

And she was.

And she saved Christmas.

Oh, and in case you're wondering, not a single ornament, candle, baby Jesus figurine or glass thingamajig was broken. Together, the two women swaddled the rescued items in bubblewrap and tissue, then packed them all away.

"You *would* miss them, you know," Daria said. "If not next year, then the year after." Grief would not maintain its stranglehold forever, she assured her sister.

Denny didn't agree, but was done arguing with people for the day. She stood and bent over to lift the storage bin, then cocked her head. A pale white scrape marred the deep blue plastic. After the lack of destruction they'd experienced until then, the scar was a surprise.

"Huh," she said.

So, sue me. I couldn't catch everything.

Chapter Sixteen: Thou Shalt Not

None of us get out of here alive. Sooner or later we all give up our earthly form and become something new. As a man who's been there, done that, I can attest it's not always the grim reaping it appears to be.

Unless you are one of the someones we have to leave behind. For you guys, grim doesn't begin to cover it.

It doesn't matter if we were your husband or wife—or your mother, father, child, grandparent, dog, cat or parakeet. If you loved us and lost us, you hurt. The stages of grief are the same: denial and isolation, anger, bargaining, depression and acceptance. But how much you suffer through each stage, for how long, or in what order? That's a miserable crap shoot. There is no get-out-of-grief free card.

That part of dying is our purgatory: watching the people we love suffer.

There wasn't much I could do but worry from the sidelines as I watched my darling Denny sail up one day, then crash the next. Cruise along like normal for a week, then become unable to function above robot for two. One afternoon, for no apparent reason, she sat down on the sofa and watched the kids play. And sat. And sat. And sat. Not moving or saying a word for three hours. Later she cried herself asleep about it.

I wanted to tell her there was no right way to feel bad and no timetable for getting to the end. But she was picking up mixed signals. My mom said it was all right to cry. Her mom told her it wasn't good for the kids. One friend told her to get out more. Another told her she was running away from reality if she went out too often. Her brother's wife insisted that after six months, Denise should be feeling better. Maybe she should get some pills or something. An article Denny read said people who'd suffered an unexpected loss still thought about their loved one with sadness every day —seven years after the death.

She was in the pediatrician's office at the time and threw the magazine onto a side table. It slid, sailed through my knees, and hit the linoleum with a slap. "Seven? Christ, I'll never make it through *one.*"

The woman sitting catty-corner to the table eyed the fallen magazine. I gave it a light kick and the pages fluttered. They settled open, the title of the article Denny had been reading bold across a two-page spread.

The woman bent to pick it up. She had a mouth wreathed with laugh lines, and salt-and-pepper hair that looked intentional but could have been earned. There was a noisy little one fussing in a carrier at her side, and an older model tussling with my kiddos at the toy table. Both had her face stamped all over them.

She gave the magazine article a once-over, then turned piercing brown eyes on my wife. "Father?" she asked.

Denise flushed. She'd forgotten where she was when she threw the magazine. "Sorry."

"No problem. I was a walking car wreck after my dad passed away."

Denny blew out a breath. "Not my father."

"Mom?"

"Husband."

Neither of them spoke for a handful of heartbeats.

Rachel shrieked, a cry of triumph as she held a sock puppet above her head, out of reach of the two boys.

The woman sighed. "And you have kids. *I'm* sorry… though I imagine that doesn't come close to helping. How many years now?"

Denise chuckled, a thick sad noise that didn't make it out of her throat. "Six months."

"Months?!" The woman shuddered, and offered the magazine back to my wife. "Want to hurl it at a wall?" When Denny only stared, she let it fall to the table and reached for her purse. "Wait. I think I have a lighter."

Denny's second chuckle was closer to the mark. "It wouldn't help. There's always another article."

"And another opinion."

"Oh, yeah."

When the woman's infant upped the ante on fussing, she tugged the carrier closer and comforted the baby with a few jiggles. "By the way, my name's Tam," she said. "You?"

"Denise."

"Hi, Denise. Nice to meet you. Have you done much screaming yet?" Her newborn quieted as Tam tucked a pink blanket around her. "When Charlie died—my father—I went out in the corn field and yelled as loud as I could until my chest hurt. Did it almost once a day—when no one was around to ask me if I'd lost my mind."

"Did it help?"

"Worked last week."

"Oh, I'm sorry. He died recently?"

"Two years last August."

Jimmy crawled over from the play area, a truck in both hands serving as roller skates. "Up!"

Denise pulled him onto her lap, and stared at nothing. "I don't think I've got years in me."

"I thought that, too. But we do." Tam leaned forward to catch Denny's eye. "It sucks. We get through it. And then it sucks some more. It gets better for a while—and a while longer each time. Then it sucks again, like it happened yesterday. Maybe it's because we have kids, but we handle it. Kids sort of make sure we do, because we *have* to."

Tam leaned back, crossed her arms, nodded. "Try screaming."

This time Denny laughed outright. "I already did," she confided. "A couple of weeks ago? When it was one of those really bad days? I put the kids in the tub for their nightly bath... and it just... I don't know... leaped out of me. I started screaming and screaming and screaming."

She gazed down at Jimmy and smoothed his dark curls. "The kids looked at me all googly eyed, like I'd invented a new game. Started yelling along with me."

Tam snorted in amusement. "Shut you up, huh?"

"Snap. Like a mousetrap."

Rachel called to her brother, and masochist that he is he scooted off his mother's lap to roller-skate his way back. "Thing is..." Denise lifted a hand to her mouth to chew on a cuticle. "When I stood up to grab a towel to dry them off? I saw my mom through the bathroom window running between the yards from her house. She'd heard me."

"Good. Sounds like you needed a shoulder to cry on."

Denny nodded. "At first I was embarrassed, but then I was thrilled. I could put the kids in bed and sit down with my mom and cry it out."

"So?"

"She ran inside and up the stairs, shouting, 'What's wrong? What's happened?' "

"And you told her..."

"Said I'd had one of my worst days ever, and couldn't hold back the scream."

When Denise didn't go on, Tam gave her a come-ahead flick with her hand.

Denny sighed. "She told me, 'Oh, thank God, I thought something was wrong with one of the kids.' "

A bell pinged from the reception desk. "Missus Meyer? Doctor's ready for you."

Tam shot the woman an irritated glance. "And?"

Denise rose, clapped her hands for our kiddos to join her. "And nothing. She left and went back home." She gave the woman a crooked smile as she lifted Jimmy and took Rachel's hand. "There was nothing wrong with her *grand*kids. So, no crisis."

Tam watched my family move toward the examining rooms, and sent a soft "aw hell" after them.

When Denise left the pediatrician's office later, the receptionist handed her a folded note. Inside was a scribbled message. *Forget screaming. Hire someone to listen. Love, Tam.*

Finally, someone had given my Denny Lou some decent advice! I wished I could take credit for it, but this time it wasn't me.

I suspect the Big Guy.

It wasn't raining the morning Denny and I drove to our first appointment with the psychologist. It was dumping out of the sky in tubfuls. Which seemed fitting. Before walking out the door, my widow had spent several minutes on the phone raining curses on the head of an ambulance chaser who'd called to chat about the cash she could wring out of St. Vincent Medical Center if she would just sue their incompetent scrubs off. It didn't matter for what. He had a list of possible infractions; just pick two from column one and one from column two.

Boy, did he pick the wrong Meyer in the phonebook.

The kids had only added to the strain by whining all morning that they didn't want to be left behind—even if it was with their Grandpa *Manski*. Grandpa was almost as whiny. "Don't see why I gotta be the one to deal with them when they're cranky." He thought he'd kept the gripe to himself, but we pesky cosmic entities hear everything.

Personally? I figured Denny could use the time away, sort of a mini vacation. But she didn't seem to agree. As we approached the block of office buildings, she glanced at the scrap of paper cupped in her hand. Then scowled in distress when she discovered she'd found the right place.

That's the spirit, sweetheart, I said, sarcasm cranked to high.

She ignored me and pulled into the back lot. Then left the motor running and the wipers slashing, so we could enjoy the zen-like squeal of rubber against glass.

Waiting for a lull? I was pretty sure we wouldn't see one this side of monsoon season.

I studied my wife's attire. The weather couldn't make it worse. She'd grabbed whatever came to hand: ratty paint-splattered jeans, black rubber flip-flops with a split sole that gave a double slap when she walked, and a baggy pumpkin-colored tunic she'd once used as a maternity smock. She'd showered and washed her hair, but then pulled it back into a stubby tail secured with a red rubber band salvaged from the Sunday newspaper. She'd brushed her teeth, but skipped makeup.

I see we're going formal for this event, I kidded. *If I'd known, I'd've rented a tux.* My heart wasn't in it, though. Denny Lou was scraping bottom.

"We're here," she muttered. "Might as well go through with it."

Oh, yeah, this was going to go smashingly.

Before I could say rinse cycle, Denise threw open the door and hauled herself out into her second shower of the morning. By the time we'd waded inside and into an elevator, a sack of drowned puppies would have looked like a party favor in comparison to my wife.

There was no receptionist in the outer office, but a brass plaque instructed us to have a seat; a consultation was in session and would conclude shortly. We followed directions and dropped onto a naugahyde loveseat to drip dry.

A puddle had barely formed when the inner office opened and a fifty-something male in a grey-flannel suit and Ivy League tie walked out. He cocked a silvered eyebrow in our direction, and pursed his mouth in distaste. I wondered if I could yank a ceiling tile down on his fifty-buck haircut.

A pleasant looking woman in a simple navy shift and black flats stepped around him. Her brown hair fell in a shiny bob to her earlobes. Matching brown eyes held their own warm shine. "Next week, Roger," she said. "Same time."

"Humph," he answered. "I will have to check my schedule."

"Please do. Your wife will be attending, as well."

The exec responded with a second noncommittal humph and headed out, but not before he sent a sneer in our direction. I hoped he didn't have an umbrella. And that he'd parked a block away.

"Missus Meyer?"

Denise tried to climb to her feet, but her wet hand slipped on the vinyl cushion. She tumbled back down with a squishy plop, grunted, and pushed up a second time. "That's me," she mumbled.

"Please, come in."

This is not my Denny, I tried to plead. *Not the way she dresses. Not the way she moves. Not the way she* is.

The psychologist gestured us to a sage-colored sofa as she seated herself in one of two upholstered chairs across from it. "Please," she said, "call me Joan. Do you prefer Denise, or is there another name you'd like me to use?"

Denny shrugged. "Denise is fine."

"Good. Would you like something to drink? Coffee?"

Yes.

"Nothing, thanks. I'm not a coffee person." There was the barest of pauses. "That was my husband's drink."

More like my daily transfusion, but whatever.

The room grew quiet, the hush of rainwater on the windows the only sound for at least a minute. Then two. My eyes wandered to the furnishings. The sofa was firm but comfortable, like a hug; the side table simple, dark wood and free of tchotchkes. A clear pitcher of water and three cellophane-wrapped glasses were centered on it within reach. Abstract acrylic paintings in thin black frames adorned two walls: soothing ribbons of pastel color that waved and drifted across creamy backgrounds. There were no photos of seascapes or mountains. No paintings of kittens or dogs. No studio portraits of family. No framed degrees. Nothing that would distract visitors from their personal thoughts. A single tall bookcase held a collection of plants and stacks of books, the titles turned to the back, unreadable. Decorative. Not meant to impress. Soothing. Restful.

I nodded. So far, this Joan had my approval.

What she said next sealed it.

"This is not you today, is it?"

The psychologist lifted a hand palm up to indicate my wife's wardrobe. "Not how you dress. How you act." She stood and moved to the bookshelf, took down a box of tissues and brought them to the sofa. When Denny didn't reach up for them, Joan placed them in her lap. Offered a sympathetic smile.

"Why don't you tell me what's happened to make you so miserable. Then we'll work out how to put things back together."

I hope Denny will forgive me, but that's when I fell in love for the second time in my life.

Once Denise had begun, the hurt and guilt and anger and fear gushed out of her like an unstoppable wave. She spoke in sobs and gulps and stammers for a full half hour, then hiccuped to a stop. "God," she gasped, mopping at her face with a wadded Kleenex.

Joan smiled. "I bet that feels better."

Denny bobbed her head and let the tissue join the others dotting the cushions and floor around her. "God," she repeated.

Joan shifted in her chair, crossed her legs, leaned forward over her knees. "Jim's been gone—what?—six months? Seven? Hasn't there been anyone you could share this with? Your mother? A friend? Someone?"

Denny lifted a shoulder, let it fall. "I've talked about it."

"But not like this. Not… fully. Why not?"

Tell her. That's why we're here.

My wife chewed her lip. "Most people don't want to hear it. You know. They, well… they *look* like they want to listen and help, but if you talk too long…"

"Share too much?"

"Yeah." Denise sighed, looked away from Joan. Placed the tissue box on the end table and nudged at it until it aligned perfectly with the corner. "Their eyes get glassy. Or they make an excuse to leave. Or to hang up. Or…" She huffed impatiently. "It's not their fault. It's not their life, is it? They thought all I'd need was a pat-pat on the head for a couple of weeks and they'd be done. So I learned not to start."

"It is your family's life, too. Their loss, as well," Joan corrected. "They must feel as awful as you do. Why haven't you unburdened to them?"

"But, see," Denise countered, her voice stronger. "That's why I can't! I'd only make it worse for them."

Say it. Come on.

"My parents want me to stop feeling bad. They want me to behave like I used to. Before."

"Well," Joan answered, her tone casual but firm. "That isn't going to happen. Not yet." She settled back, drummed her fingers on the armrest. "I'm going out on a limb here, but I'm guessing you're considered the strong one in your family. Hmm? The one others come to for advice or help?"

Denise looked startled.

Yep. Nailed it, doc.

"And you, Denise, have bought into the myth: 'Thou shalt not show weakness. Thou shalt not cry. Thou shalt not abandon them in their time of need.' They want you to be strong so they can come to *you* to help *them* feel better about Jim's death. And damned if you aren't trying to do just that."

"I am?"

"What do you think?"

Denise glanced to her right—as though she expected to find me sitting there. "Jim would have said yes."

"And Denise? What does she say?"

"That he'd be right." She blew air out of her lungs in a long noiseless whistle. "But I'm not sure knowing that is much help. I still won't wail on them like I did here." She tilted her head in thought. "Maybe I don't have to though. I mean, I feel so much better."

Joan smiled and lifted a finger. "For now. But you're grieving—and will be for some time to come. You're going to need to release the pressure again." She glanced at her wristwatch. "Which is why I want to see you next week. Does this time work for you as a regular session?"

"Next…? But I thought maybe once a month…" Denny looked crestfallen. "I'm that bad, eh?"

"You are not 'bad' at all. But you are that smart. You knew to come to me in the first place. So just think of me as your release valve for the next few months."

Resigned, Denny huffed and nodded once in agreement. "Yeah. Okay. Once a week."

Joan stood and reached out a hand. "In the meantime," she said, as my wife rose to shake it. "I want you to think about something." She closed her second hand over the top of the first.

"What's that?"

"Thou shalt not pretend Jim didn't die. Thou shalt not pretend it doesn't hurt."

I would have added another commandment to the list: Thou shalt not shut out the one person who will be there no matter how much you cry or yell. Or how ugly your flip-flops.

Chapter Seventeen: Tag Team

Once Denny began seeing Joan on a regular basis, I began wandering the house, wondering what the hell I was doing there.

Did other repurposed filaments of energy do this? Hang around, trying to be helpful? Trying to pick up the pieces with disembodied hands? Inner musings are for poets, and—outside of an occasional dirty limerick—I rhyme for crap. Answers weren't pouring in from my subconscious.

Who picks the shape of our recycled energy, anyway? Us? If the Big Guy doesn't interfere in the decisions we make in our first life, it should follow that he keeps hands off our decisions in the next one, too. So maybe some of us can choose to become heat that warms a distant planet... or light that illuminates the dark corners of this one... or a spark that triggers a chemical reaction and gives birth to a new person. Or, gee, maybe a few of us get to say, "No way am I ready to throw off this mortal coil." Maybe some of us can choose to be *sound* and *motion* so we can help the people we've left behind.

But what if those people we loved and left are ready to leave *us*?

The summer before we were married, Denise and I hopped a ferry to spend a day on Put-n-Bay, an island in Lake Erie that specializes in party bars, wineries and historical monuments. The bars not being open at ten in the A.M., we chose to sample some of the grapey goodness at one of the wineries. And sample. And sample. Then, when properly lubricated, we ascended to the top of Perry's monument, a circular Doric tower overlooking the island and lake.

At the time, the top story consisted of a small rectangular indoor lobby, surrounded by an outdoor balcony and stone parapet. I leaned out over the wall, and got a loop-de-loop view of the cyclists below. "Whoa. Look at all the li'l ants waaay down there, babe."

When Denny didn't answer, I cocked my head to the side, expecting to find two of her, wavering within staggering distance. No Denny. Of any kind. "Babe?" Standing upright without a handhold turned out to be more difficult than I'd imagined it in my head. "Sweetie?"

A helpful college frat boy pointed to my left. His frattier buddy pointed right. Denny and her doppelganger musta split up. I chose left and began to circle the balcony.

Circled it twice. No Denny. Leaned out over the wall a second time, terrified I would see a splat on the bricks below. Just more ants. More vistas of lake and island. "Denise!" I hollered. Fear kept most of the slur out of the *s*. Was that an answering "Jim?" I waited and listened for more. Nada. Only a few snickers from less tipsy tourists.

I'm guessing you've figured it out by now. While I'd been examining microscopic bicycle riders, Denise had wandered in the other direction, and lost sight of me.

Doesn't take Einstein to figure out what happens when two mildly inebriated individuals keep circling a balcony—their view of each other obstructed by a small building. Uh-huh. They keep moving—faster and faster—never catching up to each other. Eventually, Denny went down in the elevator to see if I'd deserted her. When she didn't find me, she pushed the up button. The doors opened to reveal a desperate Romeo who'd come to gather up the shattered pieces of his Juliet.

We thought it was pretty damn funny at the time. But that circling thing? Not being able to see or reach each other no matter how fast we ran?

That was how I was feeling now.

My wife still cried for me, yelled at me, and cursed her lowercase god for not saving me—but not as often. She did have a bad moment when the insurance checks arrived; couldn't look at them or deposit them for almost two weeks. But she eventually invested the money in a high-interest savings account and a mutual fund; used some of the proceeds to buy a reliable new car with a great warranty; was considering moving to a newer house with less maintenance; and had begun researching job listings in the paper. She'd even had a date or two. (Which I refuse to talk about here. Or ever. Beg all you want. Ain't happening. Jealousy, thy name is Dead Me.) Denise might be limping, but she was moving on. Should I be fishing the river for a new place to put the energy that had once animated James Patrick Meyer, Sr.?

Thoughts like these were bouncing off the walls of my nonexistent skull as I watched the kids conduct an experiment to determine which of them had the super-est superpower: evil four-year-old nuclear muscle? Or wicked twenty-two-month-old razor-sharp teeth? Jim's *My Buddy* doll would be awarded to the winner. From where I was standing, Rachel was going down. *'Atta boy, son.*

A shout from mom ended the brawl prematurely, so I wandered toward our bedroom to see what the referee was up to.

I found her sitting lotus fashion beside the bed, an open file folder in her lap, surrounded by a carpet of receipts, brochures, and other unidentified scraps of paper. The mattress held even more. It looked like the map of an undiscovered continent. Denny was growling like a pit bull. "It *has* to be here. It wouldn't make sense for it to be anywhere else."

What, honey? What are you looking for?

"I've searched under M. And W," she muttered to herself. "And N and O and V and X... in case it got misfiled one folder over," Frustrated, she shuffled the pages in her lap, snatching up one after the other to peer at the next sheet underneath. Then flipping each one over in case whatever she was looking for might magically appear on the backside. "Aw, come on, already! This is insane. I do *not* lose stuff like this."

Okay, so it's going to be a guessing game. Is it animal, vegetable or mineral?

She dropped the folder to the floor, scrambled onto her knees, and crawled her way to the two-stack of file boxes in the corner. "If I have to go through every damn folder, I will..." She slapped the lid off the top box. "But I am not going to be happy about it."

Stating the obvious, my dear. I crouched beside her, tipped my head to study the papers fluttering under her probing fingers. I could *feel* what these things were, but not why they were the *wrong* things.

Can you give me a clue, babe? How many syllables? Sounds like…?

She dropped her forehead to the box. "Grrr."

Burr? Cur? Fur?

"This is so not funny. Why won't they take my word for it? Why would I lie about such a thing?" She lifted her face, and thumped a fist against her temple. "Why, why, why didn't I change it right away? When I got the new license, updated the credit cards?"

This was good. What changes on a person's driver's license?

"Would Jim have had to go through this? Hell, no. It's never a problem for *men*. Should have talked him into letting me keep it."

Ahhhh.

Her name.

That had been an interesting—ahem—discussion. For awhile Denise Tomanski had lobbied to become Denise Tomanski-Meyer, but I'd pointed out the potential confusion for our kids. Would they be just Meyer or Tomanski-Meyer? And if it was Tomanski-Meyer and we had a daughter who married, would she tack a third name onto the mix? Or, if her husband was also the product of a two-name merger, would our grandchildren have *four* hyphenated last names? Denise had been unable to come up with a winning parry, so she'd resorted to a growl. I then pointed out how long it would take her to sign checks with a thirteen-letter surname as opposed to five. *And* how often she would be asked to "Spell that please?" In the end, I simply batted my big brown eyes, and said, "I've waited all my life for a Missus Meyer."

I didn't play the "awww" card in a lot of arguments, but when I did, it was a sure winner. First St. Louis. Then Denise's married name.

So, what was she looking for that required Denise Louise *Meyer* on it—and didn't yet have it?

Jimmy crawled through the door, looked around, and reached for the nearest scrap of paper.

"Don't!" His mom climbed to her feet and rushed to intercept him. "Mama needs that, sweetie."

She picked up the sheet and placed it out of reach on the dresser. OHIO DEPARTMENT OF EDUCATION was emblazoned across the top, under an official looking seal. Beneath it were the words Certification Renewal.

Ah-hah, Doctor Watson! A clue. Denny was renewing her teaching credentials, which had originally been issued under her maiden name.

My wife turned away from the dresser. Studied the litter that covered our room.

So, okay, can you tell me what proof they need to change it?

I saw her blink. Then she shifted her weight the smallest bit to cut her eyes in my direction... so on target, she nearly met my gaze.

Or maybe I imagined the whole thing. After nearly a year of being kept at bay by threats and pleas, was she ready to listen? *Was* listening?

Ask, hon. Just ask.

"If I'm not the one who misfiled it, Jimmy. Who do you suppose *is* the culprit, hmm?"

Our son pulled himself to his feet, using the bedspread like a climbing rope. Almost two years old and the kiddo was still refusing to walk. The first time he'd taken a step, Denise had dropped to her knees in tears because I wasn't there to see it. After that, our son had taken no chances. He would not walk if it meant making his mama cry.

Talk to me, Denny Lou. Ask for my help.

There it was again: that twitch of motion, that shift of the eyes.

"And if it *was* your daddy, where do you suppose he'd have put it?

I can help, babe. But you've got to believe. You've got to ask. And be prepared to listen for my answer.

She'd looked under M. Had looked under W. What began with M or W that would prove her name had changed from Tomanski to…?

"Where did you put our Marriage License, Jim?"

The words tingled through me, a lightning bolt of excitement. God, don't let me drop the ball. Not now! In the past, when Denise had needed my help, the answers were things we both knew, information that was already in her head—like my signature on her birthday card. She hadn't needed to hear my words. A nudge had been enough. But this was something I alone knew. I'd put our Marriage License away somewhere I'd felt was sweet. Sentimental. Denny would have treated it like the important document it was. I'd treasured it as the memento of a blessed event. If she didn't listen? Wasn't prepared to hear me?

I could use a little help here, Big Guy.

I tried to remember what it felt like to form sounds with my mouth and not my head. Leaned in close.

"Did you look in the Bible?"

No reaction.

Damn it.

I wasn't ready to give up, though. Had to try at least once more.

"I said…"

"Why in the world would it be there?" Denise murmured.

Then she smiled, a slow-blooming flower of a smile. "Of course."

She stepped away from me toward the small bookcase next to our bed where we kept the novels we read most often, the books we both loved. She reached for the brown leather volume with the engraved gold lettering. Hugged it to her chest for a moment.

Bit her lip.

Opened it.

And saw our Marriage License.

A bold red title glittered above shiny black calligraphy, affixed with an embossed seal.

I, Willis E. Ludeman, judge of the Probate Court within and for the County and State aforesaid, do hereby License and Authorize James P. Meyer and Denise L. Tomanski to be joined in marriage...

Denny's knees buckled, one leg shooting out in front of her, the other crumpling up against her chest. She landed on her rump on the floor, cradling the paper and our Bible in trembling arms.

Jimmy joined her, poked at the pretty book, looked up at her with an eager grin. "We'll read some of it later, kiddo," she told him. "Maybe a story about miracles. What do you think?"

Did this mean what I hoped it did? That Denny and I had finally caught up to each other? We could stop circling?

I could feel myself smiling. To be honest, since that day? I don't think I've stopped.

"A pen pal offer? From prison?" Joan didn't often look surprised, had probably thought she'd heard it all, but this one raised her eyebrows to her hairline.

Denny laughed. I sat next to her scowling. There wasn't one damn thing funny about it, in my opinion.

"A single handprinted page, ruled, teeny tiny letters front and back, so he could get everything squeezed in. Neat as a pin, misspellings and all. He called me 'Misses Meyer'—m-i-s-s-e-s—but hoped we could be friendlier in future correspondence. He spelled correspondence phonetically and it took two readings out loud before I figured out what he meant."

"Did his letter upset you?"

Upset? Down-set. Sideways-set. Everywhichway-set. I'd tried to shove it off the table when Denny left it there. Was aiming for the trashcan but only conjured up a draft.

"Sort of. At first. Then I called the police to ask if it was something I should worry about."

"And they said?"

"Happens quite a bit—especially if the widow is young and the death was tragic. Some cons keep scrapbooks of likely marks. Cut articles and obits out of the paper."

"They think if a woman is shattered, she's easy prey."

"Right. Not all of them, though. Some are just lonely."

I'll give him 'lonely'—with a kick to the place where he keeps his brain. That should wipe all that lonely right out.

Joan shook her head. "Six months ago, how would you have reacted to this?"

Denny shrugged. "I'm not sure. Probably kept it to myself. Fretted about it at night. Slept with a light on for a while."

Staked out all the entrances to make sure the freak hasn't been released and wants to introduce himself to my wife in person.

"But now you called the police for advice. Sounds like you've got a grip."

Denise nodded, her face empty of expression.

Joan cocked her head. "No?"

"Yeah, sure. It was no big." My wife added a self-deprecating laugh. "I just thought you'd get a kick out of some of the things we poor sorrowing widows have to go through."

"Something else happened, didn't it? Something that *did* upset you."

Denny slumped back on the sofa, propped her neck on the cushion, and rocked her head from side to side. "*Comme ci, comme ca.*" A moment passed before she continued. "Got a second letter." She straightened with a jerk. "Not from the convict," she hastened to explain. "From a friend."

Joan nodded. Waited.

"Well. A former friend. I haven't heard from her for a few years, ever since she got married."

"And—what?—she'd just learned about Jim's death?"

"No." Denny put a fist to her mouth. Chewed at a cuticle. "She'd heard about that. She just wanted to tell me she'd gotten a divorce."

"And that bothered you?"

Denny considered for a moment.

Tell her. It's not like she's going to be shocked.

"She wanted me to know... she was available."

I could see Joan considering her options, struggling to decide if she should shift to a smile or a frown. When she spoke, she was parked in neutral. "It's hard to know how you want me to respond. We haven't talked about your sexual orientation before." She leaned forward—always a sign she was reaching out without touching. "Did it intrigue you? Or offend you?"

Denny's face screwed up, like a half-deflated soccer ball. "Not at all intrigued." Then she paused and her features smoothed. "Not offended either. Just. Well. Surprised. I never knew."

"Perhaps she didn't either. Until she'd married."

Denny bobbed her head once. Then again. "Okay. Makes sense. But..." She gritted her teeth. "Did she have to come out to me? Now? Like she thinks Jim wasn't right for me...' " Her pitch had risen as she spoke, and the "*me*" shut off with an angry spit. "How *could* she? How cruel! How..."

"Self-serving."

It was my wife's turn to be surprised. "You think?"

"Absolutely. What did you think she was doing?"

"Besides the obvious hitting on me?"

Joan remained silent.

"She was... She thought... She..." Denny sucked her lips together, a taut line of rage. "She was dismissing my marriage. Like it didn't mean a thing!"

You tell her, woman.

"That... that... that *bitch!*"

Joan sat back, seemed pleased. "You tell her, woman."

"But... that's not fair, is it? I mean. I'm reading too much into it."

"Maybe. Then again, self-serving people don't think about how their words and actions affect others. Your friend didn't stop to think how her 'offer' might make you feel. Did she ask how you were doing? If she could help in any way?"

Denise shook her head.

"I didn't think so. To you? Her letter was a nasty shot at Jim. It belittled what you had together. But to her? The letter was all about her. What *she* wanted." Joan paused. "What did you do with it?"

Denny shrugged. "Threw it in the garbage with the other one." A half smile slipped out. "Maybe tore hers into pieces first. Very small pieces."

"Glad to hear it. You handled them both the way they deserved. You're not losing sleep over it, are you?"

The cuticle went back between her teeth, then Denny snatched her hand into her lap. "Joan?"

"Hmm?"

"Do I...? Am I...?" She sighed. "This sounds stupid even in my head."

Joan didn't bother to restrain her smile. "You do not look like an easy mark. *Easy* is hardly the word that comes to mind when I think of you." Then she grew serious. "You did nothing to warrant these advances, Denise. It's all on them. Does that help?"

See? Told you.

"Like I said. Sounded stupid even in my head. But yeah, it helps. Thanks."

"Good." Joan began to rise. "Our time's about up. Anything else you'd like to share?"

"Um."

Finally!

Joan sank back down. "Wow, it's been a busy week, hasn't it?"

Denise gave her a sheepish grin. "It's nothing really. Silly, actually."

"I'm guessing not." Joan pointed at us. "You saved it for last, so you could toss it out there and make a run for it. So. Spill it."

"Right."

You want to tell her, or should I?

"I heard my husband's voice."

"In a mall? At an event?"

"No. In our bedroom. And not *heard* heard. Sort of heard it in my head." Denny crouched forward, her hands curled toward each other, as though she were trying to get them around something she couldn't see. "I had this *thought*. But it wasn't *my* thought. It was a… *Jim* thought. Like his voice, but not out loud. More like the memory of his voice." Her palms turned up, ready to catch whatever fell from the sky. "And he told me something only *he* knew."

"What was that?"

"Where he'd put our Marriage License. I needed it. Couldn't find it. Tore the place apart and was at my wit's end. So, I… asked him where he'd put it."

"And was it there?"

"Yes! In our Bible. Which is so *not* where I would have stored it. But he said… or I thought he said… 'Did you look in the Bible?' " One hand dropped to Denny's knee in surrender. The other fisted and returned to her mouth. "And there it was." She was going to chew that thumb off if she wasn't careful. "Am I nuts? I mean, I'm telling you I think I spoke to a ghost."

"Nuts is not a word we toss around lightly," Joan reminded her. "But if you are, you're in good company. A lot of intelligent people have had similar encounters."

"Right."

"Seriously. Teddy Roosevelt. Umm... Sir Arthur Conan Doyle..." Joan twitched her nose in thought. "Mick Jagger."

Denny laughed. "I'd chalk that one up to chemical stimulants."

Joan grinned. "Noted. How about Sting? Or Sir Winston Churchill? Friends said he wouldn't sleep in the Lincoln bedroom because it made him uneasy."

"So you think I'm okay."

"I think you are more than okay. But consider this: maybe you didn't know where Jim put the Marriage License, but you did know *Jim*. And when the pressure was on, you put yourself in his place and thought..."

"I should look in the Bible." Denny sighed. "I'm not sure how I feel about that. It was sort of nice to hear his voice."

"No reason you can't listen for him again. But if he starts telling you to set fire to the curtains or rob a bank, you let me know. Then we'll talk."

Joan rose, held out her hands. It had become a ritual that ended our sessions: a two-handed clasp. I wished I could join them, could let Joan know how much I appreciated what she'd done for my wife.

"Have you dreamed about him yet?"

Denny shook her head.

She told me not to come to her in dreams.

"You might try telling him it's okay now. That you're ready to see him again."

Denise looked unconvinced.

"Something to think about," Joan added as she walked us to the door.

Yeah. Think real hard, babe. There's so much I could show you.

All she had to do was let me in.

Chapter Eighteen:
Don't Sweat the Small Stuff

I hear you out there: the scoffers, the realists. You're mumbling to yourselves, "Finally! It's about time someone rational like Joan pointed out the obvious."

Tough audience.

You think Denise was imagining me. That she wanted to believe I was still around, so she was hearing and seeing me in everything that happened.

As you may recall, she was right there with you, in the beginning.

I'd say you were correct. Except, I *was* around. I *was* talking to her—or trying to. I *was* making things happen. Through coincidence? Imagination? By accident? Why not? Doesn't make me less *present*. Once upon a time, people believed the world was flat—until the day they didn't sail off the end of it. So, if you Doubting Tammies and Thomases don't mind, I'm going to continue playing Let's Pretend. I make a freaking good story and I've just begun to rock and roll.

It was July third, and for the first time Denny was showing an interest in a holiday. Any holiday would have been a good sign, but the fact it was the Fourth of July was a major victory. See, when I was still warming a body, I'd been the High Potentate of Fireworks Display. It was I who purchased the first "kit" from a guy at work, a smallish box loaded down with mortars, skyrockets and sizzling fountains that shot out flaming balls of fire. It was I, armed with a long-necked lighter and slathered with bug spray, who first led the Tomanski men into the warehouse parking lot behind my in-laws' house to dazzle our womenfolk. And it was I who uttered those now famous words: "Fire in the hole!"

That debut exhibition was a rousing success, so the next year's extravaganza morphed from smallish to hellacious. Two heavy boxes of illegal (in Ohio) pyrotechnics, bought legally (in Michigan), were blasted off (again, illegally within the city limits) to enthusiastic *oooos* and *ahhhs*.

Add a couple twelve-packs of brew and you have a family tradition. The following Fourth, neighbors hauled out lawn chairs to cheer from their backyards. Cars pulled off Manhattan Boulevard into the warehouse driveway to watch and honk. One, I swore, had TPD shields on its doors. Fortunately, if he *was* a representative of the illustrious Toledo Police, he did not turn on his flashers or hit the siren; just watched us from the shadows to ensure we didn't set fire to anything important. (I guess that dumpster didn't count.)

It should be no surprise then, that when Denny packed away my clothes two months after I died, it was the battered beige T-shirt with its necklace of burn holes across the shoulders that made her curl into a ball of abject grief.

Next to Christmas, my wife should have dreaded this holiday more than any other. Yet, here she was: donating a chunk of change to the fireworks fund, tagging along with Daria and her husband Michael when they crossed the Michigan line to pick up the ammo, even baking my favorite dessert to take to the picnic.

I danced around her in our kitchen, as keyed up as the kids.

It's supposed to be hot tomorrow. How about a cold dish to pass around?

"What do you think, Rach? Should we make something to eat besides chocolate cherry squares?"

"No," our daughter declared. "No food!"

All of the blocks on Rachel's nutrition pyramid were labeled DESSERT.

What about tuna and shells?

"Not even tuna-noodle-tomato salad?"

My kiddos were underfoot, as usual, but Denny was side-stepping them to the beat of a Marvin Gaye tune playing on the radio, doing her own happy dance. Our four-year-old stopped poking her brother to consider her mother's question as if it were an offer of worldwide unilateral disarmament.

"With no green stuff," Rachel decided.

Jimmy nodded his agreement. His pyramid was weighted with edibles that came in shades of red, white, beige or brown. The expression on his face said, What is this color green you speak of?

"No celery. No peppers," their mom promised.

Celery salt works for me.

" 'Kay. Tuna noodles!"

Denise began to gather the ingredients, her hand hesitating over the bottle of celery seeds for a moment before snatching it up. I glanced at the clock on the stove. She had just enough time to whip the recipe together before she would have to get the kids bathed and ready for bed.

"On your mark," Rachel hollered without warning. "Get set." Then, jumping the gun, she leaped to her feet and sprinted into the dining room. Jimmy tumbled forward onto his hands and knees to scurry after her.

Denny laughed and lifted one foot so he could duck under it and cut into his sister's lead. "Go!" she shouted.

The Meyer 500 was off. In moments, our little racers would dash back around, through the other door from the living room, past Mom, to complete the loop. I should say, Rachel would dash. It was a foregone conclusion that she would win because no matter how fast Jimmy pumped those knees and pounded his palms, he was doomed to be lapped. It didn't seem to matter. My son would scramble after his sister with a will, certain he would catch up. He might be eighteen when he did, but he'd get there.

I pushed myself up onto the counter next to the sink, where I could watch the action and remain off the straightaway.

Are you hauling the wading pool over tomorrow? I asked my wife.

Denny skipped out of the way as Rachel shifted into second gear to complete lap one, her chubby legs leaning left as she hugged the curve back into the dining room. "Should we take the pool to Grammy's tomorrow?" Denise called as she swept by.

"Yay! Pool!"

Jimmy's palms skittered on the tile as he made the transition from carpet to smooth track, still too far behind, but not giving a damn.

Denise raised her voice. "Can you remind me to put it in the back of the station wagon in the morning?"

"Station wagon!" echoed back from the living room. "We reminding you!"

Denny chuckled. "Not quite morning. But thanks."

The song on the radio was winding down. Denny crooned along, an off-key duet that made my soul ache. "My love is alive...way down in my heart... although we are miles apart..."

Just send for me, oh baby.

You know that scene in *The Grinch*? When he hears the Whos singing? That was me. Call it a pre-holiday skyrocket. This was more than a good day. It was an amazing day—even by otherworldly standards.

"Oh, shi... *shoot!*"

What?

"Swimsuits."

Don't sweat it. You put them in the washer this morning.

"Hope they didn't get mildewy sitting in the washer all day."

Go toss the load in the dryer. I'll watch the kids.

"Slow down!" she called as lap three hit the home stretch. "Mommy's got to go in the basement. I'll be right back." She moved to the stairwell, flipped on the light, stepped down, and closed the door tightly at her back. Rachel could open it if she put some effort into it, but it was best not to make it too easy. "Keep an eye on them, please," she murmured.

Was she talking to me? Upgrade that amazing day to miraculous. *Got it, babe. No problem.*

I slipped off the counter and settled on the kitchen floor, legs pretzeled, to monitor any collisions that might require a yellow flag.

Five minutes passed, and the Meyer 500 was called on account of boredom. I got up and headed into the living room to switch on the TV. Bypassing the early evening game shows, I dialed up a cartoon featuring a lot of tiny blue men in white diapers, capering through a town dotted with mushroom houses. *Where are the women?* I asked no one in particular.

Rachel patted the patch of rug next to her for her brother to park in. "Smurfs," she informed him. "You'll like them. All boys. One girl."

Well, that sucks.

"Mama says that sucks. They need more girl animal-gators."

Jimmy turned and squinted at her. I leaned down and stared at him in surprise. When had his eyes become so much like my own?

"They need more girls to draw the pictures. Mama says."

My son turned his attention back to the screen, looking through me as if I were a ghost. Yeah, yeah, don't say it. I studied his face as it crinkled up in a smile, dimples firing on six cylinders. "All boys" seemed to work just fine for him. *You'll change your mind about that one day, kiddo.*

"That's why I'm gonna be a animal-gator when I grow up," Rachel said. "I'll draw all-girl cartoons."

You go for it, Smurfette.

A dull thud reverberated through the floorboards.

Denny?

My wife didn't answer—that would have been too much to hope for—but a second thud and a metallic clang indicated something was not going well in the basement.

You guys stay put. Daddy's going to go help Mommy.

Rachel nodded, her attention riveted to the boobtube. Sometimes I swore she heard me better than anyone.

Hang on, hon. I'm coming.

Our basement was a bit of a hodgepodge: a large rectangle made up of cinderblock walls coated with water-sealant, grey cement floors, open wood rafters, and a skeleton of two-by-four supports that bisected the center. Our plan had been to split the main space into a rec room and laundry/sewing area. We'd already added a full bath with shower in the corner under the stairs, a work room for my tool bench in the portion that jutted out under the breakfast nook, and a playroom for the kids in what had once been the coal cellar under the front porch. Unfortunately, I'd died before the stack of drywall in the far corner could be applied to finish the rec room remodel.

Denny stood on the other side of the open wall, her back to me.

It took some time to figure out the problem. She was hopping lightly on one bare foot in front of the 1930s fusebox—yet another project left undone—holding a cardboard carton of spares in her hand. Her other foot was tucked up against the back of her thigh. "Ow, ow, ow, ow."

My tool box lay open on the floor, the apparent source of a stubbed toe.

What's wrong?

"They can't all be bad," she muttered.

She placed her injured foot on the floor, testing it with a tap of her big toe. "Maybe these fuses are old."

Not likely. Why do you need them anyway?

"If it's not a blown fuse, I'm screwed! Why won't the damn thing turn on?"

Ah, the dryer. *It's not working?*

"Let us recap," my wife said in a tone that could best be described as the love child of Pissy Confusion and Max Irritation. While she grumbled, she gave a hard twist to first one fuse and then another.

Careful. They're tight enough.

"Wet clothes in. Temperature set. Door closed. Start button pushed. And pushed. And *pushed*." She raked her fingers through her hair, making her shag cut shaggier than usual. Thought back. "Pulled the plug out of the socket, waited thirty seconds, plugged it back in."

Did you screw a fuse in crooked?

"I changed the fuses on *all* the basement circuits. And I did it *correctly*. I can do this stuff. I have to do this stuff. I will *not* call my father to change a freaking fuse!"

God forbid.

"Who needs men, anyway?"

Not you, independent love of my life. But for the record, your electrician husband doesn't think it's a blown fuse.

"But if it isn't a fuse? What the hell *is* it? And how do I fix it on a holiday weekend after six-assed P.M.?"

Let me take a look.

She stalked through the skeletal wall, stepping over the 2x4 bottom plate, to get to the side of the basement where the dryer waited, taunting her.

"Okay, let's…"

…start from the top.

Denny took a deep breath, like she was going underwater and wouldn't be coming up until daylight savings time fell back an hour in October. She spoke on the exhale. "Riiiight."

I positioned myself beside her as she opened the dryer door. Bent over when she did. Studied each action as she made it. "Clothes are all in, nice and neat. Nothing's sticking out or blocking the switch."

Good. You were *watching all those years, eh?*

She shut the door—perhaps more firmly than required, but I got it. Pissy Confusion was in charge. Denny straightened and so did I. She turned the temperature dial back and forth between settings, then settled again on Permanent Press. "Dial is properly seated. Heard a click. Felt a click."

Very good. I'm impressed.

Her finger wavered over the start button. "Come on, baby. Turn on for Mama. I've got things to do, and the kids need their clothes." I shoved my hands in my pockets, resisting the urge to place one on top of hers— knowing from previous experience it would melt through, and my heart with it.

Denny let Max Irritation deliver a finger stab that began in her shoulder and landed with a knockout punch.

Silence.

"Goddamn it!" The shout had no more left her lips, than she slapped both hands across her mouth and shot her eyes to the ceiling—to where our kiddos sat above, watching television. "Sorry," she whispered. "But truly absolutely god freaking damn it!"

My wife leaned over the dryer, her elbows propped on top, face buried in her palms. "This is stupid. Jim would have known what to do."

I stood apart, helpless to comfort, and with no idea what to tell her to try next. *Okay, Denny Lou, I'm glad you can't hear me say this, but... the Jimster is stumped.*

I heard her sigh, a hiss of air sucked between her fingers. "Nothing stumped you, did it, honey?"

I hated to shatter her illusions, but if I'd been alive, I'd have told her, "Grab the phonebook, babe. We need a repairman."

But.

I wasn't alive, was I? Not in the traditional sense. I was energy off the leash. A spark. A pulse of electricity. A cloud of wandering animation in search of purpose.

And my wife had just reached out for my help. Not fully hopeful, not completely sold—but open to possibility.

Well, what the hell. Nothing tried, nothing dried.

I moved next to her, felt along the cool white surface of the dryer with formless fingertips, let my touch filter through the enamel, down past the metal, along the wires, under the switches, over each component, into the mechanical guts of it all.

Try again, babe. Ask for my help. Believe.

My wife straightened. Drummed her fingers on the dryer, a steady tattoo that spelled "Now what?"

"What the hell," she said with a scowl. "Nothing tried, nothing dried."

She leaned down and snapped open the door. "You're the electrician, Jim. *You* fix it!" Then she gave it a solid slam.

The machine roared to life.

Denny stumbled back, caught one ankle on the other, and nearly fell. With a brief flap of her arms, she righted herself. Then lifted her right hand slowly until it was directly in front of her eyes. Crooked her index finger. Stared at it. Maybe waiting to see if it would emit a wisp of smoke. Like a derringer.

"But…"

She cut her eyes to the start button.

"I didn't…"

With a slow pivot, my Denny turned her gaze on the walls and corners around her. Examining the space, studying the air, searching for shadows— or maybe for the glitter of a ghostly sparkler.

She cleared her throat. "Okay then," she said. "Thank you."

You're welcome, babe. Any time.

238

Still not convinced? The slam jiggled something back into place, you say? Oh ye of little faith. Jiggle, let me introduce you to James.

I don't know why I'm trying to prove myself to you. Then, as now, Denny was my focus. I wanted her to know she would see me again. To have hope, and be happy. But for hope to exist, there has to be belief. And, while I and the Big Guy were pretty sure she would never settle back into the same unbroken faith she'd had before, we were confident that if I stayed on the job, she would one day reassemble the pieces in a way that fit her new life.

Denise was *almost* sure I fixed the dryer, and since it never acted up again, she began to accept that my hanging around could be a useful thing. What *you* choose to believe is up to you. No arm twisting from higher-ups. Never was or will be.

You may have noticed I've been moving this story straight ahead for a bit. No sidetracking or backtracking. Hmm. I must have been smoking the drapes.

How about we change it up a bit? Do a little future-tracking.

What do you mean, I can't do that? *Pffft.* Where I am, there is no backwards or forwards, no side to side. Only *is*.

For example. While I can be with Denny in that old house on Elm Street in 1984, I can also be in it with her sister Daria and her husband Michael at the same "time" when they lived there in 1986. And with their daughter Jenny and her family when they lived there in 2006.

If I turn my attention one way, I can hear Daria fumbling about and tossing stuff on the floor of the back bedroom that once was Jimmy's nursery. She's lost some whatchamacallit and is calling out: "Jim? If you're here, can you give me a hand?" She looks so hopeful... and she's added a "pretty please." So how can I refuse? Besides. It's kind of fun to whisper in her ear: *It's right there, Daria.*

In the drawer she's already checked. Twice.

Man, I love saying, *Told you so.*

But wait!—like they insist in those infomercials my Dad loves—there's more. Downstairs, twenty years later, Jenny is searching for the remote control. Again. And blaming me. Again. Sheesh. We bodiless energy blobs get all the blame. By the way, it's under the sofa cushion.

In case you are wondering, I am not restricted to the house. If there is someone I love who could use a little support, I am there with them, as well.

Like Brooke, when she was ten-ish. You do remember Brooke, don't you? Christened on the same day as Denise's nephew Danny, and his sidekick in our wedding party three years later? She was barely old enough to remember me; I'd died when she was six. But she did have one clear memory of the day she was trapped in the bathroom, and her mom had called Uncle Jim to come rescue her.

I can see her as she was then, a trembly toddler, sandy blonde hair askew, arms raised to be picked up and comforted. And I can see her at age ten, same sandy-haired bob, and once again in a bathroom, but this time, face crumpled in distress, staring into a mirror. *What's up, Brooke? Who's made you unhappy?*

She doesn't hear the question, only sniffles. "Why are friends so mean? Why don't adults understand?" More sniffles that break my heart. "If my Uncle Jim were here, he'd get it. He'd help."

Maybe it's because she is feeling trapped and unhappy in a bathroom, but I know she will hear me if I speak. "I will *always* be here, kiddo."

She gasps and flicks her head to the side, then back to her reflection in the mirror—big blue eyes wide—as though she expects to find me standing behind her. Which I am. "Does that help?" I ask.

She bites her lip and the corners of her mouth curve. I return the smile. I've been able to lift her up and console her again. And that is enough for both of us.

Need more? Oh, I've got 'em, sweetheart. I've touched them all—parents, brothers, sisters—though some of them only looked startled, then quickly sloughed me off. Did my presence scare them? Maybe. Were they worried about their sanity? I get it. I could expect my brother Tom, the doctor, to keep our contact to himself. The smarter they are, the harder they fight anything that can't be backed up by research in a textbook. My brother Bill? He was older and my protector as a kid. Having me be the one who hovers and protects would not be easy to accept. I don't mind if they don't talk about it, or if they never noticed I was around. If they need me, I'll be there. Belief is optional.

I haven't forgotten baby brother Joe, either—the sibling who resembles me the most in appearance and personality; so much so, when he decided to grow a beard after I died, my mom asked him to shave it off. He looked too like me for her to bear. Denny was relieved when she did. The first time a bearded Joe had dropped by to visit, the image of his furry face in the door window made her lungs stop working.

My wife has never admitted it out loud, but she uses Joe as a gauge of what I would look like today if I'd lived.

Joke's on you, baby brother. I will be forever twenty-five, while you... Well, let's just say greying hair makes you look intelligent. Sophisticated. I wouldn't think of adding that you can use all the help you can get in those departments. Nah. Then again, brothers should always be honest with each other—how else will they know what areas require improvement?

No need to thank me. Happy to help.

Ah, but brother Mike—rechristened Uncle Boo after he had knee surgery and Brooke said he had a boo-boo. *You* have never doubted our contact. Well, our *almost* contact. Where were you working at the time? Oh yeah, the car dealership. Went out to lunch, and when you came back, one of the guys hollered, "Hey, your brother called. Wants you to give him a buzz."

"Which brother?"

"Jim."

I don't think I've mentioned that Mike and I shared a bedroom growing up. Uh-huh. Two brothers, a year apart in age? Sharing the same interests, the same tastes, the same *space*? (To be honest, we shared the same face, as well. Except Boo's is topped with blonde hair, and mine with brown.)

All that sameness spelled trouble from the moment Mike could crawl and get into my stuff. It got so bad, I eventually had to lock everything I valued in a black steamer trunk at the foot of my bed.

Mike took the hinges off.

Imagine the sound of teeth grinding, magnified and played through the speakers at a heavy metal concert. That was me.

Love-hate relationship pretty much described Boo and I—but always weighted to the first. So when I called him at work after I died, I wanted him to know that I didn't forget he was my brother—and if he needed something I could give, he wouldn't need a screwdriver. It was his.

"*Jim?*" he repeated to the coworker who'd taken my message. "You sure about that?"

"Yup. Wrote it down—right here."

Boo grinned, and held out his hand. "Hope you got a number."

You already had my number, Mike. You always did.

You can lower that eyebrow, Kay. I haven't forgotten my sisters. I've mentioned Jan before. She's the oldest of the Meyer Mob, Brooke's mom, and the sister with the missing contact lens. She and Boo are the only offspring with fair hair.

Kay and Beth are sisters two and three, respectively. Both of them look a lot like our mom—dark haired and bright eyed—but only Kay has mastered the questioning Mister Spock eyebrow that can stop a stampede of children in their tracks. Mom was a true artist. Not only could she have halted an army of Spartans, but she could have sent them scrambling to pick up their clothes, empty the trash, or correct whatever mistake they are suddenly certain she's spotted before she would ever have to speak their name.

"James?"

Yikes! She's settled on *you*. Goosebumps. Instant guilt.

Kay's quirking eyebrow and silent rebuke aren't quite that potent, but then again, she hasn't needed to put them to the test against a throng of eight hoodlums under the age of twelve.

I confess, Dead Me did not reach out to Kay until recently. Not because I was still irritated over some past slight. (Exactly what did happen to my shirt, hmm?) But because I was saving up for a message I hoped would set important things in motion. I will tell you all about it when the time is right —but not now. She can quirk that brow all she wants. She's going to have to be patient.

As for my remaining sister Beth, I have not spoken to her since my death— and I never will.

That's not to say I don't love her or keep an eye on her. I do, and if I thought she could handle it, I'd sit down and strike up a conversation this minute. I might not get her to shut up once we started, but it would be a lively discussion, for sure.

Beth is autistic.

I suspect her oversensitive nervous system would make her particularly susceptible to my presence—which is why I won't add to her burden.

She's a remarkable woman who has triumphed over tough odds. Beth maintains her own apartment within an adult autistic community, runs her own small engine repair shop, has obtained a limited drivers license, and has held down jobs in an auto service department and for a railroad maintenance company. She's learned to play guitar, and even now at age fifty-nine participates in Special Olympics, pulling in her share of gold and silver medals in swimming and downhill skiing. When you factor in her disability? That woman's resume puts mine to shame.

As you may have noticed, Beth shares my mechanical skills—might even surpass me at my own game. She's the only one of my brothers and sisters who takes after me in that respect. Which gives me one more reason not to bother her with advice or help from the hereafter.

Beth would scoff at anything resembling instructions.

Chapter Nineteen: Are You Listening?

It's been a crap week, Joan. She won't tell you about it. You're going to have to probe.

The psychologist nodded, almost in my direction. "Nice shoes," she said.

Denny glanced down at her feet, wiggled her toes. The chipped polish went well with the battered flip-flops. "Um. Couldn't find my tennis shoes."

"Or a hairbrush?"

Uh-oh. I scooted sideways away from my wife. *I said probe, Joan. Not punch.*

Denise's eyes narrowed. "Is this the evening gown portion of the competition?"

Nice one, babe.

Denny wasn't trying to be funny, but I made no effort to hold back a snort. Besides, even if she heard me, she couldn't jab me with one of those sharp elbows. Silver linings.

"Sorry," Joan said as her own chuckle faded. "You've been here fifteen minutes, chatting about how good this was and how nice that was…" She tipped a palm at Denny's attire. "While all the while your clothes are telling me it hasn't been a good week at all."

Denny's scowl had kittens. "I can't have an off day? Well, excuse me." She dragged *excuse* into extra syllables. "I guess I was just too busy raising two children *on my own* to waste an *hour* fancying up for a woman I *pay* to make me feel better—*not* to insult my shoes. "

Joan met my wife's glare with an easy shrug. "As long as you don't waltz in naked, I don't care what you wear. But as a barometer for your emotions? *And* as the woman you *pay* to make you feel better? I'd be doing a lousy job if I didn't point out the obvious: you're miserable."

Denny laced her fingers together in her lap. Stared daggers at them as she twisted them back and forth. "I don't get it," she muttered, nearly under her breath. "I was fine. I was over it. Why is it happening again?"

"Okay, first mistake." Joan leaned forward. "No one gets *over* this."

"I was better."

"You were coping. That's different from thinking the hurt is going to go away. You loved Jim. There is always going to be a hole where he once stood. Some people try to fill their hole with drugs or alcohol. Gambling. Spending sprees." Joan extended a hand toward my wife. "You? You're doing it the right way."

Denny leaned away from the gesture.

Joan sighed and straightened. "Look. This is not a setback. Think about where you were... and how far you've come. You said it yourself. You are raising two kids, and doing a bang up job of it. You've managed your finances in a way that makes your life easier. You're making plans... a new car, a new teaching position."

"So why...?"

Joan spread her palms. "Occasionally, something is going to happen that reminds you there's still a hole in your life." She uncurled the fingers of one hand, ticking off the possibilities. "A scene in a movie. A favorite song. A man with a child on his shoulders—"

Denny interrupted: "But it's been over a year. *Normal* women don't break down in hysterics after a year."

Joan shot up in her chair. "Normal? Who decided what normal was—and dared to say you weren't?" She huffed in aggravation. "I know *I* didn't." She eyed my wife like a disappointed school teacher. "Whoever it was, I hope you didn't pay for *their* advice, because even if it were free you were overcharged."

"You mean, I'm *always* going to grieve?"

"Not as often, not as hard, but yes. I thought we'd agreed: Jim deserves a few tears now and then."

"But…"

Joan clicked her tongue. "There was more, wasn't there?"

"It's just that…"

They were jerks, Denny. You know it. Say it.

Denise sighed and slipped her foot out of one of the flip-flops, dug her toes into the carpeting alongside it. "A bunch of us decided to have a girls night out. Drinks. Gossip. It was nice."

Joan wagged a finger. "There you go with nice again."

"It *was*. Until…"

I swear I'm going to tell her myself. Then won't you be embarrassed.

"Annie mentioned some woman they all knew whose husband had died." Denny's foot stilled. "Four months ago."

Yeah, practically a lifetime.

"And they told you she was still grieving?"

Denny nodded slowly. "The couple had two little girls, grade school age."

"Sounds a bit like you. I get it."

He was in construction.

"He built houses. One was still unfinished."

And she took her kids…

"Took her daughters to see it. The three of them—the mom and her girls…" Denny's toes were digging again. She watched them as they searched for a foothold. "They sat on the front steps of the house after the workers had gone. Held on to each other and cried."

"Sounds like an appropriate way to mourn a man they lost."

"But that wasn't all." With an abrupt lurch, Denise shoved her foot back into the flip-flop. "Annie said the mother had been taking the girls on drives every weekend. To see *all* of the homes he had ever built."

Joan waited. The silence spun out.

"The other women with us—at girls night? They wouldn't shut up about how *awful* that was. How *abnormal*. How it was a damned 'tour of death'…" Denise's voice softened, and even I had to tilt an ear to catch the rest. "How they should all get on the phone and call Child Services to report the mother as unfit."

Joan threw up a hand, palm out. "Have her kids put in foster care? Oh, Denise, tell me you didn't agree?"

Denny slouched back into the cushions. "No. I thought the visits to his houses were… well, kind of a nice way to remember him. The whole idea about reporting her? That… pissed me off." My wife lifted a shoulder and let it fall. "I should have kept my mouth shut."

She tried to tell them, Joan.

"Instead I blasted them. Told them they were wrong. That I was a widow, too, and I knew for a fact that we all grieve differently."

I could feel Denise beginning to vibrate. "They hadn't even remembered— until I defended her."

A storm was gathering around my wife, building toward a lightning strike. So close, you could smell the ozone. "Know what Annie said? What she *dared* to say? 'But, Denise, *that* woman was married for twelve years! She's having a nervous breakdown because she loved *her* husband a *long* time.'"

Denny stilled. "I'd only been married four years. I was lucky."

I kept waiting for Joan to say something.

Kept waiting.

It was Denny who broke the silence. (Smart lady, that Joan.) "They were wrong. Weren't they?"

Apparently, Joan didn't feel the question deserved even a nod.

"It has nothing to do with years, does it?" Denny's right hand fluttered off her knee, and she studied the opal that glinted there. Her voice was stronger now, no longer hesitant or questioning.

"I can't believe I went home and cried myself to sleep that night. Cried for me for speaking up. And for Jim—who they thought couldn't possibly be loved as much in four years as some men are loved in forty. For that poor woman and her girls who just wanted one last look at their father's legacy."

Denise dropped her hand into her lap, sniffed—a sound of self disgust. "Like *we* were the problem."

She shook her head. "Why in the hell did I let myself feel *bad* about *us*? I should have been crying for Annie and the others. All those foolish women who have no idea what's ahead for them."

Finally, Joan found something to nod about. "Good. That's good." She clasped her hands together and gave them a brief shake, a gesture of triumph. "You tripped. You cried. You're picking up the pieces. But more important? You recognize there is absolutely *nothing* wrong with you."

I sagged into the sofa. *I don't know about you, Denny Lou. This purging stuff is exhausting.*

But Joan was not finished. She crossed her arms. "No. Absolutely nothing. Except…"

Denny tilted her head to the side, lifted a brow.

"Your taste in footwear."

My wife laughed, the first happy sound I'd heard from her in days.

"Do me a favor?" Joan pleaded. "Before your next appointment? Burn those ugly things."

Oh, Joan… from your mouth to the Big Guy's ear.

I was spending a lot of late nights sitting up in bed with Rachel, watching classic movies in the dark while her mother slept beside us. Our daughter had stopped bawling for me in her sleep, but a month after the anniversary of my death she was still waking up around midnight wanting to cuddle.

Joan had suggested not fighting with her about it. Rachel, being a stubborn, determined little girl, would only dig in her heels and turn it into a *thing*. Instead, Joan suggested giving her a bear hug and asking her to go back to bed; or barring that, letting her climb in beside Denny until she fell asleep —at which time, my wife could trundle her back to her room. Waking up in her own bed every morning would eventually convince Rachel to stay out of ours.

I repeat: Stubborn. Determined. Previously cited digging in of little heels.

The tactic had yet to weave its magic.

Maybe it didn't help that I was enjoying the alone time with my Smurfette, teaching her the names of the great old movie stars. She was partial to Errol Flynn swashbucklers and Jack Klugman in reruns of *Quincy, M.E.*

"Mommy! Mommy! Wake up!"

Shh. Don't disturb your mom, sweetie. She's got a job interview tomorrow.

"But Mommy! You gotta look!"

Denny grumbled and turned her back on us, pulling the covers up over her chin and one ear. The room was dimly lit by the glow of the television screen. My wife's face was cast in blue shadows.

"Mommeeeee. This is important! The little girl said 'water'! She can talk."

Denny mumbled, "Tha's nice, Rach. Sleep now, 'kay?"

Our daughter clambered onto her knees, leaned over her mother's shoulder, and tried to lift an eyelid. "Hurry, Mom. You're missing it."

Denny flinched and pulled her face out of reach, rubbed a fist against a smarting cornea. "Missin' wha'?"

"Helen! She knows! She *knows!*" It was a perfect mimicry of Anne Bancroft, Irish accent and all.

Denise squinted at the portable television perched on the bookshelf next to our bedroom door. Patty Duke was dashing around a yard, patting pump handles, tree trunks, and grass—eagerly demanding the names of all the things that had filled her dark world with mystery.

"*Miracle Worker,*" Denny confirmed. "You're watching *The Miracle Worker.*" My wife was coming awake, caught up in the excitement of the movie's closing scenes. "True story," she pointed out to our daughter. "Helen Keller. She got sick when she was a baby. Couldn't see any more. Couldn't hear."

Rachel was clapping her hands with glee. "And now she can!"

Denny yawned and pulled herself into a sitting position, shoved her pillow into the small of her back. I scooted closer, let my hand fall on top of hers, where it drifted through like smoke. "No, honey," Denny said, wiggling her butt deeper into the mattress. "Helen is still blind. She's still deaf and can't hear. But she knows words now." She swallowed a few times to clear her dry mouth. "Now she can use words to *learn* what things look like. What they sound like. She can ask Miss Annie and her mom and dad to describe everything to her." She yawned again, and slid an arm around our daughter's waist.

"Teacher," Rachel corrected. "Not Miss Annie. Now she's T-e-a-c-h-e-r."

"Yup," Denny agreed.

I settled in alongside my wife and daughter and watched as the nighttime closeup of Helen and her Teacher sitting on a porch pulled back to reveal first a window, then a door, a house, then a yard, and finally hints of the hills around them: a full-screen image of a little girl's wide new world.

Together, Denise, Rachel and I listened to the closing music swell.

"You're wrong, Mom," Rachel said, her voice blurry with sleep.

Denny smiled. After four years of being solemnly corrected, we had become used to being wrong. "Am I, kiddo?"

"Uh-huh." There was a long pause, a soft inhale that took a few moments to become an exhale. "Helen *can* see again. She *can* hear."

I joined Denny in a mutual frown. *How do you figure, Rach?*

"Just." Our sweetheart's head was nodding toward her chin. Denny slid her hand up a small back to a fragile neck, tipping Rachel into the hollow between her shoulder and chest. Our baby snuggled in. "Helen sees... Helen hears... Just..." A soft yawn, followed by a valiant last struggle against sleep. "Different, Mama. Diff... rent."

I fought back tears I no longer had. Pressed my cheek against hair I knew was soft though I could not feel it. Inhaled the memory of my woman's scent, as sweet in my heart as it had once been in my life. *Did you get that, honey? What she said?*

Denny didn't answer. They'd both fallen asleep.

Are you listening?

During that week's session with Joan, the psychologist surprised us with a suggestion: Denise should consider making the next appointment her last.

"It's time," Joan assured us. "You don't need long-term therapy. You never did. You're not paranoid. Have no phobias. Aren't struggling with an addiction or other harmful habit." She shrugged. "I've been a sounding board and a crying towel while you got your feet back under you again."

Denise grinned, clicked her heels together a la Judy Garland in *The Wizard of Oz*. "Don't forget fashion consultant."

Joan gave the suede boots a once-over. "A possible backup career," she agreed. "Very nice." She cocked her head and studied my wife from bottom to top. "I like the new hair color, too."

Denny beamed. "Always wanted to try red."

"It suits you."

I wasn't sure I agreed. My Denny was a blonde—even if some of it was borrowed from Miss Clairol.

"A lot of things suit you," Joan continued. "The prospect of a new job…"

Denny sighed. "Yeah, about that. I'm not sure about going back to teaching high school."

"Oh?"

"I started looking into maybe getting my master's and working at a college instead."

Joan seemed to approve. "Familiar but different."

"Yes. Or maybe something way outside the box. I've been interviewed by the county about a public education program they're starting. They want someone to go around to community groups to talk about the new emergency system: explain about the sirens, how they work, what the signals mean."

"Sounds interesting."

Denny nodded, but I could tell she wasn't sure about the prospect—or any other career choice. She was falling back on her usual MO: making lists and checking them twice. "It's a temp position—two years only," she added. "But then I could bid into any other position offered by the county." She wiggled her brows hopefully in Joan's direction. "Would be nice to have someone to talk to about it." She lifted her hands, let them fall back together in her lap, fingers laced. "You know. While I work things out."

"I'm sure it would," Joan replied, her expression unreadable. "But at eighty-five dollars an hour, I suggest there are other individuals in your life who'd be more cost effective." She leaned forward, eyes intent. "You've got this, Denise."

Joan sat back, uncrossed her legs. "Time to dive into the deep end." Then she placed her hands on the arms of her chair, as though preparing to rise. I'd seen this pose many times—as had my wife. It was the prelaunch position for "time's up." "I was going to suggest that *today* be our last session," she said. "But I decided you should make the call yourself. This week or next, Denise. Pick one."

My wife sucked her bottom lip under her teeth. "One more week."

Joan smiled, but it was small and secretive. "If you say so."

Once again, Denise was tucking our sleeping daughter under her tulip comforter, turning off the TV, and crawling into bed. It had been one of the better episodes of *Quincy,* and I was still pumped.

Good thing. My wife's eyes glittered in the moonlight slanting through the window. She was on her side of our mattress, wide awake, staring at my empty pillow.

"What do you think, Jim? Am I ready?"

It will be tough. Maybe. But…

"Joan wouldn't turn me away if I felt I needed to go back."

Once in a while. Possibly.

"If I needed to vent."

But then again…

"There *is* Daria. And my mom."

And mine. You know she'd be there for you. She can handle a few tears. She told you so.

"Remember when your mom said I could call anytime?"

She meant it. You know she did. Strong woman, my mom.

"Am I strong like that?"

Would I have married you if you weren't?

Denise grew quiet, listened to the house creak and settle around her. Heard the distant thrum of the furnace kicking on. "Maybe Joan is wrong and I am crazy." She rolled to her back, stared at the ceiling. "I mean, I'm talking to you as if you were here and could answer me."

Oh, honey. I am and I can. You've just got to listen.

"I think I'll go back at least one more time," she decided. But when she swallowed, I heard the soft click in the back of her throat. She wanted more from herself.

Denny flicked a finger under one eye, then pulled her hand away, surprised to find that what she'd thought was an itch was a tear. "Shit, what is Joan thinking. I can't even dream about you yet. I'm doing just dandy, thanks."

She turned her back on me and let her eyes flutter closed. "There are too many pieces to my life right now," she mumbled into the darkness. "Not ready to fit them together without help." Exhaustion was beginning to pull her under. "Without *you*," she whispered.

But you don't have to! Damn it! What would it take to convince her? I hurtled over her outstretched form, landed on the floor on the other side of the bed. My back was to the door, the hall a narrow shadow behind me. I crouched near her head, formed words that felt rusty in my mouth. "You do not have to pick up the pieces alone. When things get too tough—when you think you can't manage by yourself, I will be there."

She'd been nearly asleep, but her eyes popped open as though I'd shouted at her. Which—hey—maybe I had.

"What?" she whispered.

You heard me, I insisted. *I know you did.*

She didn't move. Her eyes continued to stare through me.

When her lids began to lower once more and her breaths began to lengthen, I gave it my best shot.

"Denny Lou. Listen to me."

She stirred, started to roll away.

"The heat duct does not go down to the basement."

Whoa, that grabbed her.

"What?"

Yeah, got you wondering now, don't I?

"The heat duct?"

Does not go down to the basement. It doesn't drop straight into the furnace.

She halted her turn, and shifted her gaze to the wall where the bookshelf stood. The toothlike slats of a heat register were dark against the plaster.

"What a weird thing to say," she murmured.

I took heart. She'd said *say,* not *think.*

Not weird, I insisted. *A mechanical fact...*

"...the heat duct does not go down to the basement."

Right. I stood, excitement jittering through me like forks of lightning. *Look. Just look.*

Denny sat up, peered at me. I should have been pulsing like the Toledo lighthouse, but she saw nothing, was straining to see through the shadows. Giving up, she switched her attention to the heat register imbedded in the bedroom wall.

"The same register that opens into Rachel's room?" she asked me. "That heat duct?"

Yes!

She swung her feet out of our bed, leaped up, and damn near ran through me to get to the door of our daughter's room. She peered around the frame, careful not to wake Sleeping Beauty.

A second heat register aligned directly with the first, but on the opposite side of the wall: a second identical rectangle of ornate bars.

To the right of the grillwork sat a red, pink and green dollhouse.

"The heat duct does *not* drop..."

...straight into the furnace.

My wife would have snapped her pretty neck scrambling down the stairs in the dark if I hadn't raced alongside her, warning her to be careful. In the kitchen, she slammed into the butcher block table. Rubbing a hip that would be bruised by morning, she yanked open the junk drawer.

Grab a flashlight, I advised as she dug around for a screwdriver. *No, not a Phillip's. A straight head.*

Back upstairs, hunkered down in the dark, hands trembling, Denny missed the slots time after time. Finally she two-handed the screwdriver into place and began to turn each tiny fastener counterclockwise.

Before bearing down to make the final twists, she stopped, took three deep breaths, and forced her heart rate to slow. Then, cautiously, she removed one screw after the other and pocketed it in her pajamas.

Come on, already! Where the hell was the fast-forward switch on this woman?

If Denny heard me, she was being contrary. She slumped back on her heels. Placed the screwdriver on the floor near her thigh. Plucked the flashlight out of her lap with her left hand. Let the beam wash over the wall.

And waited.

This was entirely too zen for my taste. *Hey. Maharishi. Ain't gonna levitate off by itself, you know.*

Denise lifted the light higher, angled it from side to side. The beam flashed into the opening, picking out the shadows of our bedroom beyond. "Okay," she whispered. "Okay." She hooked a finger through the slats. "Open Sesame."

The cover held for a moment, years of corrosion locking it in place. Denise leaned back, tugged, and the grill popped off its frame with a soft crack. She placed it on the floor next to the screwdriver, where it clattered lightly before silence swallowed us again.

Denny snaked her arm through the opening, her head tipped to the side, as though she were listening to her hand slide away from her, her lips pursed in concentration. When she'd gotten all but her elbow inside, her knuckles hit aluminum with a dull clank.

"Oh."

Yeah. Big oh. Capital O.

I knew what was under my wife's fingers before she did: a small round shape, roughly the size of a beer cap, made of plastic.

And sporting a tiny handle.

Denny pinched the object between her thumb and index finger, drew it slowly into the flashlight's beam.

A Berry Happy red skillet, perfectly sized to fit the hand of Strawberry Shortcake.

"Oh god, oh god, oh god," she chanted softly.

Ten minutes later, with the flashlight now clamped under her arm, Denny knelt before the dollhouse, playing and laughing through her tears. Placing cushions. Laying down rugs. Hanging towels. Centering a red cookie jar—plus lid—on a little drop-leaf table.

Every piece was back where it belonged; the only item missing: the green bowl which had rolled farther into the horizontal section of ductwork than my Denny could reach.

It sits there still.

The next morning, Denise called Joan's office and canceled our appointment.

Chapter Twenty: Untrodden Ground

Spring inched its way into Toledo, and my family moved forward with it. Denny was called in to a second interview with the county. Jimmy decided to walk on two legs instead of four. And Rachel led a feminist uprising at her nursery school.

Oh, yeah. My tiny rebel—standing up against The Man. Those poor teachers never stood a chance.

The topic that sunny morning had been gender neutrality—tailored to the four-year-old mentality, of course, and fully toddler-appropriate. A smiling instructor had gathered her class around her, squirmy butts plunked yoga fashion on a bright red rug.

"How are little girls different from little boys?" she asked.

Sticky fingers waved in the air. "Girls have long hair." "Girls play with dolls." "Girls like unicorns and pink."

"Hmmm," the teacher mused. "Does anyone have a dad or uncle with long hair?" More waving hands, punctuated by a few giggles. "Well then," she said. "That can't be what makes girls different. And what about dolls? Do any of you have a G.I. Joe?"

Rachel didn't bother to compete with her classmates, simply shouted out the obvious: "My brother has a My Buddy. And my bestest friend's brother has a Cabbage Patch Kid."

"Very good, Rachel. So dolls don't make us different, do they?"

A pigtailed moppet in the front row pointed to the boy on her left. "Coby's wearin' pink!"

"Am not."

"Am, too!"

The teacher hid her smile, and clapped her hands for silence. "I love that color, don't you, Coby? My husband has a shirt just like it."

The group of four-year-olds fidgeted, and studied each other for telltale clues as to what made the ones with scabby knees and He-Man T-shirts different from the ones with scabby knees and She-Ra T-shirts—or the fact that none of them would be caught dead in a Skeletor T-shirt.

"Can we say there really are no differences?" the teacher coaxed. "That we all can like the same things and *do* the same things, if we want?"

Oh, man, I could see this coming a mile away without binoculars. My daughter unwound her legs from their pretzel position, stretched them out in front of her, and waggled her blue Keds back and forth. Shook her head. "Nope," she called out. "You're wrong."

Of course she is, sweetheart. I can hardly wait to hear you set her straight.

"Boys can like the same stuff. An' do the same stuff. But they're not the same." She glanced once to her left and then to her right. "Boys have got a pee-pee. I got a v'gina."

As the granddaughter of an OBGYN, my kiddo was an undisputed expert on the subject. I thanked the Big Guy she hadn't yet asked how babies got inside a mommy's tummy in the first place, or she might have been suspended from The Little Tikes Sunshine Academy indefinitely.

Rachel's nursery school teacher nearly swallowed her tongue trying not to laugh—though I don't think she was laughing once snack time rolled around. By then she had her hands full dealing with the faction of Girls Without Brothers who were demanding a session of Show and Tell.

In comparison, Jimmy's forward momentum in life was literal.

Around the same time my daughter was pointing out the anatomical distinctions between males and females, I was sitting on the counter in our kitchen absorbing the sights and sounds of a woman stirring up a batch of chocolate chip cookies. My son stood near my dangling feet, one hand propped on the cupboard, maintaining a balance he'd mastered long ago—but doubted.

I think I mentioned Jimmy had already taken his first steps, somewhere around fifteen months of age. Can't be sure, because Denny didn't note it in his baby book. Grief had taken all the joy out of such events. That's not to say she didn't cry out in delight the first time our son wobbled from one foot to the next. She did. But then she dropped to her knees, her cries turning into strangled whimpers that clawed their way out of her heart.

Our son was walking, and I wasn't there to see it. Or so she thought.

What Jimmy thought, I didn't have to guess. His mama was upset. Walking equaled tears equaled a sick feeling in the belly. Nope, he was thinking. Not gonna do *that* again.

By age two when Jimmy still refused to take another step, my brothers launched the Standing Man project. One of them, usually Mike, would pick my son up from wherever he sat and plunk him on his feet in the middle of my parents' family room. The others would encircle him, arms outstretched, voices cajoling: "Come to me, Jimmy. Come to Uncle Billtomboojoe. Come on, buddy. You can do it."

They were wasting their time. I knew this kid. All the silly faces and funny noises in the world were not going to budge him. *See?* I would say, pointing from my place in the circle. *The boy is Gibraltar.* Steady as a rock and just as immovable. Now and then, if Jimmy thought the game was over, he would drop to his knees, but one of my brothers always pulled him back up.

Instead of getting angry, he'd just blink and smile. *Oh, we're still playing? Okay.* Compared to the humiliation of the Meyer 500, *not* moving was a contest Jimmy knew he could win. Spectators could walk away, come back an hour later, and find him still there, his feet digging roots into the carpet.

"Do you think he's broken?" Bill asked.

Stuff a sock in it. There's nothing wrong with the kid. He just doesn't want to walk.

"Maybe he needs a bribe." Joe searched his pockets and found a mini Milky Way, slightly mushed from body heat.

Not up to your standards, Jimmy. Make them show you the money.

Boo did Joe one better, pulling a snack bag of Fritos from behind his back.

Oh, man. That's cheating.

My son must have decided that, as signing bonuses go, corn chips didn't cut it. His feet never shuffled enough to raise static.

Then Bill snapped his fingers, leaped up, and headed for the kitchen.

Careful, kid. This uncle plays dirty.

My brother returned, squatted, and held out a blue can with white letters and a silver crescent. Waggled it. "Hey, kid, this Bud's for you."

Nothing doin'. Jimmy would crawl across the stage at his college commencements before he'd give in to such paltry temptations.

Here's the thing. I *got* what was going on inside my son. I, too, had been a cautious child. Jimmy wasn't just afraid he'd upset his mom. He was afraid of failing. Like the old block he'd been chipped from, my boy would walk when he was sure he could do it *well.*

Right, kiddo? I asked from my perch on our kitchen counter above him.

He gazed up. Then looked away, distracted by the sound of his mother scraping the mixing bowl. In a contest with Dad, cookie dough would win every time.

Walking is cool, I assured him, as we watched her work. *Ask your mom. Chicks dig guys they can look up to.*

He frowned, unpersuaded.

Stay down there? No hot babe will notice you. You'll be just another sand-crawling Jawa. Besides. Look what you're doing to your shoes.

Jimmy scuffed his feet, looked down at his Stride Rites and the holes worn through the leather toes.

Distressed is not hip. At least not yet.

He stuck out his lower lip.

Hey, don't believe me. But I'm telling you, creeping around on your hands and knees is so yesterday. Nobody who's anybody is doing it anymore.

Denise slid a cookie sheet into the oven, tossing a quick look over her shoulder to make sure Jimmy wasn't close enough to burn a finger. "What's that serious face, little guy? Missing your sister?"

Not in this lifetime, Mom.

"We'll go get her from school as soon as this batch comes out. Okay?"

Jeez. Do we have to?

I swear my boy smirked.

It gave me an idea. *What do you say we surprise little Miss Danica when she gets back, eh?*

The smirk grew into a grin and I pressed my advantage. *Make your move, Junior. Time to explore strange new worlds. Seek out new life and new civilizations.* Channeling my inner Shatner, I shifted into warp drive. *Time to boldly go where —well—practically everybody* but you *has gone before.*

The echo faded as Jimmy looked from his mom's curious frown to my hopeful smile.

Come on, kid. Up and at 'em!

With an expression somewhere between I Don't Know About This and If You Say So, my son moved his hand away from the cupboard... tested his balance with a brief windmill... and stepped away.

Denny gasped, throwing her arms wide to welcome him.

Kiddo ignored her and took a couple of hesitant steps toward the dining room door.

Let him go, hon. He's gotta do it himself.

Our boy disappeared around the corner while the two of us held our breath waiting for his return. Or for the crash of a sturdy little body colliding with a piece of low-lying furniture.

A minute went by. Then Jimmy reappeared, this time in the doorway between the living room and kitchen. He'd completed lap one of the Meyer 500 all by himself. Giving neither his mother nor I a glance, he picked up speed, rounding the stove and exiting the kitchen once again through the dining room door.

"Oh, my god, Jim. I hope you can see this."

See it? I made it happen, toots.

It took our son less time to finish lap two. He was trotting as he banked the curve in lap three.

Then nothing. No proud handsome baby face. No patter of excited feet.

Denny twined a hank of red hair around her finger. The color was growing on me.

Liar, liar, you know the rest.

I chewed a metaphysical thumbnail while we waited. *Give him another minute,* I advised. *He'll be back.*

But I was wrong. The oven timer buzzed, announcing that the door to Tollhouse was open and taste tests would soon commence. Still no Jimmy.

Denny retrieved the cookies, slapping the tray down on the stovetop. "Okay. No more waiting. What is he doing out there?"

I jumped off the counter and followed her as she retraced our son's path. Not in the dining room. Not in the living room. For a moment I fretted that maybe he'd opened the front door and was boldly making his way to those strange new worlds. But as we approached the base of the stairway, we spied him.

James Patrick Meyer, Jr., was walking down the steps.

Without a hitch. And not two-stepping it either. Not one foot on a riser, to be joined there by the other. Not my boy, nuh-uh. He was high stepping it like he'd been walking upright on stairs for weeks. Months!

Note that I said he was coming *down* the stairs when we found him. Which implies he'd walked *up* them the same way.

My boy had made his way around the Meyer 500 circuit three times.

Had gone up and down the stairs—at least once.

No hands.

On two feet.

Like I said. That spring, my family was moving ahead. And the youngest of them was going to be doing it much faster from now on.

Poor Denny.

I played with the kiddos under the dining room table while Denny Lou sat above us, working out a career path for her future. Rachel had dragged the three unoccupied chairs to one corner, and I had helped Jimmy shove them together so we could drape them with crib quilts. The small blankets were no longer needed for sleeping, my son having graduated to a twin-size car bed with spiffy racing stripes.

Grandma Meyer had sewn the quilts by hand before our children were born: a pretty Ohio Star pattern for baby Rachel; a jazzy Card Tricks design for baby Jim. I showed my twosome how to upcycle them into walls for a fort. Rachel was a quick study, tucking the quilts up and over the slats of the seat backs. Jimmy helped by tugging the hems down so they touched the floor. It took a couple of tries before they figured out the correct amount of tension to keep the walls vertical, instead of falling in a heap to the carpet.

Some people (who will remain nameless but whose initials are DLM) would have called it a tent. Some people would be wrong. I can see how they could make that mistake, however. Tents are mostly blankets and one support. A fort is more structure, less blanket. It's a common misconception.

Childhood engineering is a very complex science.

We'd just settled in for Rachel's rendition of *Goodnight Moon* where the point of the story is to find the mouse, when a crumpled ball of yellow legal paper dropped from above. Denny's foot was doing a jitterbug, accompanied by sighs and grumbles.

Hold the fort, I ordered my troops. *Major Dad has to go on a recon mission.* I figured I had fifteen minutes before one of them staged a coup and tried to exile the loser to Malta.

Whatcha doin'? I asked my wife.

Denise answered by ripping a second sheet of paper from the pad, strangling it between her hands, and tossing it over her shoulder. Denise? Making a mess? Answer enough.

Still no decision?

She gathered the pages spread before her, shuffled them, then repositioned them around the blank pad. One page was titled WHITMER. Another, MASTERS. A third read COUNTY. She propped an elbow on the table, her palm cradling her chin and cheek. A number-two pencil waited next to the legal pad. She picked it up with her free hand, twiddling it like a miniature baton.

After a moment's study, she steered her head from right to left, her palm acting as a rudder as she examined each list in turn. With a flick of the pencil, she nudged WHITMER out of first place, used the eraser end to select COUNTY and slide it into the preeminent position.

There was more studying. More steering. More twiddling. Then a faint grumble. "Temporary. Not a good thing."

Different though. Not teaching for a change.

"Still teaching—but without all the grading and testing."

I leaned over her shoulder. *That falls under the Pros column, I see.*

Denny had sailed through her second interview with the county on wings. The panel composed of all men had been impressed by her demeanor and her background in education. She would have no problem organizing meetings with local Kiwanis clubs, VFWs, AmVets—any organization willing to gather its membership and sit through an explanation of the new emergency warning system. It would be up to my wife to educate the masses about the sirens, what to listen for, what to do if they went off— stuff you guys take for granted today, but was a brave new world in the mid 1980s.

Denny expected to get a call offering her the job. The head of the hiring committee had admitted she was the only female applicant and they had an Affirmative Action quota to fill. He'd beamed with relief. Not only was Denise a woman, she was an over-qualified woman to boot.

So what's the problem?

"Whitmer is the best option for the short term. I can go back as a sub next week. My old boss is still head of the English Department. The first full-time opening is mine for the asking."

The pencil morphed from baton to drumstick. Denny tapped it firmly against the sheet farthest to her right. Shave and a haircut, but no two bits for MASTERS. "Working for the university is the best choice for the long term. Better pay. Great benefits. But I'd have to complete my degree. Two years at least, assuming the kids give me time to write a thesis." The pencil tapped again, this time slower. "But it would be worth the effort."

Still, my wife made no move to shift MASTERS out of last place.

It's because it's teaching again, isn't it?

She dropped the pencil, added her other elbow to the table, and covered her face with both hands. "It feels like going backwards. I want to move forward, move *to* something…"

More exciting. More challenging.

"Something *new.* Ground I've never covered before." She lifted her face, scrubbed her eyes with the heels of her hands. Let her arms fall to the tabletop. "Something that won't constantly remind me of the past."

So the county, then?

She raised one hand and slapped it on her first choice. It was *not* a pat of approval.

"They asked me what kind of painting I did," she muttered.

The hiring committee?

"Saw on my resume I painted in my spare time."

Yeah. So?

Denny barked a laugh. "I told them acrylics mostly. Usually landscapes—mountains, forests, farms." The laugh caught her again. "They looked at me with these blank expressions."

I don't get it.

" 'You mean barns?' one guy asked. 'You paint barns?' "

" 'Paintings *of* barns,' I told him. 'You know. Not the barns themselves.' " She crossed her wrists on the table in front of the legal pad, rested her chin on the X. "I thought I was being funny."

No way. They thought you painted buildings?

I moved next to my wife, put my back to the table, and pushed myself up so I could watch her face.

They wanted *someone who could paint buildings, didn't they?*

Denny blew a steam of air across the legal pad, her breath ruffling the pages. "Maintenance. They don't just want someone to do public speaking. This is the *government* we're talking about. Employees need to multitask."

You'd be painting equipment when not speaking to the Lions Club, huh?

Jimmy's dark head popped up alongside his mother's knee. Denny stroked his cowlick back where it belonged. "Mommy shouldn't be so elitist, should she, kiddo?"

"What's *leetish?*" our daughter called from the depths of our fort.

"It means stuck-up, babe. Mommy shouldn't be so picky about what she does for a living. She shouldn't think she's too good to brush on a little paint. I bet *you'd* love painting metal boxes, wouldn't you?"

Rachel didn't deign to answer. I concurred. I couldn't see my wife switching from a pinstriped suit to speak at a retirees breakfast into plaid flannel to slap Rustoleum on a meter box.

So what are you going to tell them when they call?

"So what do I tell them when they call?"

I asked first.

Jimmy squatted and scooped up one of his mother's discards, the paper ball begging to be tossed. Probably at his sister. He disappeared under the table.

I slid off my perch, and bent to study the crumpled wad he'd left behind.

What's this?

Denny didn't answer, was mulling over what steps she ought to take next.

I could make out only a handful of words: *On a paneled wall far beneath...* The rest was too wrinkled to read.

My wife's pencil scritched and scratched as she added new pros and cons to her lists. I swung around to see what they were.

Denise was doodling on the legal pad, her chin still propped on one wrist, lying flat on the tabletop. She paused to study what she'd written, peeking at the words through her lashes. Then she flicked a look to her left. Another to her right. Like she was afraid someone would catch her doing... hell if I knew what.

She looked...

Guilty?

Denny thought a moment, then scribbled some more.

On a paneled wall far beneath the rolling English countryside hangs a tintype of five men. One sits ramrod straight in a low-backed chair, his hands clasped in his lap. He is flanked by the remaining four, their heads held high in the noose of nineteenth century collars.

She raised the pencil, left the tip poised over the period that followed "collars."

"It's a crazy notion," she said. "I need steady income. The insurance money won't last forever."

A novel? Is that what this is?

She'd never told me.

I mean, I knew she could write. She'd promised she could get me through composition if I went back for my bachelor's. She'd worked on the school newspaper in high school, and I seemed to recall one of her stories rating a feature and photo spread in the local paper. She'd written articles for trade publications once or twice. Had won a couple of writing awards.

"Freelance is so unreliable."

My wife might feel guilty about the idea. But me? I felt... interested. Okay, more than interested. Proud.

You want a challenge? Something that moves you forward, *not back?* I grinned and scratched my head. I could see her doing this. Writing stories. Books even. Hell, it sounded like fun to me and I didn't know a dangling participle from a fly strip.

Plus... I really *could* see her doing this. If I let myself dissolve into bits of electrons and neutrons, allowed myself to reach out in all directions in the river...? Well, there were a lot of maps out there with my wife's name penciled in the margins.

Professor. Politician. County supervisor.

There was an office in an ad agency with her purse tucked in a desk drawer. There was a cubicle at a newspaper with stacks of project folders tagged with sticky notes initialed to her. There was a classroom of adults at a continuing education college waiting for her arrival. Camera men were unloading equipment from trucks, asking where she wanted them to set up. A composer sat musing as he jotted down notes to suit her lyrics.

I saw one mayor hugging her, kissing her cheek; listened as another spoke her words in his State of the City Address.

Talk about roads less traveled! My Denny had so many ways to move forward I might be forced to use a TripTik after all.

But what would make her happy? I didn't think any of her current lists were going to put a smile on her face for long. *Hold off,* I advised her. *Put this all away until Monday. Sleep on it. The county isn't going to call on a weekend.*

Denise lifted her head from her arm, placed the pencil diagonally across those few timid sentences: a Do Not Enter symbol denying the dream. "I can't think about this anymore," she said to herself, then raised her voice so it could be heard in a fort far off in the wilderness. "Who wants to go out for ice cream?"

"Me, me, me!"

"Strawberry!"

I would let them go without me. I had work to do. I'd seen something else in the river: an advertisement that needed to be called in to the Classifieds department before end of day.

No, no, I promised the Big Guy. *Not a push. Just a nudge. An arrow pointing out a more interesting road. That's all.*

Besides, the copy was already written. I just had to make sure it made it into print before the county called.

> WANTED: WRITER/EDITOR
> Local monthly magazine seeks qualified professional to write human interest features and investigative articles; proofread and edit submissions; develop headlines and photo captions; and assist in all other aspects of production. Educators with a background in Communications or English welcome. Apply with resume and cover letter to…

My wife wanted new ground? New challenges? A new direction?

It didn't get more untrodden than this.

Chapter Twenty-One: If She Builds It

What is it about women and Kevin Costner? I don't get the attraction myself, but there was a definite gleam in my wife's eye the first time she noticed him in *Silverado*. That was the same year Denise began working at *Toledo Metropolitan Magazine*—and the same year she began taking baby steps into the dating scene. No problem. I'm secure in my manhood. But if she wanted to stay home and crush on a screen star instead of going out for drinks with the latest Denny groupie, I was more than happy to have her curl up in her flannel PJs to watch *The Untouchables* on pay-per-view.

For the third time.

Didn't bother me an inch. She could drool over Kevin; I would focus my attention on Sean. Sans any drooling, of course.

But when *my* Denny began quoting the Crash Davis monologue from *Bull Durham*? Swooning over those "long, slow, deep, soft, wet kisses that last three days"? When she went so far as to buy a VCR so she could *own* the stupid thing? Well, that curled my hair—and it already leans toward the Brillo side of coiffure as it is.

I mean, seriously? How could I fall behind on the score card of love to a guy who technically didn't exist?

Well, okay, neither did I. But still.

Anyway. Denise had a thing for Kevin Costner. Remember that. It's going to be important later.

Speaking of.

When last we saw *my* wife (italics intentional, by the way), she was mulling over the pros and cons of various job options—none of which were right for her. Not in my opinion. So with a nudge here and a poke there, I'd opened her up to a new possibility: working as a writer and editor for a local magazine.

You should know up front, the Want Ad Denny saw that Monday had materialized against all odds. There was only one major newspaper in Toledo at the time, and few specialty publications. Even if you'd expanded your search for a writing position into outlying areas, ten times out of ten, you'd have found zip, zilch, nada. Years later, an executive placement service would locate only one similar opening in the entire state—working in the marketing department of a Columbus hospital three hours away.

Like I said. Against the odds.

Toledo Metropolitan Magazine was a new publication in 1985, funded and launched by a feisty thirtysomething woman named Morgan Lawrence. Name ring any bells? What if I tell you Morgan Lawrence was married to a doctor? A neurosurgeon? One of the best in the region, and a prominent physician at St. Vincent Medical Center?

Uh-huh. Morgan Lawrence was the wife of Dr. Ned Lawrence, the man who'd wished he could save my life.

Neither she nor Denise recognized the connection at the time. Editor-in-Chief Lawrence was more focused on finding an eagle-eyed proofreader who could lend a hand writing an occasional article. As a former English teacher, Denise was a perfect fit. And when Morgan asked how my wife felt about doing interviews or a little investigative reporting? Denise mentioned a state supreme court ruling that was slated to be released that year, and wouldn't it make an intriguing story? That hit Morgan's sweet spot. A lawyer as well as a publisher, she too had been eager to cover the outcome of that case.

The job had been Denise's before she'd walked out the door.

She hadn't know that at the time, however—and wouldn't for five more days.

They call it a "leap" of faith for a reason. It's like diving off the high board in the dark over a swimming pool that may or may not contain water. Which might, in fact, be filled with gravel and broken glass. Did my wife have the courage to execute a swan dive?

I paced circles around Denny the morning after her interview for the Writer/Editor position. When the phone rang, I could have jumped out of my skin. If I'd had any.

I pressed my ear to the back of the receiver.

If Denise Meyer was agreeable, the department of community education for the Emergency Early Warning System of Lucas County would be happy to welcome her aboard. Would she be willing to visit the administrative offices on Wednesday to fill out the paperwork?

I ducked out of the way as Denny tangled the phone cord around her hand and cast a glance at *The Blade* Want Ads, still open on the kitchen table..

Don't do it. Don't do it. Please, honey. Lawrence will call. I swear. At least stall them.

She turned her back on the newspaper. "I'm afraid this week won't work for me," she demurred. "Could we make it next Wednesday?"

You couldn't miss the disapproval in the man's pause.

"We really need to move forward in a timely manner, Missus Meyer. Thursday would be the latest we could wait to finalize your employment."

Denny's shoulders slumped. She bobbed her head, short bird-like dips of acceptance. "Of course. I understand."

No. Damn it.

"Shall we say ten? Ten thirty? It shouldn't take long. I'll have your file ready."

"Ten thirty. Right. The suite number again, please?" Denny shuffled away from the wall phone, stretching the cord to its limit as she reached for a note pad and pen on the opposite counter.

How the hell was I going to stop this?

I heard the man's answer echoing from the earpiece. He had a tinny voice, but understandable. I snapped my fingers and it was suddenly wrapped in static.

Coincidence. Honest.

"The admin office is on the…" Crinkle, crackle, pop. "Two-ten, where we met for your first… It's to the…" Garble, muddle, slur. "…of the stairs."

"Got it," Denny answered. Her arm was outstretched the remaining distance to the counter, hand scribbling at an awkward angle. "Second floor." She rotated the mouthpiece away from her face to gain a few extra inches, raised her voice to compensate. "Two-ten. Uh-huh." The pad skittered to the side. Denny skittered sideways with it. "Was that right or left of the stairs?"

I won't say I was making it difficult for her to take down the information. Nope. Won't say it. To borrow a quote from somebody somewhere someplace in the river of time: *I didn't do it. Nobody saw me do it. There's no way you can prove anything.*

"Oh, and Missus Meyer. Please bring your Social Security card. For verification purposes."

Denny's hand froze in mid scribble. "Um."

Remember the break-in? When burglars got away with a paltry haul of our possessions: a small chunk of cash, half of an intercom system, a birthday card filled with love and nothing more?

And, oh yeah, Denise's drivers license and Social Security card.

Oh, now, isn't this an unfortunate dilemma? What will she do, what will she do?

I can be such a bitch.

Denny did not have a Social Security card. She'd replaced the license, but had decided it was a lot of fuss to drag our kids with her to the Soc office and wait in line to fill out a form. Did she really need the piece of pasteboard, as long as she knew the number? She'd lived without it for so long she'd forgotten she didn't have it. Until now.

"Er," she added.

Careful, babe. Your eloquence is showing.

"Uh."

"Missus Meyer? Are you there?"

Come on, hon. You can do it. Point your toes. Lift your arms. Give the board a couple of bounces.

A sneaky breeze slipped through an open window in the breakfast nook, rattling the newspaper.

"Shit, shit, shit," she muttered.

Bounce? Bounce? Bounce?

The tinny voice came again. "I'm sorry?"

"What? Oh. Excuse me... Mister Franklin?"

"Yes, yes. I'm still here. We seem to have a faulty connection."

I laughed and my wife rolled her eyes. Almost as if she'd heard.

Finally, she spoke. "I'm afraid this isn't going to work out after all."

Is that a push off the board?

"I do appreciate the offer, but another... opportunity has come my way."

"Oh?"

Pike position. Touch your toes.

"Thank you for considering me for the job..."

Extend. Reach.

"I'm truly sorry it didn't work out."

I took a deep breath. Held it.

The man cleared his throat. This had never happened to him before. "You do know we cannot offer it again? Missus Meyer? Should you change your mind, I'm afraid it will be too late."

"I do understand. I… You…" My wife paused. Took her own deep breath. "…won't hear from me again." She moved the receiver away from her face, crossed the kitchen and began to place it back into its cradle.

Before I could let out a whoop of success, she hesitated and jammed the phone back to her ear. "Sorry. And goodbye."

Splash.

Postscript (So much easier than saying, "Let's take a detour down this alley, shall we?"): the article Denise wrote about the Ohio Supreme Court's ruling in the case of *Sawicki versus the Village of Ottawa Hills* would be featured on the cover of *Toledo Metropolitan Magazine*. She would write dozens of other articles, as well, on a variety of subjects, over the course of her four-year tenure with Lawrence Publications. Six would grace the front. One would garner a personal thank-you from the woman featured in the interview.

> *In 33 years of reading stories written about me I have never read one that topped yours for truly fine writing. You have a great talent.*
>
> *Love,*
> *Phyllis Diller*

I give that dive a 9.9.

Have you seen some of those surveillance videos on reality crime shows? They aren't actually recordings of the events, but cameras that capture single shots, every few seconds, not the full footage. So, one moment you may see a guy in a ski mask enter a quickie mart, the next you are rocked by the flash of a gun he wasn't holding a moment before. You never see the entire sequence. Just guy, flash, and explosion of Little Debbies from what is left of a snack rack.

I don't want to detail every event my family experienced after their own world was rocked in December 1983. Let's just say they faced ups and downs, moments of sorrow, stretches of success, and clusters of problems, lightened by random gifts of peace and prosperity.

You know. Life.

But I would like to share a few snapshots—especially since they ultimately lead to where you are today: reading the words on this page.

Ready? Frame the first shot and click. There she is—my Denny, packing up our possessions for the big move. She's gone all-in with her parents on the purchase of a bigger house in a newer suburban neighborhood. She's thinking it will be nice to share the fun and frustrations of single motherhood with her mom, that Jimmy will benefit from having a male role model on the premises. A legal pad rests on top of our dresser, outlining what you expect will be my wife's usual lists: things to store, things to toss, things to donate.

The top sheet is wrinkled and half filled.

On a paneled wall far beneath the rolling English countryside…

She's scratched out some of the sentences that follow, has written an additional sentence in red with an arrow pointing to where it ought to go.

Tell me about the photograph, his boy says without speaking.

Don't bother to try and read it all. It's a series of haphazard notes, half-formed thoughts, fragmented ideas, and run-on sentences. A jigsaw puzzle of scraps that might or might not fit together into a whole one day.

The thing to notice is that the legal pad is *there*.

Grab your camera and move ahead. Wow, great new house, but not as happy a home as hoped. Denise's mother sits in the luxurious family room watching old movies, her father in the elegant living room watching a sitcom, the kids in Jimmy's sprawling bedroom, playing tag with a gerbil. Everyone is settled into a pretty but separate space, too set in their ways to blend easily into a whole.

Denny sits hunched over a desk in the formal den, pecking at a Selectric, stopping now and then to slather Wite-Out over something she's decided is unworthy. Rachel runs in, grabs a piece of candy from the dish Grandma insists should be fair game any time of day. My kiddo approves. Her mother does not, but is tired of arguing with the household's second mother about the care and feeding of children. A tiny rectangle of silver paper lands on the floor at Rachel's feet.

"Uh-uh, young lady. Where does that belong?"

Rachel bends and retrieves the discarded candy wrapper, holds it on the palm of her hand, then grins the grin of devils everywhere. "Curses," she intones, Snidely Whiplash without a mustache. "Foil again!"

Denny laughs. Tips her head to the side to consider. Then returns to her tap tap tapping.

Treece was more comfortable with wisecracks. "Gee, you look nice today, Marlie. What happened?"

Capture that image, if you will. Then let's move on.

Denny is surrounded by boxes again. But this time she is unpacking. She and the kids have moved to a smaller house with fewer amenities and two fewer parents. Just in time. She and Mom and Dad have agreed to part ways. Another six months and there would have been harsher words, more permanent wounds, fewer chances to reconcile. For now, there are smiles, strained, but firmly in place. Denny's mother is unwrapping glassware, asking where it ought to go. Her dad is on the floor, head under the sink, grumbling that the house should have come with a garbage disposal in the first place. Jimmy crouches alongside him, fingers twitching, butt bouncing on the back of his heels. "Let me try, Grandpa. Let me."

"He can't do any worse, Len," Esther says.

Denny chuckles. "He does have smaller hands, Dad. Besides, I'd like him to learn—if you don't mind teaching?"

Leonard slides out from under the sink, scrubs his palms on his pants. "Sure. Okay. Give it a shot."

My son scoots inside the cupboard, a wrench already clutched in his hand.

"What you want to do," my father-in-law tells him, "is tighten that flange. See it? Just above…"

"I got it," Jimmy assures him.

"According to the instructions…"

"Don't need 'em," my boy cuts in. "I see what to do. No biggie."

He didn't. He did. And it wasn't.

I beam at him unseen from a shadowed corner. Jimmy is six. A couple more years and he will ask everyone to stop calling him that. He will insist on being Jim. Lucky for him, no one will mistake him for Peter Brady. Hairstyles have changed and the show has been off the air too long. One day friends will compare him to NASCAR driver Jimmie Johnson. Like I said, lucky.

Denny slips her legal pad from under a stack of dishtowels. Grabs a pen from behind her ear. Dashes off a few words:

Her brother smiles at her in the dark. "I can't do the stuff you can. So's I'll just have to get real good at somefin' else."

Frame and click. Time to move on.

Denise has left Lawrence Publications and is hard at work at Mitchel & Company, writing promotional materials for national clients: a poster for a million-dollar Discover Card sweepstakes, a do-it-yourself roofing manual for Owens-Corning, baseball cards for a Mister Turkey promotion.

Another shift. Another snap.

She has her own office now, at Fruchtman Marketing, an ad agency where she is the Creative Director, writing and producing ad campaigns—mostly for the jewelry industry, but some for politicians seeking election. Ah, so that's what that hug from a mayor was all about.

Then a quick edit. My wife has made a jump to *The Blade*—writing advertising to increase the newspaper's circulation. But keep that camera ready. Before you know it, she will make the return jump back to the agency.

All those roads I once saw in the river, pointing to the different directions my wife's career might take? She's skipped and danced along most of them, growing bolder and more competent as she goes.

But where is the legal pad? It's not showing up as often as it once did in our gallery of snapshots. Probably because there are too many photos of a busy single mother trapped in her car, driving her kiddos from baseball practice to skating lessons, from Cub Scout meetings to theater rehearsals.

It's not all wasted effort, however. There's a fabulous shot of Rachel, grade school age, stepping into the spotlight for a surprise rendition of *Locomotion* during a school recital. And another from a community theater production of *The Wizard of Oz*. My budding Shirley Temple has nailed roles as a Munchkin in the Butterfly League and a Flying Monkey. Denny does go home that evening and dig up the battered old legal pad, pens a few new sentences.

"When I was a boy, my father took me with him to New York. He saw a lot of people about business. I saw a lot of Broadway plays."

When she finishes, she tucks the pad back in a file drawer. It will be a long time before it sees daylight again.

Can you see her there? Have I given you a clear enough picture?

Denny is poised on a ladder, but no longer climbing. She is walking through life with all these *people* living and breathing inside her... all these stories demanding to be told. But she's too busy—or says she's too busy—to finish the job.

What was it going to take to nudge her off the high board again?

That unfinished manuscript was driving me bonkers. I mean, I'm no reader, as you may recall, but the story had me hooked. It would do the same to our daughter one day. I could see Rachel—a faint outline in the distance— waiting to play her part in getting my wife's first novel from head to paper. But if Rach had to stand out there in the far-off future for too long, that stack of typewritten pages could easily end up in a trash barrel during Denny's next Spring purge.

I figured we had one chance. The more time and paper my wife had invested in the book, the less inclined she would be to throw it all away. At the moment, she had less than fifty pages. Not enough to survive one of my wife's cleaning frenzies.

What, you are wondering, could Dead Me do to get the novelist back to the typewriter? Relax. I had an idea. It began with K and ended with Costner.

The movie *Field of Dreams* was released in 1989, and I could have made millions of dollars betting my wife would not only watch it, but own it. How will a movie about baseball help? you ask. Because *Field of Dreams* is not about pitchers, batters or taking me out to the ballgame. It's about second chances and pursuing dreams. As a message to someone with a novel gathering dust in a file drawer, I couldn't have written it better myself.

Truly couldn't. Ask my ninth grade composition teacher.

If you don't know the story, bear with my faltering attempt to summarize.

The movie's hero Ray (who looks remarkably like Kevin Costner) is a struggling Iowa farmer who begins to hear nocturnal whispers from his cornfield. That ought to be enough to make any man wonder if his gumball machine is short a few chews, but not Ray. The voice (which sounds remarkably like Ed Harris but is listed in the credits as Himself) repeats to Ray night after night, "If you build it, he will come."

What would you do? Start thumbing through the yellow pages under shrinks, right? Not Ray. He follows directions. (Hey, when Himself speaks, you probably ought to listen.) Ray's father had played professional baseball for a time, so for sentimental reasons Ray mows down some of his corn and builds a ball diamond. Soon after, the ghosts of former baseball greats, led by "Shoeless" Joe Jackson, start filtering out of his field of corn to play ball on his field of dreams.

Before you even think about arguing this could never happen, remember who you are speaking to.

Ghostly apparitions are not the point of the story anyway. *Field of Dreams* bats you over the head with its theme so you can't miss it. There's even this great visual at the end, where night is falling over Ray's baseball diamond, and a winding road leading to it begins to fill with cars, one after the other

—a long line of twin headlight beams shining in the darkness. Ray built it. And against all odds, they came.

What better way to poke my wife than with Kevin Costner and a cursive line of cars that practically wrote it out for her? Finish It, Denny, and They Will Read.

Would it be enough, though? Or would my wife be distracted by dreamy eyes and shaggy hair?

I was wound around her on the sofa the night she cued up *Field of Dreams* on the VCR for a second time. (By the way, pay up. I told you she'd buy it.) We were halfway through the flick when I couldn't hold back any longer. I raised up on one elbow and looked over her shoulder at her rapt expression.

Seriously, babe? I bitched. *What do you see in this guy?*

She sighed. Long and dramatic. Like I wasn't there, for God's sake. Well, okay. But come on. Look at me? I slid one leg over her hip, tried to tug her onto her back. She rolled over obligingly, as though I'd succeeded. I shook my own shaggy hair at her, batted my big ol' baby browns. *When did you stop swooning over dark and sultry?*

Denise sighed again. But before I could take heart, she twisted her head to the side to look past me to the television.

Oh, for crying out loud. He isn't even on the screen right now.

The ghostly baseball team was vanishing into Ray's cornfield for the night. I stopped complaining long enough to catch the next bit of dialogue. It was among our favorites and important to my plans.

Shoeless Joe is shouting across the diamond: "Hey, Ray! Is this heaven?"

Kevin Costner grins—damn the guy's cuteness factor all to hell. "No," he answers. Then, after a teasing pause, adds the punchline: "It's Iowa."

The line is a showstopper, and I was prepared to capitalize on it. But this was our second viewing of the movie and Denny had yet to notice my message.

The credits were rolling when she began to stir on the sofa, sliding out from under me and the afghan, rubbing at her eyes.

Stop that, woman, Pay attention.

She turned away from the TV for a moment to fluff the throw pillows, and tugged her pajama top down over the waistband where it had wandered.

Damn it, she was going to miss it again. *Please, honey. Don't make me sit through another Kostnerfest.*

By the time she turned back, she'd missed the cast of characters, the director, the producer, and all the bigwigs. The names of lesser production members were beginning to roll up from the bottom of the screen. She moved toward the television, prepared to shut it off for the night.

Wait! Stop! Not yet. Look!

The title slid up to the middle of the screen. She was less than three feet away, hand reaching for the OFF button. One more second. Just one. She couldn't miss it. Could she? Not again.

My wife stopped. Leaned forward, eyes sharpening—then widening.

The credits read: CASTING ASSISTANTS, IOWA.

The title was followed by three names. But it was the one in the middle that grabbed her attention. Nothing fancy. No Burgess W. Farthington, III, or Marylin Ladyfish Crawford. Nothing to make a person gasp or wrap their arms around their waist.

But my wife did both. Because one of the guys who helped pick the cast for heaven? JIM MEYER

It wasn't me, of course. Another Jim Meyer. But that didn't matter. Denny got the point, without Cliffs Notes. The next day, she pulled out her old manuscript and started from the top. She wouldn't finish her novel—not yet —but over the next few years she would crank out an additional two hundred or so pages. She'd taken the plunge off the high board for a second time.

Rachel, babe. You're up.

Chapter Twenty-Two: Hell Hath No Fury

...like a Rachel scorned.

Our daughter is in high school when she digs into her mom's stash of old manuscripts.

What, you don't see her? She's right there. Yeah, the toddler is all grown up... and at a glance, she could have been born to any number of parents.

But not us.

On Planet Tomanski, most family members look like my father-in-law Len. In Meyer World, the majority of inhabitants resemble my dad. It's easy to tell which surname belongs to which face. Rachel? She is what you get when worlds collide. She has her mother's curves, but in a shorter package. She has my nose, but she nearly broke it when she was ten and it now has a cute little bump. I figure she did it on purpose so it would be hers alone. Her hair color is no longer towheaded, but clocks in halfway between midday and midnight (when she isn't having it painted in purples and blues, that is). Again, not quite Denny, not quite me.

But when it comes to curiosity, she's Daddy's girl all the way.

When Rachel discovers the dusty, tattered stack of paper her mother has forgotten even exists, she dives right in. Long hours of reading ensue, the pages turning as fast as her sort-of-Denny eyes can scan. When she comes to the final incomplete sentence—the thing doesn't even have a period, for heaven's sake—she goes in search of her mom.

"Hey!" she demands. "Where's the rest?" (Okay, some things about my princess have not changed.)

Denise is fine-tuning a proposal for a client Fruchtman Marketing is courting, and barely glances up. "Where's what?"

"This." Rachel waves the paper. "*Fellowship of The Guild.*"

"Oh."

Denny continues to chew on the pencil she is holding like a bit between her teeth.

Surrender, Dorothy, I wisecrack. *Your mom's not coming up for air anytime soon.* But I'm hoping Rachel will ignore me. I'm as curious about how the story will end as my daughter. Have been for about ten years.

"Where in the world did you find that?"

"In your file. It is yours, right? You wrote this?"

"Uh-huh," Mom answers, with zero interest. She's intent on highlighting a paragraph in her copy so she can cut and paste it in a more advantageous spot. "Ages ago."

"Okay, so where did you put the rest?"

"Honey, I'm really busy here. Can we talk later. Deadline."

Rachel plunks down in an adjoining chair. "Just tell me where it is. I'll get lost."

"Sorry, kiddo," Denise says. "That's all there is."

Should have asked me. The rest is in her head.

Are either of them listening to me? Nope. A debate follows. To hurry things along, I'll give you the bullet points:
- No time for personal writing.
- The plot is dated.
- No one would care to read it (outside of a loyal daughter with a passion for fantasy and her deceased but ever-hovering father).

"Besides, it's three-hundred typewritten pages," Denny argues. "Who has time to enter all that into a computer?" The rest of her argument is an irritated mumble. "Some of us don't have time to finish the work we get paid for."

I can see the calculation in my daughter's eyes. Nothing. Noth Ing can stop my stubborn dynamo when she puts her mind to it.

Go get her, tiger.

As Denny should have known when she threw down the challenge, our daughter will damn-well *make* time. It takes months. I reiterate: the unfinished manuscript is a whole lot of pages long, and was drafted on a typewriter, with additions and edits penned in red in the margins. But Rachel perseveres. Even the typos and misspellings make it onto the disk.

Denny is throwing together a fast supper of tomato soup and grilled cheese —Jim has a ballgame—when Rachel tosses the blue square of plastic onto the counter.

"Here you go."

Denise glances down, reaches for a plate. "What's that?"

"*Fellowship of The Guild.* On disk. Like you wanted."

Her mom lowers the plate back onto the stack, turns off the skillet. Picks up the blue plastic floppy. "I didn't want this."

"Okay. What *I* wanted. The thing is, you've got it now." Rachel shoulders her mom out of the way, grabs a spatula and slides the sandwich from pan to plate. "So no more excuses." She swivels away toward the dining table. "Jim! Supper is served. Light a fire under it. You're going to be late."

My wife is still standing near the stove, turning the disk round and round; a slow rotation, as if she expects it to start whirring between her fingers. "You entered it? The whole thing?"

Rachel shoots her a look over her shoulder. "I did."

"But…"

"No buts. I want to know what happens to Dina. And Scott. And even Zach—the murdering bastard."

"Language," Denise scolds, but her heart isn't in it.

Rachel grins. Then scowls, instantly serious. "And, Mom? If you die before you finish it, you are going straight to hell."

Fellowship of Psys—the name changed over the course of the rewrite—would be my wife's second completed novel. The first, *jon.com,* would beat it to the finish line by a month. All those characters living in my wife's psyche had been clamoring to get out for years. Only a fool would have bet on one over the other.

D. L. Meyer would write and publish three novels and an illustrated novella between the time our daughter issued her fire-and-brimstone warning and 2018. My wife's lungs were still inflating regularly when she began novel number four, so I figured she was safe from the everlasting torment of hell.

I'm telling you all this because I want you to know what brought you here, to page 287 or thereabouts of story number five.

Yes, this is *my* book, but I couldn't have written it without Denny. Without her belief in me and her willingness to listen—really *listen*—to a persistent voice speaking from the hereafter.

Can we talk about that word a moment? Here. After. Not the other way around, mind you. It would make more sense for it to be afterhere, wouldn't it? A clear description for a place beyond the physical world. A plane of existence (or nonexistence) that comes *after* the life we've left behind.

But that's not how we say it. Not in English, in any case. We—or our subconscious, maybe—says something quite different. We imply there is a *here* after we've given up our bodies. That we continue to exist in some way, shape, or form right *here*, after.

I'm not a theologian. I'll let them and the realists duke it out. I know one thing with certainty. I continued. I did not leave my family behind, only my body. I stayed where I needed to be. I was there for them then. I am here for them now.

It took a lot of poking and prodding and hinting and outright shouting to convince my darling wife of that one essential fact. But I did it. (Hmmm, maybe that's where Rachel gets her stubborn streak.)

In the meantime, my children grew up. Attended college out of state. Rachel at the Savannah College of Art and Design, where she'd intended to become an animal-gator, but succumbed to the lure of photography. Jim at Full Sail University in Orlando, where he degreed in recording arts.

After graduation, Jim had a chance to interview for a job at a studio in Memphis. Denny had contacts in the industry. He gave it a pass, said he wanted to come home—to be close to family and old friends. That's all right. I know his nature. My son was never going to be walking in Memphis, or to New Orleans, or even like an Egyptian, until he was sure he could do it without falling. He's got a lot of roads to choose from yet. I can be patient.

He and Rachel both married. Jim to Katie Barber, a tall bombshell blonde he met in high school. Kate is a nurse now, and Jim builds Jeeps—not to mention, a mean Mac and Cheese. Rach married Mathew Peterson, a sergeant in the Third Infantry Division of the U.S. Army, whom she met while living in the same apartment complex in Savannah.

The first time I saw Rachel and her soldier boy together, I thought, *salt and pepper shakers*. They were the same height, the same build, the same coloring —even the same oval wire-rim glasses. He proposed before he was deployed to Kuwait to take part in Operation Iraqi Freedom. Remember all those news reports about the Bradleys storming across the desert, the fighting at Bagdad Airport, the taking of Saddam Hussein's palace? Matt.

When he returned home, safe and sound, he followed Rachel back to Toledo to plan the wedding. During a get-to-know-him dinner, Daria asked how he first met my precocious daughter. Matt's dry reply: "Well, actually, I *heard* her before I saw her." And while setting up their bridal registry, when Rachel asked which silverware pattern he liked, he answered, "I don't know, honey. Which one *do* I like?" My first impression had been spot-on: Matt and Rachel didn't just look alike, Matt *got* her. They were a matched set.

The newly minted Petersons lived in a house near Denise for a time, but eventually transferred to Minnesota, where Matt's family lives. Jim and Katie bought my in-laws' rancher in Sylvania, Ohio, after first Len and then

Esther died. Denise moved to a condo overlooking Lake Erie. Retired. Bounced grandchildren on her knee, one after the other: Rachel's tribe of Noel, Ariel and Rose; Jim's twosome of Lydia and Jim (who seems to prefer being a *Buddy*). Then Denise, too, pulled her roots out of Ohio and followed Rachel to the Twin Cities. To borrow a line from one of Lydia's favorite movies: the cold never bothered her anyway. Denny's new apartment still overlooks a lake—how could it not in a land that boasts ten-thousand of 'em—but it's smaller, more peaceful. She continues to write, having more time to devote to it than she did when she was juggling a job and kids. A pleasant corner holds her desk and laptop, which is open for business daily.

Denny Lou never remarried. I won't lie and say I'm sorry. But if she'd found someone who made her smile the same way she did for me? Well. I would have stepped back and let her say those vows again. But I *might* have tried to trip the new guy up so he forgot a few crucial words, giving him—okay, *me*—a loophole.

Sue me. I loved the woman. Still do.

Along the way, I continued to tell her where lost things could become found things: like the missing cable equipment receipt, proving she had indeed returned that stupid box and most definitely would *not* pay for it. And a photo of us taken the day Rachel was born—a snapshot Denny had kept in a wallet she lost in a parking lot when she worked at *The Blade*. Rachel would find a duplicate while cleaning out her desk in Minnesota years later. Nobody knew how it got there. Except me.

And Denise.

Yeah, she believes now. Doesn't question how or who or why. That wasn't the case in the beginning, as you may recall. Denny was positive that the ashes in her dad's wood stove were a combination of air currents and wishful thinking, a product of imagination and grief. Finding our Marriage License and Rachel's dollhouse furniture? Well, she knew *me*, right? Knew me so well, she'd been able to think like me, see things through my eyes—figure it out without help from an interfering, ectoplasmic husband. And those dives off the high board: the Want Ad for a perfect job, appearing in the nick of time? The static on the phone and the shoulder block to the man from the county who would have led her down a different path? My name in the credits of a movie? Coincidence. All of it. Coincidence. After coincidence. After coincidence.

Hmm, perhaps Rachel was doomed to be stubborn from the womb—what with all that obstinance built into her DNA.

Logically, you're thinking it must have been my persistence that finally wore my wife down. Forced her to accept I hadn't really gone.

But you're wrong.

It would take nothing less than a missing glove and a traffic jam to seal the deal.

Chapter Twenty-Three: Believing

I sit on the stairs, a few steps up, where I can watch her move around the room. She's been doing this off and on all day: running her hand over a countertop, stroking a finger across the woodgrain of the built-ins, pausing to listen to a floorboard creak. Once, I caught her pressing the curtains to her face to inhale the scent—the same curtains she spent too much money on the year we bought the place.

I get it. I do. It's going to be hard to leave Elm Street. There's time yet; she and her parents only applied for the loan on the new house today. But it's coming.

It's going to be all right, I say. *We won't have to quit cold turkey.* Daria and Michael have asked to rent the place while they put together a downpayment to buy it. The home Denny and I shared is going to stay in the family a while longer. *We'll be back. To visit.* And one day, I know, we'll be able to walk away without regret.

She's moving from lamp to lamp now, toggling switches, dropping the living room into darkness. She disappears from my sight for a moment as she checks the deadbolts in the kitchen and the basement stairwell. Then she drifts past me to the front door to give it a final tug for the night. All is secure.

She climbs the stairs and I stand to go with her. *It's just walls and floors and ceilings,* I tell her. *The stuff that made it a home? We won't leave any of that behind.*

Denise has spent a lot of time outdoors today, too, walking the perimeter, gazing at the windows, the airing deck, the place where an antenna tower once stood, before she had it ripped down. She spent an eternity studying the front eavestrough with its telltale dents.

Do you think you're running out on me?

She slips into Jimmy's room. Bends low over the shiny white car bed, kisses his closed eyelids one at a time.

Ain't gonna happen, babe.

She brushes past me on her way to Rachel—rubs a chill from her arms, as she does.

Our little girl has fallen asleep, half in, half out of her canopy bed, her bare toes dangling over a cluster of Berry Happy playmates and the picnic she put together for them. The front yard of Strawberry's home is littered with pots, skillets, dishes, and towels. Denny spends a few minutes collecting first Rachel and then Rachel's toys, putting each back where it belongs. When she climbs to her feet, she pauses to lay a hand on the heat register. But she doesn't linger. She's convinced herself that finding the missing dollhouse pieces was a lucky happenstance. That she knew me, understood me, so she'd been able to make an intelligent guess.

You're wrong, you know. About a lot of things.

Denise strips off her clothes, piles them on the floor near the door where I used to discard mine. It's her one concession to messiness. They will be the first things she picks up in the morning to deposit down the laundry chute. She drops a nightshirt over her head, lets it fall to her thighs. Pulls back the covers.

But she doesn't sit down. Makes no move to crawl into bed.

What?

I wonder if she's having second thoughts about the new place.

"I was never meant to have this."

She lifts her hands palms up, spreads her arms to indicate the room, the house, the memories. "If we'd never moved here. If I'd never met you."

I step around her, crowding against the bed so I can get close enough to look into her face. *You're being ridiculous. Stop it.*

Doesn't she realize? If she'd never met me, there'd be no Rachel. No Jimmy. No Denise as she is now.

She drops her arms, and her head follows. "Will I forget you?"

She isn't asking. She's decided.

Is this why she's chosen to move? To punish herself?

Short of clubbing me over the head and tying me up, Denny could not have prevented my fall. I could show her, but she refuses to believe in me.

"Oh, Jim. I'm so sorry. I should never have put that goddamn list up. Should have thought about the weather. Should have stopped you. Why didn't I do something—anything—to keep it from happening?"

Now just wait one damn minute.

She turns away from me, perches on the edge of the mattress, wraps her arms around her chest. Stares at the floor. Finally she lies back, legs dangling, half in, half out—much as she found our daughter.

"It was my job. I screwed up."

I shove my hands deep in the pockets of my jeans. I will not cry. I will not cry. I will not cry.

"I just," she begins to say, her lids sliding closed, "wish."

What, babe? What do you wish?

She rolls onto her side, pulls her feet off the floor, curls into a ball crosswise on top of the bed. "I wish I could see you one more time." Her mouth opens in a deep yawn. I hear her jaw crack with the strain. She's so tired, she can barely murmur the rest. "To say goodbye before we move."

Finally!

Goodbye is not in the cards. Not if I can help it. But the other? I've been waiting years for this.

My wife is asleep.

I step into her dream.

"Guess what I got?" I chant in a sing-song as I come through the door.

I wave a four-pack of varicolored replacement lights at my wife as she pulls her mom's best-recipe-ever Mac and Cheese out of the oven. It's topped with bacon and smells like crispy slices of heaven.

Jimmy and Rachel are playing in the living room. Correction: Rachel is playing. Jimmy is wondering what to do with the dishrag she traded for his xylophone.

My wife looks up as she hefts the casserole out of the oven and onto the stovetop. "Seriously?" she says. "*Now* you remember? I thought it was going to snow."

I move into the kitchen, pass the refrigerator list, and give it a grin. "Not yet. Getting colder though." To prove it, I wrap my arms around her from behind.

"Yikes! Stop that!" she complains. But not really.

I release her from my hug, and take her hand, not bothering to remove my jacket. "Come with me."

"What? Where? I'm about to set the table."

I tug her from the kitchen toward the stairs. "Gonna change into my work boots. These tennis shoes will be too slippery."

"But, Jim…" The space between her eyebrows is crinkled in confusion. "You're going to do it now?"

"Yup. Waited too long already."

She thinks I mean the lightbulbs.

I smile at her, and keep tugging. Up the stairs, into our bedroom, inside the closet, to the boot drawer—pulling her ever closer to the truth.

"There's something you need to see."

I drop her hand and slide open the bottom drawer of her repurposed Goodwill dresser. I haul out my battered brown work boots, flip one upside down and present it to her. "Thick crepe soles," I point out. "Ribbed to grip."

Denise leans against the doorjamb, crosses her arms and smiles. "You're nuts."

I give her an uh-uh wag of my finger as I toe off first one tennis shoe and then the other. "Nope. I'm safety conscious." One boot drops to the floor with a heavy thud. I wiggle my foot down inside it. "You know that about me, right?"

She shrugs and nods. "Sure. Always."

"Good." The second boot lands on its side and I have to crouch to stand it upright. I repeat the process of inserting my foot, and wiggling it firmly in place. "So what makes you think I couldn't make a sound decision for myself?" I pull the leather laces taut, fasten them with square knots to ensure nothing can come undone once I'm out on the roof. "What could you have told me to do or not do that I didn't think of first?" I stand and present each foot heel down, toe lifted—left boot, right boot—showing off my handiwork. I put a hand on my hip, and lift the other over my head. Vanna couldn't have done it better.

Denny laughs, a sound of genuine pleasure. It lights me up like—well, like Christmas. I've brought the replacement bulbs with us, and they're on top of the dresser. I tear open the cardboard sleeve, unzip the pockets of my new jacket, and place two bulbs in each. Zip them closed.

I thrust a hip in her direction. "Wanna check? Zipped tight. Nothing to fumble with later."

I step out of the closet, my hand on her shoulder to turn her around and hustle her along. "As for your list? The one you're so sure *forced* me to do something that was unsafe... that maybe I didn't want to do?" I flip a middle finger at the staircase as we pass it, heading for Jimmy's nursery. "I saw your squiggle, and flipped you off."

Her footsteps slow and she starts to pull back, glances down the stairs. "You did?"

"Yup. Saw it. And ignored it." I slide my hand off her shoulder and down to her elbow, spin her toward me. "Even if we'd never put it there in the first place—or you argued with me it wasn't necessary?" I duck my head to catch her gaze and hold it. "I would have done it anyway."

She opens her mouth to object, but I cut her off. Toss my hands in the air. "I mean, come on, woman. It was Jimmy's first Christmas! The first one where Rachel believed in Santa. *Ordered* the fat man what to leave her under the tree."

Denise starts to tear up. I huff at her, twist my mouth up on one side. "Think about it. We built a dollhouse that should have required a team of contractors. You made so many cookies, we could have shared with a homeless shelter and still gained weight on the leftovers. And I hung lights —hundreds of them. I would have bought more, if not for that Berry Happy mansion. It's my thing. You *know* that."

I kiss her nose. "So, no tears. We—you'll note that includes two of us, not just one—wanted to make this Christmas as colorful and fun and crazy and perfect as *we* could."

"But the weather…"

"Nope. No buts. No questions. Just follow." I steer her across Jimmy's room toward the airing deck. "And pay attention."

I unlock the deadbolt, lead her out through the storm door onto the flat tar-paper roof above our breakfast nook. "Close that behind us, will you? And double check that it latches." I stop to make sure she does what I've asked. "I did the same thing before I climbed up. Didn't want one of the kids to push it open after I'd gone out."

"Being careful," she says, more to herself than to me.

"Right." I place a booted foot on a rung of the antenna tower, reach inside the sleeve of my jacket and pull out my gloves. They're black leather with a grey fur lining: stocking stuffers from Denny from our first Christmas. I keep them on my person starting in November and don't put them away until March has gone out like a lamb.

"Watch your step," I warn my wife, as I tug them on. "But note. It's not slippery out here. The deck is dry as a bone. The weather you are so worried about? It's holding."

I haul myself up, hand over hand toward the peak of the roof. "Tower is dry, too." I cut a look down to where she stands, dressed in jeans and a white "boyfriend" shirt, her feet bare as they always are when she's indoors. If this were real life, I'd be sending her back for a coat and shoes. Instead I holler, "What are you waiting for? Come on up. And try not to snag my only dress shirt, will ya?"

She hesitates, then follows, clambering skyward like a monkey. I am standing on the roof peak when she gets to the top. "See. Easy peasy. No slips. No slides. And *you* have never been up here before. Me? I've done this dozens of times. Piece of cake."

I turn away and start walking along the ridge, one foot in front of the other. The shingles are made of asphalt. The black grit crackles with each step, pulling at the crepe of my soles before letting go. It's like walking on heavy-duty sandpaper.

"But, Jim…"

I stop, turn sideways, strike an A-frame stance—confident and sure-footed, as always.

"Why didn't you use the ladder?" She's standing where I left her, the look in her eye telling me she won't move another inch if I can't give her an acceptable answer.

"I know, I know. Shoulda done that, right? Shoulda worn a hard hat and safety harness, too—if we had a safety harness. Shoulda piled mattresses in the driveway. But, babe, only hindsight is twenty-twenty."

She scowls. I ought to look ashamed, but she is so damn cute when she's trying to scold. I crouch down to hide my grin, resting my elbows on my knees. "Did you know you can see the downtown skyline from here?"

"James Patrick Meyer."

Uh-oh. Full name. My grin escapes. "Sorry, honey."

How do I explain to her I hadn't been cocky or indifferent to the danger? It was all… just… too *familiar* to be scary. I'd hunkered down in this same spot countless times, admiring the view, waving at neighbors, calling a *halloo* to my brother-in-law Len.

I give her an answer I think she can handle. "Lot's of reasons. The driveway is cracked and lumpy. There are tree roots poking up everywhere. Hard to get a firm base so the ladder doesn't rock." I gesture with one hand toward the garage behind us. "Hauling out the ladder would take time, and I wanted to get done and back inside before it snowed."

I stand back up, keeping my hand extended. I'm not sure she will come to me, but I'm determined to wait her out.

To my surprise, she takes a few barefooted steps and puts her hand in mine. We begin to walk the peak, me in front, our fingers linked. "Besides. See how easy this is? Nice and flat. Non-slip surface to walk on. If I prop the ladder up nearer to the porch? I have to scale up the roof from the eavestrough. That section is steep." I look back. "Not nice. Not flat. *Not* easy."

We reach the front of our house, overlooking the street, before I speak again. "So, really? I did exactly what I thought I should. There was nothing a worrywart wife could have said to change that."

I release Denny's hand, crouch, and lean back—one hadn't extended behind me like a kickstand. My ass settles on the roof and my legs straddle the peak. "Not enough room for you to sit beside me," I tell her. "Cop a squat back there. So you can see what happens."

She gasps.

"What?"

"I don't want to see."

I consider this for a moment, then pat the shingles behind me. "Okay. You won't have to. Just the important part. Sit."

Denny tucks her lower lip beneath her teeth, and looks out over the edge of the roof to the ribbon of concrete where I was found.

Studies the driveway, so far away.

Lifts her eyes to study me, so close and warm and resurrected.

My Denny Lou. Stubborn and predictable. Even in a dream.

Lifting her chin, she gives a short nod, then inches her butt down until she is straddling the roof at my back. I hear her grunt softly as she tucks herself against my spine, grips my hips with her thighs, and wraps her arms around my waist. Tight.

I give her hands a pat. "My guardian angel?"

She puts her lips next to my ear. "Just a woman who loves you."

"I love you, too." Though I know she won't get the reference for years yet, I can't resist adding a variation on our usual. "To infinity and beyond, babe. To infinity and beyond."

I reach down to unscrew one of the three blown bulbs on the string of lights. "Now, pay attention."

I halt just short of touching it.

"What's wrong?"

I lift my hand so she can see it over my shoulder, waggle my fingers. "Gloves. Leather. Thick lining. Awkward."

"Oh."

I grasp the tip of the index finger between my teeth and pull. The glove slides off, and I take it from my mouth, lay it on the peak between my legs. "See where I put that?"

"Uh-huh."

"Keep an eye on it."

Denny tips to one side so she can crane her neck around my shoulder. I unscrew the first of the burnt lightbulbs, lift it to my mouth, and grip the metal base with my teeth. Then I unzip my pocket. I do it all with my bare hand. The other one, still encased in leather, maintains a hold on the roof edge. I swap the dead bulb for a fresh one. "Huh. Well, look at that. Same color. Coincidence. But it's why you couldn't tell if I'd started the job or not."

I pause a moment. This part is difficult, even for me who knows it's coming. Maybe especially because. Instead of continuing on to the next light, I keep my eyes downcast, my head bowed. "Denny?"

"Hmm."

"I was busy. Never looked up… at the horizon, I mean. I should have. Will you look for me now?"

I feel her breath heat the back of my neck as she straightens and lifts her head.

I ask, though I know what she will say: "What do you see?"

She doesn't answer right away, and I don't blame her. I know what's out there. Coming for me.

"Clouds," she finally says. "Thick. Dark. A band of them—just visible behind the tree tops on the far side of the street."

"Right. It's the storm front. Coming quicker than expected. But still a long ways off. Plenty of time yet, before the sleet begins to fall."

A high-pitched whistle pierces the silence, rattling the bare branches of the maple. A ripple of wind lifts the hair off my forehead. "But I felt the breeze kicking up."

"What?! Stop. Come in! Now!"

"I was going to, babe. Honest. I thought about those other two bulbs. How it would only take me a minute longer." I shrug. "But decided, nah, forget it. One would have to do. Watch." I zip the pocket closed. "See? I was done."

I lean forward, breaking Denny's hold on my waist. Then pull one knee up under me, dig in to the shingles with the toe of my other foot—and wonder what it would take to alter history.

Instead, I say, "Sorry, sweetheart."

I let go of the roof.

Begin to stand.

With a guttural howl, the first blast of wind hits me like a pillow swung by a giant. It comes and goes in an instant. In another time and another existence, it will take me with it.

"Jim!"

"It's okay," I call out. "It can only happen once, hon."

A second howl begins to build. "Hear that?"

With a weather system like the one that rolled into Toledo that day, wind is the first sign of its arrival. The warm seventy-degree temps of the previous system are about to clash with the thirty-degree air sweeping snow into the region.

I teeter, caught off balance, not quite crouching, not quite upright. The glove that had been resting on the rooftop, whips into the air and slaps me in the face, then is snatched away toward the maple overhanging our driveway.

Denise cries out, but when I don't fall, she steadies.

"What did I do, honey?" I holler over the encroaching storm. "Think about it."

Her sigh mixes with the wind whining around us. "You reached for it."

Yeah. Instinct. Damn knee-jerk instinct. I reached for it.

Everything in our dream stops—no sound, no motion—like the freeze-frame in a movie. I pull myself out of the crouch, sit down sideways on the peak, and wrap my arm around my wife's waist. We shiver, but not from cold. "The roof was dry. No ice. The sleet wouldn't start to fall until after you found me."

She hides her tears in the fold of jacket between shoulder and neck.

"The wind hit me during the one moment I wasn't holding on. During the one freaking second I didn't have my feet planted. There's no way I or you or *anyone* could have expected that."

She wipes her eyes on the soft grey fabric. Lifts her face. "But the dents."

"I was twisted sideways when I fell, made a grab for the eavestrough. Got a decent hold, too, just as I was swinging out into space. But the hand with the glove?" I wiggle it again to remind her. "No grip." I gesture with my chin at the ground below. "Lost my hold, spun around one handed. Shot out feet first."

I turn back to gaze at her face. Her eyes are wide and gray in the gathered gloom. So sad, but dry. "You wondered why my knees were bent? Why I looked like I was about to sit up?"

She nods, and lifts a hand to stroke my beard.

"Landed on my feet, hard. Felt the shock ricochet up my spine. My knees collapsed, but these crazy-assed boots? They did what they were meant to do. Grabbed the concrete like superglue." I touch the spot where my skull met concrete. "Fell backwards. Then lights out."

We sit there silently for a couple of minutes: Denny watching the cloud bank grow purple and begin to move closer once more; me looking out through the branches of the maple to the last things I saw in my old life. The fingers of the storm front begin to twist around us again, ripping at our hair, trying to strip away our clothes.

"I think you should go back to sleep now, babe," I tell her at last. "You're going to have a big day tomorrow."

She tightens her hold to keep me close.

I let her, and wait.

It doesn't take long.

As soon as I feel her go loose in my arms, I stand, bend, and shift her under the covers. Pull them up, tuck her in.

In the morning, while Denise scrambles eggs for breakfast, Rachel dashes outside to retrieve the mail. She is gone longer than usual.

When Denny steps out on the porch to track her down, she finds our daughter trotting up the driveway. "Mom! Mom! Look what I found."

Cradled in Rachel's hands like a wounded bird is something small, scrunched, and faded—previously black, now grey. She launches herself up the steps, presenting it proudly. "It was lying on the ground."

It's a glove: the leather cracked from years of exposure, the fur inside matted and moldy. "Somebody lost it," Rachel crows. "And I found it. Can I keep it, Mom? Can I?"

Denny drops straight down onto the steps, struggles to drag air into her lungs. "Where did you get this?"

Rachel hugs her prize against her tummy with one hand, and points with the other. "Right there, Mom." She waves all five fingers. "Under our tree."

My daughter looks down at the glove she is sheltering, and ponders her good fortune. "No more snow. No more cold. Who loses their fuzzy glove in springtime? Huh, Mom? Who?"

Things are not going as I'd imagined. Denny is stomping around the kitchen, clearing plates, and dashing them into the sink. Normally she rinses them and places them in some mysterious pattern inside the dishwasher that she insists is the only way they can be properly cleaned. Today? Cleanliness has been abandoned in favor of...? Cussing out her late husband, apparently. The smash and clash of tableware masks her mutters from the kids, who've raced from breakfast to *Care Bears* with barely a breath between. But I hear her words clearly. Denny's anger is like a third person in the room.

"What in the Sam heck am I supposed to do with this shoot? Hmm? Buy into the whole freaking package? Son-of-a-gun husband didn't die? The illegitimate creep is haunting me? Risen from the golldarn dead? And dropped a stinking arse glove in my lap to prove it?!"

Only she isn't saying heck, shoot, freaking, son-of-a-gun, illegitimate, golldarn (so, that's how that's spelled), stinking, or arse. But this is a family book, so substitute as you see fit.

I am back on the kitchen counter again, which feels suspiciously like a doghouse today, my head in my hands. *Yes. Sort of. Not the words I would use, but yes. Would if I could, but no. Technically in Rachel's lap, but whatever.*

She snatches up the jug of juice, the butter dish, the unfinished plate of toast from the kitchen table, and hauls them to the fridge. Grumbles as she yanks it open; swears as she slams everything inside—including a dishtowel; spits out a string of expletives as she bangs it shut. I'm not sure I've heard some of these cuss words before. I'm not sure a longshoreman has.

Then she falters. Puts her back to the refrigerator door, slumps until she is halfway between standing and arse-on-tile. "This cannot go on," she says.

Swallows. Says it again. "Cannot go on."

I roll my eyes heavenward—where help is not forthcoming. *Why is this so hard for you, babe?* I just don't get it. Haven't I done enough to prove myself?

"Coincidence," my wife says. "Probably not even his glove."

I push myself off the counter and cross to her side. *But Jesus you saw it! You know it is. You bought the Goddamn things for me, for Christ sake.* Under the circumstances, I am not inclined to self-censor. The Big Guy is going to have to plug his ears and chant *na na na na naaaa* if he doesn't want to hear me take his name in vain.

Denny! It is me. I am here. I'm shouting at her, getting no reaction.

She opens her mouth, snaps it closed, opens it once more. "Besides. Jim would never do it this way."

Huh?

"He knows me better than this. What I'm like."

You mean fanciful? Creative? Open-minded?

"Logical. Analytical. Anal."

Double huh? *Well, sure. But the other, too.*

My wife *is* the thinker and planner in our family, but she's also the one who can discuss hypotheticals until the cows come home to milk themselves. She has always been the half of our partnership that comes up with outlandish ideas, so that *moi*—the handy guy—can make them happen, can turn the impossible into reality.

Haven't I been doing that?

"If Jim really wanted to speak to me, he'd know how to do it right."

Well call me Spanky and turn me over your knee, woman, but I'm clueless. What more could I possibly do?

She straightens, pushing her spine up along the refrigerator door until she's balanced again on both feet. Looks to her left—right through me—to the digital clock on the stove.

"Half an hour, Rach," she calls out. "Are those the clothes you want to wear to school?"

Our daughter has attired herself in a Pee-Wee's Playhouse nightshirt, Calvin Klein kiddie jeans, purple jelly sandals, and a Toledo Mud Hens baseball cap. If she's heading to Woodstock, she should be fine.

A sweet soprano voice bellows back. "No!"

"Then you better go change."

" 'kay!"

Kindergarten is in session for my daughter, but Jimmy's nursery school is only open three days a week. Still, a stampede of tiny feet follows. Our son feels obligated to follow his sister's lead and replace the color-coordinated ensemble his mother picked out for him this morning with something more on trend.

I can trace their progress above us. Slamming drawers. Squealing laughter. The buzz of treasonous plotting as our kiddos compare fashion notes to see which of them can shock Mom unconscious.

"Jim?"

Denise is still standing in front of the fridge. She stares straight ahead, angry tears shining in her eyes. But I feel encouraged. As long as she keeps talking to me, there's hope. She drags a hand through her hair.

"Jim, if you're out there. Really, really out there? You've got to stop this."

Hell, no.

"I can't keep riding this rollercoaster."

I've heard this someplace before, but can't quite recall.

"Climbing a mountain one minute. Crashing to the bottom the next."

Belief on Monday. Doubt on Tuesday. Helter skelter every day of the week.

She pushes off the refrigerator, lifts her face to the ceiling and hollers. "Twenty-five minutes! Then we've got to hit the road."

She moves to the sink, turns on the faucet, begins to rinse the dishes.

Tell me what I can do, Denny. Short of leaving you. But I know with a sinking heart I might have reached the end of my options. I will not keep poking and prodding if it's making her miserable.

For several minutes, forks rattle against stoneware, then my wife slaps a palm against the faucet, shutting it off.

Her knuckles turn white as she clutches the edge of the counter. "No more hints and maybes and could be's," she demands to the sink filled with dirty dishes. "If you can't tell me in no uncertain terms that you're still here? If you can't—I don't know—write your name in ten-foot letters on a wall…"

Well, they weren't ten-feet tall, but I did write my name for you. She just hadn't stuck around to see it.

She sputters as her rant picks up speed. "In day-glow paint. Or something that—well—screams it at me?" She spins around to address the room. "Then it's not you. Not the Jim Meyer I knew. And loved. And want back. With every fiber of my body and soul."

She looks magnificent, strong. Standing up against her grief. Against me, if that is what it will take. She wears her jeans and red-flowered shirt like Joan of Arc wore armor. But her tears are falling fast, a waterfall of furious weeping that she wipes away with the hem of the blouse. The roses darken like blood stains. "My Jim Meyer would tell it to me straight. In a way that even a freaking nit-picky list-making pragmatist can't possibly explain away."

I stare at her, dumbfounded. My message? In ten-foot letters? My signature on it? All over it, so she can't mistake it for anyone's work but mine?

The Big Guy can take his fingers out of his ears now. *If you would, please? Sir. With all due respect? Could use a little help here.*

Denise is still standing at the sink. Waiting. Perhaps for spray-painted graffiti to appear on the wall above the stove.

She inhales. Holds it. Lets it sigh away. Hollers. "Fifteen minutes!"

I hear my kids giggle, their feet slapping the floor above as they rush to meet Mom's deadline.

And then I pick out something else, underlying the everyday clatter. A rushing noise. Or maybe it's more like a roar. I glance at my wife to see if she hears it, too, but she pads out of the kitchen toward the front room and the coat closet.

I turn an ear toward the sound, like a satellite dish, shifting from right to left in a semicircle to see if I can pick up where it's coming from. *The backyard?* No, farther out than that. But the direction is correct, I think.

The roar hesitates, pauses briefly, then deepens. A second hesitation, and it increases in pitch. More *re* on the musical scale than *do*.

I face it head on, straining to pick out the clue the Big Guy has handed me. A heaviness presses against my chest, not unlike the blast of wind that knocked me from the roof. Like a line of churning storm clouds, something is coming for me.

And then I know. *Oh, holy God… and I mean that with absolute sincerity, Big Fella.* If this doesn't work, nothing ever will.

My Denny's message is already written. I just have to get it in front of her. I glance at the clock.

"Ten minutes," my wife calls out, her loudest warning yet.

Man, this will be cutting things close. *Get the lead out, kids! Move it, soldiers! Move it! Mommy and Daddy's happily ever-after is on the line.*

I race after my wife, who is on the staircase landing, scuffing her feet into leather mules. She pulls small coats out of the closet, holding each up in turn, trying to decide which would be appropriate for this fine spring day.

Anything, I shout at her. *Or nothing. They're healthy little tikes. They can take it.* What's a sniffle or two, compared to the windy roar that is bearing down out of the north? Or it might be out of the east. Two possibilities... but just as unimportant as which jacket will be selected for the day's festivities.

"Mommy," Rachel calls. "I can't find my blue sneaky shoes."

"In your closet."

Under your bed. Damn it, we have to go. Now.

"Got 'em," our daughter calls. "They was under my bed."

She and Jimmy come clomping down the stairs. Denny sighs. "Rach, honey, those pants and that top don't match."

Who cares!

"Nobody cares, Mommy. You're a old fudgie duddy."

Five minutes! Get 'em moving, fudgie duddy. Snap it up.

Jimmy beats everyone out the door. It's like he hears me and is leading the charge. Rachel is on his heels, and I've never been happier that she's determined to beat him at everything. She yanks open the rear car door, and they push and shove at each other as they clamber in. Rachel holds one blue sneaker like a club, the other flops around on the end of her foot, barely covering her toes. Denny hasn't noticed. Thank God... *again, Big Guy.* If she had, we'd be stopping to get our daughter properly shoed. Instead, Mom is on the porch, fumbling to lock up the house.

Leave it! Four minutes. We aren't going to make it.

A screech of metal echoes up from the expressway at the end of our block.

It's followed by a hollow thud, and a blast of car horns.

Gracias, danke, grazie! There is no official language in heaven, but I am anxious, and figure it's best to cover my bases.

Come on, I holler at my wife. I might be able to hurry things up by opening the car door for her, but that would cause all kinds of shock and debate. I have to settle for jumping into the front passenger seat and warming up the starter.

Denny meanders—yes, freaking meanders—down the porch steps, carefully selecting the correct key out of the many on her keyring, pausing to hoist the strap of her purse higher on her shoulder. "Buckle up," she tosses into the backseat as she finally finally finally climbs into the car. Closes the door. Checks it. Opens it and closes it again.

I try not to scream, instead tracing the upcoming route in my head: left out of the driveway, right at the end of the block onto one-way Expressway Drive North. A half block down, we'll grab a left over the short bridge that spans Interstate 75, then make another left onto one-way Expressway Drive South. I was hoping there would be a clear view of the traffic as Denise crosses the overpass, but I realize with a gulp and a swallow that the timing will be all wrong.

And if she doesn't look out and down at all… well, no ten-foot message from me to her with love. She will continue down Expressway Drive South to Lagrange Street and hang a right toward Sylvania Avenue.

I am bouncing forward and back in my seat like a two-year-old, as if my rocking motion can make the car move faster.

More horns are blasting as Denny approaches the end of our block. She and I both stretch our necks to see what's going on. A U-Haul has copulated with a Wonder Bread truck on the other side of the expressway.

"Well, shi… shoot," Denny mutters. "Of all days, when we're running late." The accident is tying up traffic at the junction of Lagrange and Expressway Drive South.

I pump both fists in the air. *Yes!*

Jump on the e-way, babe. Take it down to the Phillips Avenue exit.

"If I detour up Seventy-five," she says to herself. "It's just a couple miles to the next exit."

"We going to school, Mom?" Rachel asks.

"Yep, sweetie. Just taking a different road today."

One less traveled, I say, grinning like a loon. I look to my right as we cross the bridge, and have a straight-on view up I-75 toward I-280 and the Michigan border. One day, Denny will ask the same questions: *What was it doing there? Where was it coming from?* There's no reason for it to be anywhere in this region, let alone this state. For now, all I care about is how heavy is my wife's foot and how hard can I step on the gas without risking life and limb.

The roar has become a thunder of sound inside my head. Mixed with it? A faint overlay of music. I can almost pick out the lyrics.

Denny weaves through the traffic jam on Expressway Drive South, merges onto the entrance ramp to the interstate.

I lean back in my seat, cross my fingers, and say a prayer. Hey, when it's something as important as this, you take no chances. Left up to me? I'd've had a rabbit's foot in my pocket, a rosary around my neck, and a four-leaf clover clenched between my incisors.

Denise stays in the righthand lane. The Phillips exit is just ahead. It's a quick jump on and off I-75, and my family will be back on its way toward Rachel's school.

I see my wife glance in the rearview mirror, then swivel her attention to the driver's side mirror. She cocks her head.

The roar is audible to more than me now. Even with the windows rolled up, she cannot miss it. She frowns, no doubt wondering why a semi is passing on the left. She is going over the speed limit. How fast must he be driving if he's catching up? "That guy's cranking it," she mutters under her breath. I can't help but be grateful. Two minutes slower or faster, and I'd have been in the unemployment line at the pearly gates.

The truck is about to thunder by, but at the last second, the driver downshifts, changes gears, before picking up speed again.

It's more than enough. For a full ten seconds, the semi hovers alongside our car, the name of the trucking company in bold on its cab. But Denny barely notices that. She is fighting to keep one eye on the road and the other on the trailer.

Where a camel named Snortin' Norton is blowing a steamy hello out of both nostrils.

Jimmy laughs and waves, and the driver blasts his air horn.

The slogan *Humpin' to Please* sails past our windows. Ten-feet tall and impossible to miss. Not day-glow, but who's quibbling?

Denny gasps and instinctively presses her foot to the gas, speeding up a few more precious seconds so she can memorize the image. So she can capture every detail, to take out, and turn over and over in her mind far into the future. For the rest of her life.

She can't stick alongside the truck for long, though. The exit is racing toward us. She watches for as long as she can as Norton disappears around a bend and into history.

I can still hear the music playing in the trucker's cab, so I flip on our radio and crank the dial until I find it.

Denny glances at the dashboard, but instead of the frown of confusion I've grown to expect? She smiles. And begins to sing along.

About mountains high and valleys low. About rivers that will never be so deep, so wide or so raging they can keep people apart. Not so long as those people have love. Not so long as they believe.

I join in, no longer in doubt that she's listening.

Rachel laughs from the back, melding her pretty voice with ours. Jimmy tosses in an "ain't no!" now and then, but doesn't try to sing. He can't carry a tune in a Radio Flyer wagon. Instead, he adds a peppy drumbeat with the toes of his shoes against the front seat.

We boogie. We clap our hands. And we shout the last word all together—as we are meant to be, in any life.

"Babe!"

The song ends, and Marvin drops out of our quartet. But I turn off the radio and we start again from the top, repeating the lyrics a cappella in a happy loop all the way to Rachel's school.

In the river of non-time, we are singing still.

Afterword: Denny's Turn

In January 2019, on an ordinary morning when the only things on my mind were breakfast and the day's to-do list, a Jim Thought popped into my head.

Not sure what a Jim Thought is? Take a listen: "Hmm, egg white omelet or oatmeal? Vacuum the carpets first or go fetch the mail?" *Oh, and wouldn't it be great if you let me write the story of my life and afterlife?*

A Jim Thought is other. Not my own. It sounds like my memory of Jim: has his timbre, his barking laugh. The words are out of context to anything I am thinking or doing at the time, so I usually recognize his voice. And when I do, I pay attention. Anyone lucky enough to hear Jim "speak" can bet their last nickel the Marriage License is in the Bible and the dollhouse furniture is an arm-stretch away in the heat duct.

Still, on that January morning when my late husband told me he wanted to write this book, I wondered if it was really him. I mean, my slow-reading, composition-flunking (or almost flunking) Jim? Saying, *Me? I want to write it?* I'm sure he understands why I doubted.

This would not be the first time I considered telling the story of Jim's death and the events that followed, but I'd always vetoed the idea. It would be too emotional for me—and, frankly, embarrassing. I didn't have a problem writing about psychics or ghosts in my novels, but that was fiction. Jim was fact. One part love story, one part ghost story, and all parts true story. There was no way I could tell it without sounding like a raving lunatic. Ahh, but now, the "ghost" was offering to write it for me. Lunacy could be laid on the narrator's shoulders, not mine. So to speak. Hmmm. Gee, what a brilliant idea. Good thinking, honey.

So, how much of what the ghost has told you can you trust? An honest estimate: about ninety percent. This story was not written by a novelist, but by life. I've tagged it *creative nonfiction* out of necessity. It is *nonfiction* because I'm the spouse left alive who experienced these events firsthand, making it largely autobiographical. It is *creative* because the narrator is dead and—while Jim has proven to my satisfaction he can do a lot of things from beyond the pale—he cannot plunk himself down at a keyboard.

But perhaps I was wrong about that. When I took a stab at that first chapter, I had one goal: to stay faithful to my husband's personality, his idiosyncrasies, his *Jim-ness*. It turned out to be easier than I imagined. After a while, I could almost hear him whispering over my shoulder: not short cryptic Jim Thoughts, but whole paragraphs. If I forgot and lapsed into my own voice, he corrected me: "I would not have said that. Say it like this. Don't hold back. Tell it like it was, Denny. What *I* felt. What *I knew.*"

By the way, I never liked being called Denny or Denny Lou, and Jim seldom did after we were married, out of respect for my feelings. But in this book? He insisted on it. Hardly seemed fair. If he didn't want me to use the *P* word, why did I have to put up with the *ny* one? But it was hard to say no to a guy who continued to love me from his grave. Three-hundred or so pages later, I've grown fond of the endearment.

That makes names part of the ten percent of this story that was "fictionalized." There was a Joan, but that was not her name. There was an Annie and she was a thoughtless gossip, but that wasn't her name either. There was a woman in the pediatrician's office who suggested I "pay someone to listen"—but I never learned her name at all, and she did not tell me she screamed out her grief in a corn field. That advice came from a friend years later when we were comparing the emotions that tore us apart following the loss of our loved ones. I borrowed Tam's name and melded her story to the office encounter so I could segue to my own screaming experience with my mom. In short, anytime I renamed someone, it was to protect their privacy or to give them an identity when needed.

There are a few other alterations, as well:

For the sake of brevity, a handful of events that occurred months apart in real life were combined into a single day—such as the request from the hospital to get Jim's signature on an insurance form and my request that they correct their invoice and remove the charge for TV usage. If I had not consolidated here and there, this book would have rivaled a George R. R. Martin novel.

In addition, any dialogue that took place in real time between living individuals was recounted based on my best recollections. The wording is not verbatim, but it's as close as I can come and remain honest. Also, if there are inaccuracies about hospital procedures, *mea culpa*. I described what was said during those horrible days in ICU to the best of my ability, but I do not have a medical degree.

For the record, my memory is exact on two important occasions. That *is* how Jim proposed. That is how he told me I was beautiful. Those moments are engraved upon my heart and made it to the page precisely as spoken.

As for dialogue that takes place between Jim and others after he dies? It is conjecture based on how well I knew the man—how clearly I remember the quips and asides that made him dear to me. I believe I have done him justice. He's had no complaints—at least so far. Jim's wisecrack about the complexity of childhood engineering was borrowed from his son. Jim Junior shares his father's wit, and was happy to put words in his dad's mouth.

Please note there are exceptions here, as well: Brooke, Daria, and Boo believe Jim spoke to them after he'd passed on. And my husband did tell me to look in the Bible. He did wake me up in the middle of the night to say the heat duct did not drop into the basement. What we each heard is what I wrote.

Finally, there really was a Campbell 66 trucking company, and one of its trailers was Humpin' to Please along I-75 the day I demanded Jim tell it to me straight. I later learned deregulation had allowed the firm to venture into Cleveland, Ohio, and Toronto, Canada, but that attempted expansion had done little to save the dying business. By 1985, the famous camel was nearly extinct, and there was scant chance of anyone seeing it in our area at any time, let alone during the dozen or so seconds I shared with it on that two-mile stretch of road. But it happened. It, too, is true.

The only fabrication of a real-life event is Jim's fall.

No one witnessed the accident, and I was too traumatized at the time to recall with accuracy what I did or did not hear after Jim left me to climb up on the roof. But Rachel did find his missing glove years later under our tree. There were two dents in the eavestrough which could have been made by his hands or the heels of his boots as he slid off the edge. And I did have a dream after Jim died, where I found myself sitting behind him, straddling the peak, watching him tug off his glove with his teeth and place it between his legs. He did tell me, "Pay attention."

Many people hold theories about what must have occurred. For me, there were always holes. The weather had not yet turned. The roof could not have been slippery or Jim could not have walked across it so easily. How did the missing glove end up in our tree for two years, caught in branches at least fifty yards away from where he'd been sitting? Then a friend with a background in construction pointed out to me it was less likely Jim slipped, and more likely something startled him: a bird, a shout from a passerby below. Or the wind—which would have been much stronger two stories up than at ground level.

That one detail filled in the gaps to my satisfaction, so I expanded on my real-life dream to create a fictional one that completed the puzzle of how my husband died.

That brings us to the question I've asked myself most often. Why did Jim want to write his story in the first place? For one: I believe it was for family who are still alive. He has an adult son and daughter, their spouses, five grandchildren, brothers and sisters—by birth or marriage, nieces and nephews: all who still think about him, and many who never had a chance to meet him. Boo's son, Justin, texted me, "I was -4 when it happened. It was never a moment that was talked about in great detail. I was only told the basics." I figure Jim wanted to share his story with the people he loved, before I, too, was gone and those details lost.

But I sense there was more on Jim's mind than family history.

I'd written only a handful of chapters, when his sister Kay sent me the following message: *"Okay, so today... possibly a coincidence, but I don't think so. Before Mass starts, our music director asks us all to close our eyes and picture someone standing behind us. And how with our eyes closed, if that person speaks, we are tuned in, and can tell who they are from the sound of their voice. While the director was obviously trying to point out that we need to quiet ourselves so we can hear the voice of Jesus when he speaks to us, I believe we certainly can hear others who we love, as well. We just have to be in the right place and right state of mind to listen to them."*

I used to be a card-carrying Catholic, attending Mass, being active in the lay community—the whole ball of candle wax. Then Jim died, and an emotional earthquake tore apart my religious landscape. There was the person I was and what I believed before his death; there was who I became and what I fought against believing after. I was angry at myself and at God for letting a bad thing happen to a very good man.

That wasn't fair to either of us. It wasn't God's fault I expected more than he provides. But he was a handy target for my rage and despair. This is not unusual for people who are grieving. I make no apology for it, and I don't believe God expects one. He knows what we are going through. If we discard him, he will wait however long it takes for us to find him again.

The thing is: disbelief didn't make me feel better. Only lonely. Over time, I began to envy those survivors on reality crime shows who told horrific tales of murder or violence, and were able to forgive their attackers. Worse were those who claimed they survived because God had intervened. I couldn't do the first, and I no longer believed in the second. Either God did not exist, or he didn't care. It doesn't get any lonelier than that.

Then I began writing Jim's story for him, and I realized that by staying true to my husband's personality and beliefs, he was teaching me something. He was telling me how things worked on the other side—and that he wanted others to know it, as well. He was trying to give something back to people like me who'd been brooding by ourselves for too long.

I used to say, "I no longer believe in God. But I will always believe in Jim."

"Silly you," Jim whispers even as I type this. "You can't believe in one without the other."

Denise L. Meyer
April 3, 2019

Death Is Nothing at All
Henry Scott-Holland

Death is nothing at all.
It does not count.
I have only slipped away into the next room.
Nothing has happened.

Everything remains exactly as it was.
I am I, and you are you,
and the old life that we lived so fondly together is untouched, unchanged.
Whatever we were to each other, that we are still.

Call me by the old familiar name.
Speak of me in the easy way which you always used.
Put no difference into your tone.
Wear no forced air of solemnity or sorrow.

Laugh as we always laughed at the little jokes that we enjoyed together.
Play, smile, think of me, pray for me.
Let my name be ever the household word that it always was.
Let it be spoken without an effort, without the ghost of a shadow upon it.

Life means all that it ever meant.
It is the same as it ever was.
There is absolute and unbroken continuity.
What is this death but a negligible accident?

Why should I be out of mind because I am out of sight?
I am but waiting for you, for an interval,
somewhere very near,
just round the corner.

All is well.
Nothing is hurt; nothing is lost.
One brief moment and all will be as it was before.
How we shall laugh at the trouble of parting when we meet again!

Made in the USA
Coppell, TX
26 January 2020

14997035R00185